THE
NEBULA

A Political Murder
Traces Back to NWO's
Absolute Power

WALTER J. BAEYENS

THE NEBULA: A POLITICAL MURDER TRACES BACK TO NWO's ABSOLUTE POWER
COPYRIGHT © 2017 WALTER J. BAEYENS

Published by:
Trine Day LLC
PO Box 577
Walterville, OR 97489
1-800-556-2012
www.TrineDay.com
publisher@TrineDay.net

Library of Congress Control Number: 2017936717

Baeyens, Walter J.
–1st ed.
p. cm.

Epub (ISBN-13) 978-1-63424-106-9
Mobi (ISBN-13) 978-1-63424-107-6
Print (ISBN-13) 978-1-63424-105-2
1. Conspiracies. 2. Corruption. 3. New World Order. 4. Conspiracy theories. 5. Political culture. 6. Politics and government. I. Baeyens, Walter J. II. Title

FIRST EDITION
10 9 8 7 6 5 4 3 2 1

Printed in the USA
Distribution to the Trade by:
Independent Publishers Group (IPG)
814 North Franklin Street
Chicago, Illinois 60610
312.337.0747
www.ipgbook.com

I am settled and bend up,
Each corporal agent to this terrible feat.
Away, and mock the time with fairest show.
False face must hide what the false heart doth.

– William Shakespeare
The Tragedy of Macbeth
Act 1, Scene 7

FOREWORD

In an era of the disclosure of sensitive government and private documents and computer files – from WikiLeaks' dissemination of classified U.S. State Department cables and Edward Snowden's release of above Top Secret files from the U.S. National Security Agency to the "Panama Papers" describing the world of offshore corporate entities, an overlooked release was that of the ATLAS report. Dated November 21, 1994, the ATLAS report is a "Confidential – Not to be used for trial" Belgian police report describing a criminal syndicate known as "Nebula."

In this book, *Nebula: A Political Murder Traces Back to NWO's Absolute Power,* Walter Baeyens delves into Nebula, beginning with what the ATLAS report describes and into a deeper and darker world of corrupt politicians; arms, nuclear, precious gems, and drug smuggling; religious cults; counterfeiting; child prostitution; and political assassinations. Once consigned to the world of "conspiracy theories," Deep State manifestations like Nebula, Gladio, the Bilderberg Group, the Trilateral Commission, Le Cercle, and other groups and networks with covert agendas are now part of the political vernacular in the United States and other countries. U.S. President Donald Trump accused a Central Intelligence Agency-directed "Deep State" of trying to undermine his presidential candidacy and presidential transition with damaging leaks of information to the media.

Associate Justice of the U.S. Supreme Court Antonin Scalia, an influential member of the Catholic Opus Dei sect, died from a heart attack while among members of the powerful International Order of St. Hubertus at a remote Texas hunting lodge. The Order of St. Hubertus was founded in 1695 by the Habsburg kings of Austria-Hungary and Spain as a hunting society. However, St. Hubertus has a more secretive connection with the Bohemian Club of San Francisco, which annually gathers the world's most powerful political and business leaders for a pagan ritual held at the Bohemian Grove, north of San Francisco. After Scalia's death, information on the connection between St. Hubertus and the Bohemian Club was not found on some obscure website specializing in dark conspiracies, but on the pages of the elite-friendly *Washington Post.*

It should be noted that "conspiracy theorist" was a pejorative term developed by the U.S. Central Intelligence Agency to disparage, first, those researchers and officials who questioned the findings of the Warren Commission on the assassination of President John F. Kennedy. The CIA and its agents-of-influence then expanded the conspirators' universe to include anyone who questioned anything pushed by the Deep State. One does not have to pawn off as conspiracies what occurs rather naturally among power centers. As the great novelist and observer of history Gore Vidal once noted, those in power "don't have to conspire, because they all think alike. The president of General Motors and the president of Chase Manhattan Bank really are not going to disagree much on anything, nor would the editor of the *New York Times* disagree with them. They all tend to think quite alike, otherwise they would not be in those jobs." Vidal later said of himself, "I'm not a conspiracy theorist - I'm a conspiracy analyst."

The story of "Nebula" begins with the assassination in 1991 of Belgian Socialist Party Minister of State André Cools. As with several political assassinations involving large conspiracies, the Cools assassination helped lead to the exposure of Nebula and all of its intertwined and intermeshed connections. Baeyens's research into these criminal networks opens one's eyes to the political and corporate underworld that actually calls the shots around the globe. The murder of Cools in 1991 was reminiscent of the assassination of the promising Minister-President of the German state of Schleswig-Holstein in 1987. Uwe Barschel was a rising Christian Democratic Union star in West Germany. His likely assassination in a Swiss hotel by members of the Israeli Mossad opened a can of worms that became known as the German "Watergate," or "Water-Kant Gate." The murders of Barschel and Cools set off political firestorms in West Germany and Belgium, respectively. Both deaths, along with the assassinations of former Italian Prime Minister Aldo Moro in 1978 and Swedish Prime Minister Olof Palme in 1986, pointed to the covert world of arms smuggling, political blackmail, and other unsavory operations involving intelligence agencies, corporations, and the most obscenely wealthly families on the planet. For those in positions of covert power, there is no difference between pontiff or prince or business tycoon or army general. They are all quite expendable in furtherance of the goals of the Deep State.

False flag terrorist attacks blamed on leftist and right-wing fascist groups thoroughly penetrated by NATO intelligence agencies are part and parcel of the Nebula's activities. These range from the 1981 Bologna train station bombing to some of Europe's and America's present-day massacres blamed on various public villains.

Baeyens provides a road map that takes the reader on a walk through the secret world – one that involves the Russian-Israeli Mafia, or "Red Mafia," and Mossad, twin evils that have nested themselves inside the Trump White House. They have been part of Donald Trump's calculations since his early friendship with Jewish gangster Meyer Lansky's attorney Roy Cohn. This conjoined Mafia-Mossad octopus, with its many tentacles, connects to some of the most outrageous scandals in modern times, including the Banco Ambrosiano – the major partner of the Vatican Bank – affair that may have also involved the assassination of a sitting pontiff, Pope John Paul in 1978. It was the same year as the murder in Rome of Aldo Moro. These deaths connect to the London murder in 1982 of former Ambrosiano chairman Roberto Calvi by assassins reportedly hired by Propaganda Due (P2), the secret Masonic lodge in Rome and key player in NATO's underground Gladio "strategy of tension" operations. The strategy of tension involved Western intelligence services carrying out "false flag" terrorist attacks and assassinations in order to blame them on other parties, including the Soviet KGB, Western European Communist parties, and Palestinians.

Readers of this book will likely be exposed for the first time to characters worthy of any gangster-land movie, including Felix Przedborski, also known as "Don Felix," a Jewish syndicate godfather with holdings from Costa Rica to Congo (Kinshasa) and Israel to Belgium. The reader will also be led through a labyrinth of corporations and crooked politicians. It should not be surprising that in these pages are found such ne'er-do-wells as former Italian Socialist Prime Minister Bettino Craxi, Saudi intelligence chief Prince Turki and his friend the Saudi arms dealer Adnan Khashoggi, smuggler and financier Marc Rich, the corporate team of the failed Wall Street junk bond house Drexel Burnham Lambert, Belgian blood diamond merchant Maurice Tempelsman, and the most nefarious of them all, Henry Kissinger.

There is practically not a single political or corporate collapse, including the U.S. Savings & Loan failure, the mid-2000s banking and Wall Street near-failure, or the financial bedlam faced by post-Soviet Russia, as well as Greece, Argentina, Mexico, Brazil, Italy, Iceland, and others that has not involved the dark players who nest in their hidden lairs inside the Nebula. Baeyens charts a course from Nebula to Bilderberg, Gladio, Opus Dei, P2, Freemasonry, the Skull and Bones, the Muslim Brotherhood, the Houses of Rothschild and Bronfman, the Bush political dynasty, and the Fourth Reich of Nazi revivalists. Although this course is a bewildering one, it is also eye-opening and after the journey the reader can look upon the world as it is, not as the corporate media or the agents of the Deep State wish to portray it.

Wayne Madsen
May 5, 2017

CONTENTS

List of Abbreviations

ABS	Alex Brown & Sons
ADL	Anti-Defamation League
ADFA	Arkansas Development and Finance Authority
AEG	Allgemeine Elektrizitäts Gesellschaft
AESP	Académie Européenne de Sciences Politiques
AG	Aktien Gesellschaft (Stock Company)
AIG	American International Group
AIPAC	America Israel Public Affairs Committee
AP	Aginter Press
ATCO	Azur Trading Company
ATT	Amrican Telephone and Telegraph
BCCI	Bank for Credit and Commerce International
BIP	Banque d'Investissements Privés
BIS	Bank for International Settlements
BKA	BundesKriminalAmt
BND	BundesNachrichtenDienst
BNL	Banco Nazionale del Lavoro
BONY	Bank of New York
BURAFEX	Bureau des Affaires Extérieures
CCC	Cellules Communistes Combattantes
CCF	Crédit Commercial et Financier
CCTV	Closed Circuit TV
CDU	Christlich Demokratische Union
CEDI	Centre Européen de Documentation et d'Information
CEO	Chief Executive Officer
CFR	Council on Foreign Relations
CGE	Compagnie Générale des Eaux
CGER	Caisse Générale d'Epargne et de Retraite
CIA	Central Intelligence Agency
CIC	Counter Intelligence Corps
CNN	Cable News Network
CP	Communist Party
CSIS	Centre for Strategic and International Studies
DC-3	Douglas Cargo Type 3
DD	David Dubinsky
DDT	dichloro-diphenyl-trichloroethane (insecticide)
DEA	Drug Enforcement Agency
DGSE	Direction Générale de Sécurité Extérieure
DIA	Defense Intelligence Agency

DINA	Dirección de Inteligencia Nacional
DMI	Dar Al-Maal-Al-Islami
DVD	Deutsche Verteidigungs Dienst
ECB	European Central Bank
EDOK	Einsatzgruppe D zur Bekämpfung der organisierten Kriminalität
EH	Eric Hufschmid
ELF	Essence et Lubrifiant de France
ENI	Ente Nazionale Idrocarburi
ERT	European Round Table (of Industrialists)
ETA	Euskadi Ta Askatasuna
EU	European Union
FBI	Federal Bureau of Investigation
FDP	Freie Demokratische Partei
FDR	Franklin Delano Roosevelt
FIOE	Federation of Islamic Organizations in Europe
FJ	Front de la Jeunesse
FN	Fabrique Nationale (d'Armes de Guerre)
FOIA	Freedom of Information Act
FRG	Federal Republic of Germany (West-Germany)
GB	Grand Bazar
GBL	Group Bruxelles Lambert
GDF	Gaz de France
GDP	Gros Domestic Product
GE	General Electric
GIA	Groupe Islamique Armé
GO2	General Operations section 2
GPS	Ground Positioning System
GRU	Glavnoye Razvedyvatel'noye Upravleniye
HBC	Hudson Bay Company
HMS	Her Majesty's Ship
HQ	Headquarters
IAEA	International Atomic Energy Agency
IATA	International Air Transport Association
IBEL	Investerings- en Beleggingsmaatschappij Lacourt
IBM	International Business Machines
ICBM	Intercontinental Ballistic Missile
IDB	Israeli Discount Bank
IEPS	Institut Européen pour la Paix et la Sécurité
IG	Interessen Gemeinschaft
IOS	Investors Overseas Services
IRA	Irish Republican Army
IS	Islamic State
ISIS	Islamic State in Iraq and Syria
IT	Information Technology
KG	Kay Griggs
KGB	Komitet Gosudarstvennoy Bezopasnosti
MAUE	Mouvement d'Action pour l'Union Européenne

MB	Muslim Brotherhood
MF	Mossack Fonseca
MGM	Metro Goldwyn Mayer
MI6	Military Intelligence 6
MJC	Militia of Jesus Christ
MK	Mind Kontrol
MP	Member of Parliament
NATO	North Atlantic Treaty Organisation
NBC	National Broadcasting Corporation
NEFA	Nine Eleven Finding Answers
NEM	Nouvelle Europe Magazine
NRC	Nuclear Research Centre
NSA	National Security Agency
NSDAP	Nationalsozialistische Deutsche Arbeiterpartei
NSU	National Sozialistische Untergrund
NV	Naamloze Vennootschap
NWO	New World Order
NYT	New York Times
OAS	Organisation de l'Armée Secrète
OSS	Office of Strategic Services
OTRAG	Orbital Transport and Rockets AG
PAC	Political Action Committee
PFLP	Popular Front for the Liberation of Palestine
PIO	Public Information Office
PLO	Palestine Liberation Organisation
PRB	Poudreries Réunies de Belgique
PSC	Parti Social Chrétien
PV	Procès Verbal
SABENA	Société Anonyme Belge d'Exploitation de la Navigation Aérienne
SAVAK	Sāzemān-e Ettelā'ăt va Amniyat-e Keshvar (Iran Secret Service)
SBA	Société de Banque Arabe
SCK	Studie Centrum voor Kernenergie (Nuclear Research Centre)
SDRA	Service de Documentation, de Recherche et d'Action
SGB	Société Générale Belge
SGR	Service Général du Renseignement (Military Intelligence)
SHAPE	Supreme Headquarters Allied Powers Europe
SICO	Saudi Investment Company
SIPO	SicherheitsPolizei
SIS	Special Intervention Service
SMAP	Société Mutuelle des Administrations Publiques
SO	Special Operations
SOFINA	Société Financière (de Transports et d'Entreprises Industrielles)
SP	Socialist Party
SPD	Sozialdemokratische Partei Deutschlands
VDB	Vanden Boeynants (Paul)
VDV	Van De Voorde (Etienne), (Norbert)
VDW	Van de Weghe (Eric)

VUM	Vlaamse Uitgevers Maatschappij (Flemish Publishing Cy)
VW	VolksWagen
WACL	World Anti-Communist League
WJC	World Jewish Congress
WMR	Wayne Madsen Report
WNP	Westland New Post (Ultra-right group)
WTC	World Trade Centre
WW	World War
SRC	Space Research Corporation
SRCI	Space Research Corporation International
SS	SchutzStaffel
STC	Section Training and Communication (of SDRA)
SWAT	Special Weapons and Tactics (Team)
UFC	United Fruit Company
UK	United Kingdom
UN(O)	United Nations (Organisation)

INTRODUCTION

On a bright July morning of the year 1991 the tiny nation of Belgium woke up to the news of the murder of Minister of State André Cools, the big-mouthed leader of the socialist party. He was shot in the chest and the neck by two men on a motorbike when boarding his car in the vicinity of Liège. His girlfriend was badly wounded too but she survived. The ex-minister died in a pool of blood next to his car just two weeks short of his 64th birthday.

Belgium had just lived through the bloody 1980s when the skies over Flanders Fields and over the Ardennes had turned pitch black under the brutal point-blank executions of women and children by the Brabant Killers; and the bomb attacks of the Communist Combat Cells. Belgium, the poster child nation hosting the EU and NATO headquarters in the very heart of Europe, seemed to have turned into a banana republic. The killing of Cools – a political murder – topped it all off. The Dutroux scandal was still a few years away. Belgium went into a state shock once again. The press went mad. The incident revived unpleasant memories of the killing of the popular Swedish prime-minister Olof Palme in 1986 and of the liquidation of Italian premier Aldo Moro in 1978.

This was the second political murder in Belgium in the post-war era. Forty-one years earlier, in 1950, Julien Lahaut, the leader of the popular Communist Party, had been murdered. Just like in Italy and France the Belgian communists had been in good standing after the war. They had massively joined the "Résistance" and had fought the Nazis tooth and nail. And after all it was not the Allies who had won the war on the Western front, but the Russian Red Army on the Eastern Front, at a terrible cost.

Lahaut's funeral was attended by 300,000 people. He was blacklisted by the Belgian Catholic royalist elites after he had the gall to shout "Vive la république" while attending the crowning ceremony of young King Baudouin. Blasphemy! Barely a week after the incident he was gunned down by two men near his home in a suburb of Liège.

The Belgian justice department was not at all eager to solve the case. By 1950 the Marshall plan was already upon us and Baudouin's willing little kingdom was well under way of being colonized by the fiercely anti-Marxist Wall Street gang. It was decreed that henceforth communism was the enemy, and so the only good communist was a dead communist.

Although State Security had collected enough evidence to identify the killers within two weeks of the attack, the murder would officially remain unsolved for six and a half decades. The case was finally wrapped up in 2015, not by the police but by a group of stubborn historians who had at long last dug up some conclusive evidence.

The Lahaut murder had been organized by André Moyen, whose involvement with high-level collaborators during the war was well documented. At the time of the murder Moyen must have been very confident that he had nothing to fear. As was the case in Italy, France and Germany, the fascists, supported by the American liberators, had returned to their positions of power. André Moyen proved to be a big friend of America. He gladly mediated between his rich and powerful right-wing Catholic mentors and the US intelligence services. In later years Moyen was found to have laid the groundwork for the Belgian branch of NATO's secret army called Gladio. In the late 1980s he attempted to derail the investigations into the Brabant Killings and into the child abuse cases labeled "Dossier X." Who was he protecting?

The Cools murder investigators submitted a bizarre report that came to be known as the ATLAS Report. This report – the starting point of this author's research – was leaked to the press in 1994. It painted an unexpected picture of a criminal organization that was obviously above the law. According to the reporting officers this organization controlled half of the global economy and held "Absolute Power." (Appendix 1)

The report came on the heels of a 1990 paper by Judge Schlicker who had been investigating the case of the "insane" Brabant Killers who had massacred at least 28 men, women and children in and near shopping malls in the mid-1980s. Even today the exact number of victims remains unclear. Several unsolved liquidations may or may not have been linked to the case. The Brabant Killers are still at large to date. In his report judge Schlicker had warned the political leaders of a new kind of organized criminality that had taken root in Belgium. Not surprisingly, people started to speculate about similarities to the Italian "Strategy of Tension" massacres, organized by the intelligence services and NATO-Gladio.

In his September 2-4, 2011 edition, investigative journalist and ex-NSA agent Wayne Madsen published an online article on the subject titled "Classified Belgian police report on Nebula receives another look." The article reads in part:

> "In the mid-1990s, a report prepared by the Belgian police, which looked into the assassination of former Belgian Deputy Prime Minister and Belgian Socialist Party leader Andre Cools, in a gangland-style murder in 1991, is getting a fresh look after reports have surfaced about Mossad links to neo-Nazi, anti-Muslim gangs, some

with criminal underpinnings, that are masquerading as legitimate political movements in Belgium, the Netherlands, and other countries. The renewed interest in the Belgian police report, known as the ATLAS Report, is of special interest following the recent massacre of Norwegian socialist youth on Utoya island and a deadly bombing in down-town Oslo carried out by pro-Zionist, neo-Nazi Anders Behring Breivik.

The ATLAS Report's detailed investigation of Zionist players in global financial scandals dovetails with recent comments by officials of Egypt's Muslim Brotherhood that the former corrupt regime of Hosni Mubarak represented a "Talmudic dictatorship" imposed on Egypt by international players. The comments made by the Brotherhood were highlighted in a recent seminar on Islam and democracy held in Jakarta by the Jakarta Foreign Correspondents' Club.

Before Cools' murder, Belgium had been wrecked by Italian Gladio-style "strategy of tension" (or, as in Turkey today, Ergenekon) right-wing terrorist attacks, including death squad hits and bombings, which were initially blamed by authorities on leftist guerrilla groups such as the Communist Combatant Cells. Cools' home town of Liege was the center of the nexus of organized crime syndicates and the right-wing Gladio cells. However, it was not the revelation that Cools and other top Belgian politicians were involved in Belgium's right-wing "deep state" that brought down their house of cards but the infamous Agusta helicopter scandal.

Agusta, the Italian helicopter manufacturer and a licensee of Bell helicopters of the United States, bribed Socialist Party leaders, including Cools and then-NATO Secretary General Willy Claes, a friend of Cools, to cement a Belgian Army contract for 42 helicopters, which would replace the Army's aging French Alouette helicopters. Cools was to have received $10 million in bribes but the cash he received turned out to be counterfeit. Cools, in retaliation, threatened to tell all he knew about the Agusta deal and much more. It was Cools' threat to go public that earned him two bullets while he was sitting in his car next to his girlfriend. One bullet struck Cools in the head, the other to his chest. His girlfriend was also hit but she survived. What Cools threatened to expose was an intricate network of terrorists, nuclear smugglers, drug dealers, diamond and gold smugglers, and weapons merchants who were ultimately tied to Mossad and a shadowy network of influential European Jewish Zionists, a network known as "Nebula." The details on Nebula are contained in the ATLAS report. The ATLAS report is also the main subject of a 400-page book on Belgium's deep-state politics to be published in Belgium in the Dutch language in 2012.

The Confidential "Not to be used in court proceedings" ATLAS report was issued by the Special Investigations Unit of the Belgian Gendarmerie in Liege on November 21, 1994. It is clear that the authors of the report realized the problems they faced in pointing to Jewish criminal networks as a major force behind Europe's "strategy of tension" and the financial contrivances established to support acts of terrorism and other illegal acts. The report in its introduction states ." . . some information is still being cross checked. Several files have already been examined by various police services, who have been able to corroborate some data, even if Justice [Ministry] has not always followed-up on them. Day to day events show us that some files never go anywhere and some others will no doubt never lead anywhere, for various reasons. The report states: "To understand 'Nebula,' one has to abandon the established path of logic as far as finances and politics are concerned. No longer can there be mention of nation states, of political party colors or of any economic coherence. Our conclusion would be that, over 20 years, some economical forces, some of which are of the mafia-type linked to the political power and organized crime structures, have reached the 4th level of money laundering, in other words: Absolute Power."

[...]

WMR [*Wayne Madsen Report*] has reported extensively on the activities of the Russian-Israeli Mafia but, thanks to the ATLAS Report from the Belgian police, the Mafia now has a proper name: Nebula.

PART I

What's Left?

1953 Police mugshot of Felix

Pictures of Felix are rare and small. (1979)

CHAPTER 1

DON FELIX

THE TICO CONNECTION

The ATLAS Report issued by the Special Investigations Unit of the Gendarmerie of Liege was peculiar in more than one way. At the top it was marked "*Confidential. Not to be used in court proceedings*" and it continued, "*To understand this 'Nebula,' one has to abandon the established path of logic as far as finances and politics are concerned. No longer can there be mention of nation states, of political party colors or of any economic coherence. Our conclusion would be that, over 20 years, some economical forces, some of which are of the mafia-type linked to the political power and organized crime structures, have reached the 4th level of money laundering, in other words: Absolute Power.*"

The spider in this web, the report said, was a Belgian national of Polish-Jewish descent by the name of Felix Przedborski, aka Don Felix.

"*We have been informed about a person who appears to be one of the mysterious top leaders in several countries, (including ours). This person is portrayed as being the 'éminence grise,' the de facto director of most of the big multinational companies whose structures are being used to launder large amounts of capital.*

This person is: PRZEDBORSKI, Felix, born 12 December 1930, 'stateless' ..."

The police document was never really taken seriously. It was considered "too outlandish" and conspiratorial. Indeed, the Nebula seemed to have a lot in common with what others called the New World Order. How had "ordinary" police investigators been able to identify "absolute power" when accidentally stumbling over it? Still, the report listed many names of individuals and companies. Its content became a lot more plausible to those who were willing to research its backgrounds.

Also noteworthy was the fact that Costa Rica was identified as a major nexus for the worldwide network. In more recent years Russian-Israeli Maffiya control of Costa Rica has indeed been confirmed. Here is what Wayne Madsen wrote about Costa Rica and Przedborski in his September 2011 report:

> "The ATLAS Report also identified who the Belgian police believed was a kingpin of Nebula. It is also noteworthy how Costa

Rica is identified as a major nexus for the worldwide network. The information about Russian-Israeli Mafia control of Costa Rica has been verified by recent information obtained by WMR from Costa Rican sources. The ATLAS Report states:

"We have been informed about a person who appears to be one of the mysterious top leaders in several countries, (including ours).

This person is portrayed as being the "éminence grise," the de facto director of most of the big multinational companies whose structures are being used to launder large amounts of capital. This person is: PRZED-BORSKI, Felix, born 12 December 1930, 'stateless,' husband to Helène KRYGIER, formerly living in TERVUREN.

On the subject of this person, we have been told that:

-He has a double nationality: Belgium + Costa Rica.

We have been able to confirm that he obtained Belgium nationality on 6 September 1978, a few days before his emigration to Costa Rica. His wife, born 5 June 1931, obtained Belgian nationality on 28 December 1950.

-He is Ambassador of Costa Rica to IAEA in Vienna (anti-nuclear commission) and allegedly also holds the position of minister pleni-potentiary of this same country at the European Economic Communi-ty as well as to France (where he has offices on Avenue Wilson, Paris).

-He actually lives in Costa Rica, where he owns the property BELLA VIS-TA in the San José Country Club, Escazu/San José-Costa Rica.[...]"

On November 2, 2010, WMR reported on the strong Israeli and Mos-sad influence on the government of Costa Rica:

"On October 28, Nicaragua accused Costa Rica of staging cross border raids by Costa Rican paramilitary police into Nicaraguan territory. Costa Rica has been warning Nicaragua against dredging the San Juan River inside Nicaraguan territory. Costa Rica, which fancies itself as an ecological 'green haven,' claims the dredging of the river is causing environmental damage. But as WMR previous-ly reported, Costa Rica, which is backed by George Soros 'civil so-ciety' agents of influence, as well as Israeli intelligence agents, is trying to paint Nicaragua as an aggressive destroyer of the envi-ronment.

On November 1, Costa Rica claimed that Nicaraguan troops had taken up position on Calero island in the San Juan River and which is claimed by both countries. Nicaragua claims that its troops are in the area to control drug trafficking from Costa Rica, which WMR previously reported involved Costa Rican police and intelligence personnel. In a statement published by the *Washington Post*, Nicaraguan Army chief of staff General Julio Aviles confirmed WMR's previous report stating the drug trafficking from Costa Rica is controlled by an expatriate Nicaraguan family operating from San José, the Costa Rican capital.

WMR has also learned that the paramilitary operatives operating out of Costa Rica, including CIA and Mossad agents, are now looking at extending their destabilization operations into El Salvador, now governed by the leftist Farabundo Marti Liberation Front government of President Mauricio Funes, an ally of Ortega in Nicaragua. The tactic being used by the Chinchilla-Lieberman regime in San Jose is the same as that being used against Nicaragua: flood El Salvador with cocaine to increase drug gang warfare and instability.

Most of the drug smuggling from Costa Rica into Nicaragua and El Salvador is being conducted by Russian-Israeli mafiosi figures operating under diplomatic cover at the Israeli embassy in San Jose. Others officially operate in San Jose as "Russian Martial Arts" trainers, however, they are actually Israeli defense Force "Krav Maga" trainers.

One of the Mossad suspects, now wanted by INTERPOL, in the assassination of a Palestinian official in Dubai was suspected of making death threats and engaging in an attempted kidnapping in Costa Rica but the Costa Rican government declined prosecution. The Israeli suspect's false identity in the Dubai assassination is Kevin Daveron, born 2/2/1972, Ireland Passport 980975, alias Jonathan Lewis Graham (stolen identity from a United Kingdom passport.

Ex-Israeli commandos operating in Costa Rica with the blessing of Israeli Foreign Minister Avigdor Lieberman (not known to be a relation to Costa Rica's pro-Zionist Vice President Luis Lieberman Ginsburg; Avigdor hails from Moldova while Luis is of Polish descent) operate under the cover of the Mossad-linked security firm Bitajon Shar, which has been connected, according to WMR's Central American sources, to the destabilization efforts on the Costa Rican borders with Nicaragua and El Salvador."

In updated information provided to WMR from Costa Rican sources, the Costa Rican charged with the assassination of popular Argentine folk singer Facundo Cabral in Guatemala in July is tied to the Mossad-linked criminal drug smuggling network operating throughout Central America and Mexico. Alejandro Jiménez Gonzalez, charged in the killing of Cabral, is the Costa Rican leader of a Central American money laundering syndicate. The actual target of the assassination may have been Cabral's driver, Nicaraguan Elite night clubs owner Henry Farinas, who reportedly received protection from the Nicaraguan government of Daniel Ortega, a prime target of the Israeli syndicates in Costa Rica. In addition to Guatemala, Farinas owns night clubs in Costa Rica, Nicaragua, and Panama and he has, in the past, been linked to the CIA. However, because of his links to Ortega, Farinas may have had a falling out with Langley, which used friendly Mossad operatives to target him in Guatemala, but ended up killing Cabral instead.

THE INSIDER

The report was essentially based on the statements of an insider by the name of Michel Verdeyen. He had been involved in shady real estate deals with the Jewish-Russian Maffiya, from Brussels to New York. As a consequence he had spent some time in jail. His term in prison, so he said, had helped him to return to an honest life. And he was now willing to talk. One of his contacts had been the cousin of Hélène Krygier, Don Felix's wife. Michel V described what he had learned about the machinations of Przedborski, Grand Master of the Jewish Lodge B'Nai B'Rith, as "simply unimaginable."

"Let's theorize for a minute," he said, *"that there is this structure that is well organized, well equipped and well trained. Its existence is justified by the paramount interests of the nation states. For a number of reasons, this structure is accountable to no-one. This structure had its origins in history and it is so well established that nobody really directs it any longer, while nobody knows all the intricacies of it any more. The more so because anyone in the know keeps silent or lies about it. Now imagine the enormous power available to the persons who can put this structure to work for themselves. And then, some day, someone pulls the lever and sets the machine in motion, confident that everything is under control. Who would have the guts to do it? Who was in a position to do it and exactly what levers could be pulled? That's what we should focus on."*

In the same vein, Michel V continues: *"Let's consider Andreotti, the Divine! At the time when he was indicted, I remember one of my Italian friends telling me that Andreotti wasn't linked to the mafia. No, he was the mafia. But by the time we realized that, he had been protected for years. Or this: who has any idea of the magnitude of Craxi's fortune when he fled to Africa? Let's imagine that this really happened somewhere in the world, then why not in Belgium too… or, for all we know, everywhere…like some universal law of nature. Like Mitterrand and his forty thieves. Because the enthronement of Mitterrand in '83 has had a great impact.*

"As early as 1981 there existed a European caste that was confident it could take control of Europe and that had set out to do exactly that. Belgium was already split up.[…]Politics: don't look for any differences in ideology there, it's all just about getting hold of the instruments of the 'democrature' in order to grab power. As I said, let's stop dividing the world in left, right, socialist, catholic, democratic… on the level we are talking about, they all fight the same fight. Give and take. In essence, it's always about three things: weapons, money, corruption. These three are so omnipresent that we don't even notice them any more.[…] Yet, for sure, there have been way too many dead already.[…] I am beginning to realize that there is this giant international structure that is anchored in Belgium and that politics and finances are submerged in it. For their criminal operations, they call on the best lawyers, the biggest banks and the major business consultants, in order to walk away scot-free. Just imagine

what this means in reality, taking into account that the highest rulers of many countries either belong to this structure or support it. Those who keep looking at the world through left-right glasses are stuck on this one tenth of an inch of the time-scale. The only real divide is that between having money and having none, having power and having none. And besides, below a certain depth, all fish have the same color. I know what I'm talking about."

THE DISCRETE MILLIONAIRE

Oddly, despite the fact that he had been living in Belgium for several decades, nobody had ever heard of Don Felix until the publication of the ATLAS Report. Now his name had popped up in the Cools murder file. Przedborski, born in 1930 in Zgierz, Poland, allegedly had known Cools' deported father in a Nazi concentration camp during the war. Many years later, in Belgium, Don Felix and Cools junior had become friends. The picture Don Felix painted of his concentration camp years was quite vague and full of contradictions. Fajbusz Najman, one of Felix's 1950s friends, claimed that Felix was "the biggest fraud on the face of the earth." Felix, Najman said, never showed up at Jewish ex-Kz gatherings for fear of being exposed. Be that as it may, thanks to the testimonies of Najman and Lejbus Szampaner, whose name was on the prisoners' list of the Lodz ghetto, Felix managed to extract reparation payments from the German government.

But how could Don Felix, a poor Jewish refugee who had made his way to Belgium by the end of WWII, have gained such enormous wealth and power without being noticed?

One of the reasons he had remained unnoticed was that he had ways to silence critics and nasty investigators. Most of the time a letter from his lawyers would suffice to shut them up. If required Felix would sue in Court anyone who portrayed him in a negative way.

That is what happened to investigative journalist Walter De Bock back in 1995 after he published a series of critical articles about Felix in the Belgian newspaper *De Morgen*. The same thing happened to journalist Mauricio Herrera in Costa Rica. Both journalists and their newspapers lost their case.

The said articles condensed the info collected by a group of "Felix Watchers" in several countries. In Germany, where Felix had been involved in a scandal involving Lufthansa that had taken on gigantic financial and political proportions, Felix-watcher Jurgen Roth had taken it upon him to publish a book, titled *The Grey Eminence*, about the wheeling and dealing of Przedborski. The book was soon taken out of circulation.

According to the authors of the ATLAS Report this international group of journalists was determined to expose Przedborski by simultaneously publishing their findings in their respective newspapers. The investigating officers seem to have been of the opinion that these revelations could destabilize the Belgian nation. For that reason they had submitted their report before being able to double-check the data. However, it was crystal clear that the Belgian ruling class was not going to allow the press to embarrass them. Witness the gagging of MP [Jean-Pierre] Van Rossem in Parliament. The journalist revolt quickly ran aground and fizzled out. Citing from the ATLAS Report:

> Item 16. The reasons why we submit this report now, without having had the time to double check certain items, are several:
> -the most important reason, or so it appears to us, is that a group of journalists has obtained information similar to ours through channels and by means differing from ours which results in their information being more complete and verified in several countries.
> -these journalists allegedly are very determined to bring it all out in their respective newspapers [...]
> -we have been told that they would go so far as to cause a national strike of the journalists (note from the undersigned: which could eventually cause an uncontrollable government crisis) if they were to be prohibited to publish their articles.
> In case the pressure on the on the Belgian press would prove too strong, other journalists (French, Italian, American..) would take over and proceed to get these informations published. (note of undersigned: again situation uncontrollable).
> -we are in a position to get in touch with these journalists without really knowing what their demands are.

AMBASSADORS

Don Felix obviously wielded a lot of power in high-up circles in many countries. He was a force to be reckoned with in Costa Rica after he had wormed his way into the Tico diplomatic corps in the early 1970s. His diplomatic status as Consul of Costa Rica allowed him to travel unhindered and to penetrate the top of the international political and business milieus. With the help of Felix Przedborski shady figures of the Mikhailov gang, many of them Jews, obtained the same status. Their diplomatic immunity had incited some of them to start their own cocaine business. When they got caught the affair snowballed into a political scandal in Costa Rica in the mid-1990s, triggering an official investigation into the Przedborski haggling of diplomatic honorary titles.

Costa Rica, one of the first nations to have declared war on Hitler, had long been the favorite destination of fugitive Jews, in particular of Polish Jews. There had been a massive immigration of Polish Jews in Costa Rica after the failed January Uprising in Russia in 1865. Teodoro Picado Michalski, son of a Polish immigrant, was Costa Rica's president from 1944 to 1948. Costa Rica was the first nation to open its embassy in the newborn state of Israel, not in Tel Aviv but in Jerusalem! For this Israel had repeatedly shown its gratitude toward the Tico nation.

In his October 2015 Special Report titled "A little known Israëli-Zionist Power Syndicate Exposed," Wayne Madsen likens the uncanny power of Don Felix in Costa Rica to that of the [Jamie] Rosenthal gang in Honduras. Madsen, who confirmed and documented the virtual takeover of Costa Rica and other Central American nations by the Jewish mafia, wrote:

> The Przedborski syndicate in Costa Rica is similar to the Rosenthal criminal family in Honduras. Headed by former Honduran Vice President Jaime Rosenthal, who is of Romanian Jewish extraction, the syndicate owns Banco Continental, part of Grupo Continental. On October 7, 2015, Rosenthal was named by the U.S. government as a "specially designated narcotics trafficker." As it is normal with the Zionist-founded and -controlled Wikipedia, Rosenthal's close connection to wider Jewish global gangsterism is not to be found in his Wikipedia entry. Rosenthal, who once met President Ronald Reagan in the White House, owns over 20 businesses in Honduras, including cattle ranches and alligator farms. Rosenthal's Inversiones Continental controls banking and financial services companies, as well as real estate, media, agriculture, and construction interests in Honduras as well as three off-shore firms in the British Virgin Islands. On October 7, 2015, Rosenthal's nephew, former Honduran Investments Minister Yankel Rosenthal, was arrested, along with his lawyer, at Miami International Airport and charged with providing "money laundering and other services that support the international narcotics trafficking activities of multiple Central American drug traffickers and their criminal organizations." His uncle Jaime and cousin Yani were similarly charged although Jaime remains in Honduras. As with the Rosenthals, who used Honduran government and diplomatic offices to further their criminal operations, Przedborski relied on the help of Costa Rican officials, including the former Costa Rican ambassador to Belgium and Austria.

Don Felix had spent huge amounts of money to provide his friends with Tico diplomatic passports. Next to Colombia no country worldwide had more Consuls on its pay-list than Costa Rica. Obviously, the local regime had turned the Tico diplomacy into a lucrative business. Felix must have been their biggest client. A student at the San Judas Tadeo University in San Jose, outraged by this state of affairs, published a thesis on the subject under the title "The Price of a Diplomatic Passport: Felix buys Costa

Rica." The title of the paper alluded to Tico senator Julio Sunol's 1974 book, *Vesco buys a Republic,* in which the author accused the government of selling out his country to Robert Vesco, a top US criminal.

THE VESCO CONNECTION

Vesco was Meyer Lansky's lieutenant who found refuge in Costa Rica in 1972. Lansky was a Jewish immigrant who had made it to the top in the crime jungle of Lower Eastside Manhattan in the 1920s and '30s. Vesco had his fingers in many pies: booze, drugs, casinos, prostitution and blackmail. He became close friends with [Richard] Nixon, whose campaign he had financed, which was illegal at the time. Vesco, hunted down by the US tax-man, was eventually forced to flee the US. In Costa Rica he was welcomed by president "Pepe" Figueres, whose rise to power allegedly had been sponsored by Don Felix via the German top-criminal Ekhard Peters, the Tico consul in Bonn. It was Figueres' successor Daniel Oduber who had granted diplomatic status to Felix in 1974.

After the arrival of Vesco in his private 707, Costa Rica had become the main transshipping point for tons of Colombian cocaine, on their way to the USA. By the end of the 1970s the north of the country was turned into a bulwark against the Sandinista forces operating just across the border in Nicaragua. As the ATLAS Report pointed out, Don Felix had a big stake in the pristine northern region of Santa Elena, near the Nicaraguan border. The Papagayo tourist project in the area promised rich returns on investment. Other investors in the Santa Elena region were, not coincidentally, Leon Deferm and the Italian Agusta family.

The project however had no chance to succeed without an airport. In the early 70s that airport found its humble beginnings in a dirt strip that was being used by Colonel [Oliver]North to supply weapons to the Nicaraguan Contras. On their way out, the CIA aircraft were loaded with cocaine. Costa Rica, just like Belgium, found itself in the midst of the Iran-Contra operations in which the Mossad was also deeply involved. Israeli top agent Mike Harari was the Jewish point of contact for both aspects of the operation – weapons in, drugs out – in Central America. Harari was the puppet master who pulled the strings on Manuel Noriega, the CIA-recruited strongman of Panama. All of this had a lot to do with Don Felix as we will discover later. Suffice it to say now that in 2015 Harari was one of the names on the list of Facebook friends of Daniel Przedborski, Don Felix's son and successor. Old friendships never die.

WAR STORIES

Faidor "Felix" Przedborski was born into a poor family on December 12, 1930, in the village of Zgierz, a few miles north of Lodz. The Polish people had somehow managed to struggle through the First World War. In the 1930s, when conditions were at last improving somewhat, Poland had to face yet another devastating war. Felix was nine years old when the Nazis took the city of Lodz and renamed it Litzmannstadt, after the German general who had died there in WWI. Its Jewish inhabitants were forced to move to the Lodz ghetto.

Young Felix, as he himself declared after the war, was sent to the labor camp of Auschwitz-Birkenau, ignorant of the fate of his relatives. In 1945 he was liberated by American troops. Very few people could acknowledge Felix's story. His name did not show up on the Auschwitz prisoners' lists. Swiss records showed that a young man by the same name – date of birth January 22, 1930 – was arrested near the Swiss border on September 11, 1943.

An "atheistic Jew" by the name of Fajbusz Najman, four years older than Felix, had also made it to Belgium after the liberation. His name did figure in the Auschwitz prisoners' lists. He confirmed Felix's story – to a certain extent. It was not unusual for Jews to tell convenient lies about each other's past so they could file reparation claims. It worked for Felix. In 1954 the German government would pay him close to 11,000 mark. Quite a lot of money at the time.

According to Najman, Felix had served as the errand boy for Mordechai "Chaim" Rumkowski, the Jewish head of the Lodz ghetto. Rumkowski was appointed by the Nazis to run the ghetto and provide for its inhabitants. "Rumki" yielded enormous power within the ghetto. He issued his own currency, postal stamps, conducted wedding ceremonies and – most importantly – drew up the lists of Jews who were to be sent to labor camps. He later died in Auschwitz, allegedly killed by his own people.

After a journey into the Russian sphere of influence, the 15 year-old Felix fled to Belgium where he found refuge at the center for Aid to the Israeli victims of the War in a Brussels suburb. In 1946 young Felix was officially registered as a citizen of the commune of Tervuren, a few miles east of Brussels. Profession: diamond cutter.

This was the start of Felix's meteoric business career.

Najman and Felix had met in Brussels "by chance" and had become friends. In the late 1950s they, their wives Malka and Hélène and their children used to go on holidays together and enjoy life. Later on, as Felix all of a sudden had become very rich, their friendship petered out. Indeed, by the early 1970s Felix owned a villa in Tervuren. Soon thereafter he was known to be "the biggest taxpayer in town."

Najman now complained that "Felix was the biggest crook in the world" and that he never attended Jewish war victims gatherings for fear of being exposed. True, Felix did seem to have a natural talent for setting up grand-scale scams. Although he could barely write his own name, so the story goes, he could express himself in six or seven languages. He was said to be a very persuasive person who could "sell sand to an Arab."

In the early 1950s Felix got caught up in black market smuggling. He learned all the tricks of the trade. The demand for goods, from cigarettes to cars, in bombed out Europe must have been gigantic. 1953 proved to be an important year. He married Hélène and started operations via his Tradin company. This company, incorporated in tax-free Liechtenstein, would serve him well for the next half century. He was often seen in Café Old Vienna in the Rue du Pont Neuf, Brussels, where he discreetly "manufactured" documents on request. Counterfeiting identity papers, export documents and even money, proved to be big business. In that same year 1953 Felix was arrested, convicted and briefly jailed in 1954 for forgery and the illegal use of aliases. Young Przedborski used to do business under the name Hancart, Hankard or Finkelstein.

MAURICIO

Felix teamed up with an adventurer from Paris by the name of Mauricio Ungar, alias Maurice Gonzales, who turned out to be a relative of the aristocratic Borbon family of Costa Rica. Ungar was a sweet talker in his own right, a connoisseur of antique art and jewelery. He could go on for hours about the origin of some piece of art he put up for sale. Mauricio claimed to have studied philosophy in Paris and to speak fourteen languages fluently. His grandfather had been a jeweler in the court of the Austrian emperor in 1860. During the war he had joined the French Resistance and had helped many Jews stay out of Nazi hands. After the Liberation Mauricio had focused on what he knew best: diamonds and antiques. He sold some diamonds to the staff of the Chinese embassy in Bonn, which was illegal. This earned him the sympathy of Mao who invited him to Peking.

The duo traveled through Europe in grand style, from Yugoslavia to Paris and Trieste. Their black Plymouth caught the eye wherever they passed. The expensive car was no doubt a big help in luring gullible victims into their web. Trieste at the time was a free state, divided in a British-American and a Yugoslavian zone. It was the ideal setting for contraband deals and the smuggling of expensive watches, diamonds and counterfeit money. Felix and Mauricio were caught spending phony $100 US bills.

EASTBOUND TRAVELS

At the age of 17 Felix had started to travel from Belgium to the Eastern Bloc, allegedly to find out what had happened to his relatives. His travels soon aroused the suspicion of the Austrian intelligence service. Was he in contact with Polish spies behind the Iron Curtain? The question remained unanswered. Whatever the reason for his trips to the East, Felix was soon found to be well connected to various Western intelligence services, the Vatican, various heads of state, the White House and the mafia.

Was young Felix recruited by the American CIC or the OSS in the early post-war years? Ted Shackley, of CIA fame, who spoke fluent Polish, had spent time in Europe scouting for Polish agents. By 1976 Shackley was a key figure of "the Enterprise," a parallel CIA secretly set up by Bush senior to compensate for the decimation of the Agency by President Carter. The Enterprise was also a main player in the Iran-Contra operations.

By the start of the 1960s Felix had set up shop near the Koekelberg basilica in Brussels, where he sold stationery and groceries. It is said that he became friends with Albert Kalondji, King of Kasai province in the Congo, with whom he concluded some lucrative diamond deals. From his Brussels shop he started selling gadgets to large companies as promotional gifts to their clients. One of his early clients was the Belgian airline SABENA. Felix had always been and would remain fascinated by travel, tourism and transport.

In 1981 Don Felix clashed with the Belgian tax-man over his huge profits in the SABENA and Lufthansa deals. After Felix had returned from a short escape to Tel Aviv, a fiscal inspector by the name of Stockmans was dispatched to the Przedborski villa in 1982. Both gentlemen would agree on a tax settlement of about three million dollar. After their meeting Stockmans admitted being very impressed by Don Felix, whom he deemed very powerful. His words were *"It is not the politicians you see on the screen that hold real power. These people are being controlled by people who are never seen in political circles."*

He also stated that Felix was quite influential within the Socialist Party. And indeed he was, as would be clearly demonstrated a decade later, in the wake of the Cools murder. Felix proudly had his picture taken rubbing shoulders with his socialist friends ministers Andre Cools and Guy Mathot, also known as "Mister Five Percent." Mathot was one of the most corrupt well-known politicians of his era. Yes, Stockmans was right about Felix pulling some strings on the socialists. The Polish tax dodger even had the nerve, Stockmans recalled, to offer him a job in his Saint Hubertus real estate project, but he had wisely declined. Asked whether Felix was in the drug trade Stockmans replied that he had the impression that Felix was not personally involved, but that he might have financed it.

CAVIAR FOR THE VATICAN

In a 1977 Interpol telex from Washington, Mauricio and a character by the name of Bela Rabelbauer were being linked to arms and drugs trafficking. Reportedly there had been an unusually large influx of shady figures from the Hamburg crime scene into Costa Rica. Their local liaison man turned out to be Mauricio.

Big Bela Rabelbauer was another close friend of Felix. He was an Austrian lawyer-businessman who would come to be known as the "man with the suitcase," the key figure in a political corruption affair. Big Bela had been recruited as an "economics advisor" by Tico president Figueres. He was on minister of Foreign Affairs Gonzalo J. Facio Segreda's staff for an official visit to Persia, in 1975. Facio was a very influential Tico lawyer who had both Robert Vesco and Felix Przedborski for friends and clients. This suggested that Felix was involved in Vesco's cocaine operations, as would indeed be confirmed later.

Rabelbauer had found his way into the diplomatic milieu of Costa Rica. In fact he was Felix's predecessor as the Tico representative at the IAEA in Vienna. He was born and raised in Voralsberg, Switzerland, in a Catholic family with Hungarian roots. As a boy he went to school in Hollabrun, just across the Austrian border. One of his teachers was Hans Hermann Groer, who was to become the archbishop of Vienna. However, Groer, a proven pedophile, would soon fall out of grace with the Vatican.

At the age of sixteen young Bela was already on the run from the police. Between 1957 and 1964 he was convicted four times for fraud. He managed to stay out of prison by moving to Switzerland. There he used to pose as a director of Radio Vatican, driving around in a black limousine featuring Vatican banners. This set the stage for some remarkable scams. Before long the Swiss authorities ordered him to leave the country, back to Austria. This did not stop him from worming his way into the Vatican. He would have fifty kilos of caviar delivered to the Pope on a regular base. "Dear Bela, cordial greetings from the Holy Father. The caviar was of excellent quality as usual" was one of many messages he received from Rome.

Caviar was by no means the only base of Rabelbauer's friendship with the Pontiff. The Vatican held ten percent of the shares of Bela's company Teston Finanz, which made exceptional profits by selling German bonds, legally available to German citizens exclusively. Bela had figured out a way to sell these titles to his international clientèle. The demand for the rock solid German bonds was huge. Teston made a killing. The financial guru at the Vatican in those days was the infamous Archbishop [Paul] Marcinkus, director of the Vatican bank. He got caught up in the Banco Ambrosiano scandal which culminated in the murder by hanging of Ambrosiano banker [Roberto] Calvi in London. The affair laid bare the Vatican connections with the Italian mafia; the Italian Lodge P2 and its leader Licio Gelli; and the Latin American death squads. Links with the Belgian Roman Catholic elite were not hard to find either. Kredietbank of Belgium and its holding Almany, both staunch Catholic institutions where lots of "old money" was stacked, were major shareholders of the Vatican bank Ambrosiano.

Like the Vatican, the Belgian noblesse had always been a supporter of the fascist movement that they hoped would shield them against the communist threat. What had happened in Belgium in the run-up to WWII mirrored the events in France. Fascism and Nazism had been welcomed in by the industrialists and their bankers. They embraced fascism because it promised to be the cure for the depression of the 1920s and 30s. At the same time it would eliminate evil Marxism that preached the abolition of private property and religion. Mussolini, whose rise to power had been heavily sponsored by J.P. Morgan, was portrayed as the hero who had led Italy out of the economic morass.

SYMPATHY FOR THE DEVIL

In the 1930s both Hitler and the "Duce" were hugely popular throughout the Western hemisphere, from Brussels to Washington. Hitler, who had the full support of the Vatican and Wall Street, made the cover of *Time* magazine as "Man of the Year" in 1938. The dictatorial fascist system guaranteed high profits for the upper class in times of recession by crushing the workers' wages. Leftist unions were outlawed, strikes illegal. And so it was that the clique of bankers and captains of the coal and steel industry of Northern France – later called the Vichy government – had colluded with the German Ruhr industrialists since the late 1920s to bring about the longed for French-German synergy. Belgian industrialists and bankers were in on the deal. The German invasion of 1940 was greeted with enthusiasm and sparkling champagne in red velvet salons from Brussels to Bordeaux. German General Walther von Reichenau declared *"We have not conquered France. The country was handed to us."* That summed it up quite nicely.

So there you had it. A convenient convergence of interests had brought together Big Business, the Vatican and the fascists. Many high-level Catholic aristocrats throughout Europe, nostalgic for the glorious days of Charlemagne, were dreaming of a new empire under the flag of the Vatican. They too joined forces with this alliance of opportunity. Nearly eight centuries earlier they had fought the Moors and saved Europe from these "barbaric heathens" in bloody battles. Now they were prepared to safeguard Western Catholic values and mount a new crusade against communism. One of the last remaining members of the old Hapsburg dynasty, Otto von Hapsburg, had taken it upon him to lead this battle. In essence this new European Catholic empire really looked a lot like Hitler's Thousand Year Reich. In turn these "Europeanists" joined the fascist endeavors. The military, the intelligence services, organized crime and thousands of useful idiots would be the tools used by the elites to make it all come true. Before, during *and after* the war.

PONTIFICAL CONTACTS

Felix was presumably introduced in the highest Roman circles by Rabelbauer. Things turned for the best when Polish cardinal "Woityla" was appointed to the highest office in the Holy See. The Vatican timing was excellent. At the start of the 1980s the Solidarność rebellion in the Polish port of Gdansk promised to be a great opportunity to undermine Soviet power. The new Polish Pope John Paul II supported the uprising wholeheartedly. Felix visited Woityla in Rome. They had their picture taken together. Felix cherished the picture like a big-game hunting trophy. It served him well. People who visited Felix came away convinced that he was a very powerful man who could call the Vatican or the White House any time of day or night.

Rabelbauer had a similar Papal picture. German magazine *Der Spiegel* published it in 1976 after the German bonds scandal had erupted. The article made it clear that Big Bela was very close with the archbishop Giovanni Benelli, the most powerful man in the Vatican next to the Pope..

CHAPTER 2

JEWISH DOUBLECROSS

ANOTHER DEAD MINISTER

The investigations triggered by the Cools murder opened not one but several cans of worms. Cools was involved in the Agusta helicopter bribery scandal that would lead to the resignation in 1995 of NATO Secretary General Willy Claes, a Belgian socialist ex-minister and close friend and colleague of André Cools. It became known that the Socialist Party had been bribed by the Italian company to decide in favor of their Bell-type attack helicopters as a replacement for the outdated Alouette of the Belgian Army. However, part of the money apparently ended up in the wrong hands – the Jewish Connection – which infuriated André Cools. He threatened to spill the beans and reveal some secrets "that would turn the kingdom on its head." He was silenced quickly and permanently. Two Tunisian hired killers were arrested. They soon confessed and were convicted for murder in their home country. Had they known their target was a top politician, they would have refused the job. They were told that Cools was a big-time drugs dealer. To be honest, he looked like one. The arrest of the two left open the question of who contracted them.

The investigation focused on socialist minister [Alain] Van der Biest, Cools' competitor for power in the Liège area. To the amazement of the public, the police discovered that his ministerial cabinet was actually being run by Italian mafiosi who were dealing in stolen bonds. Van der Biest denied the murder accusations. Obviously the poor guy had been steam-rolled by his corrupt entourage. The affair escalated. Cars went up in flames, shots were fired ... The "Ardent City of Liège" had turned into "Palermo on the Meuse." Van der Biest could not handle the heavy burden of the charges against him. He started drinking heavily and became depressed. He killed himself in March of 2002.

The justice department now turned on the mafiosi who had hijacked the minister's cabinet. They were blamed for the Cools murder, but the mystery of who really was behind it remained.

IRAN-CONTRA

What was Cools about to reveal? One could only guess. At least half a dozen hot issues came to mind, one of which was the Iran-Contra affair that had left its marks on Belgium. The illegal arms deliveries to Teh-ran via Tel Aviv had started in Belgium in the early 1980s. Phased-out Bel-gian Air Force J-79 fighter jet engines were sold to Israel. From Tel Aviv the engines were shipped to Iran as spare parts for the Iranian Air Force F-4 jets. The airport of Liège was at the center of the arms shipments. Cools was known to watch "his airport" like a hawk. He must have known.

The direct cause for Cools' rage appeared to be the fact that he and his party had been double crossed. The bonds handed to him in the Agusta deal had turned out to be worthless. Who had made the switch? All agreed that Cools had not acted out of self interest. He used to be a socialist of the old school, a hard-headed activist union man who had supported the miners and steelworkers of the Liège coal belt in the 1960s and 70s. He had grown up among hard-working men and their families. His father had perished in a Nazi concentration camp. And yet Cools had become very powerful. He had obviously been in the process of building his own little empire in an attempt to bypass the establishment. One of his preoccupa-tions was the high price of drinking water in the Liège area. He was trying to circumvent the existing monopolistic providers. And he was running his own private intelligence service, keeping files on many important fig-ures. Cools' ambition, projects and methods worried many of his friends even inside the SP.

THE JEWISH DOUBLECROSS

The Agusta investigation in turn opened several other Pandora's boxes. One of which could be labeled "the Jewish Connection." It became clear that a middleman by the name of Leon Deferm had presented him-self to discretely funnel the Agusta millions into the coffers of the Social-ist Party. Deferm's proposal really sounded too good to be true. Yet the socialists fell for it. Here's how it went.

It just so happened that the American Unisys computer company near Liège was planning to close its doors. Hundreds of jobs were about to be lost. This of course was a big concern to the local unions. Deferm, a rich businessman, stepped forward to offer a solution. He promised to hire the laid-off Unisys workers for his new IT-venture Trident. The deal was sweetened by the fact that Trident offered to discretely funnel the Agusta bribes to the Socialist Party. The SP hoped to kill two birds with one stone. The jobs would be saved and the Agusta millions silently trans-ferred into socialist hands. But then, of course, after the deal had been signed and the money had been paid, Trident never materialized. The jobs, as well as the money, were lost. The Agusta millions and Deferm re-surfaced in Costa Rica shortly thereafter. This Central American country obviously found itself right at the center of the whole affair.

George Cywie, the lobbyist who originally had set in motion the Agusta deal with the Belgian SP-dominated government now found himself in the line of fire. Cywie's wife was Jewish. He had become a "friend of Israel" who had successfully lobbied the Belgian institutions in favor of the Israeli Elbit and Israeli Aircraft Industries companies. It was obvious that Cywie was in cahoots with Deferm.

Who was Deferm really working for? He was certainly involved with "Don Felix" Przedborski, the Belgian-Tico dual nationality businessman of Jewish-Polish descent who was the main figure of interest of the ATLAS Report. Deferm was found to be involved in the gigantic Italian-Swiss SA-SEA fraud, in which billions of francs had found their way into the coffers of the Italian Socialist Party of Bettino Craxi in the 1970s. The scandal involved the infamous financial magicians [Florio] Fiorini and [Giancarlo] Parretti, the Italian national oil company ENI, the Vatican, Banco Ambrosiano, Opus Dei and the Lodge P2. The SASEA affair mirrored the gigantic "sniffer-planes" fraud in France that left a huge crater in the balance of the national oil giant ELF.

THE SASEA SCAM

The bribing of the socialist parties in Europe was financed by at least three massive frauds that generated billions of dollars in the 1970s. There had been the 1969 Matesa state subsidy affair in Spain that had exposed the nefarious preponderance of Opus Dei in Franco's government. In France, the Matesa scam was topped in the 1970s by the absurd but well documented case of the so-called "Sniffer Planes." It involved president Giscard d'Estaing, prominent sympathizer of Opus Dei and ex-finance minister under de Gaulle.

It all started when the "crazy Italian professor" [Aldo] Bonassoli claimed to have invented a device that was able to detect petroleum trapped within the geological layers of the earth. Bonassoli's contraption was mounted on a DC-3 aircraft overflying France, the Channel, the Mediterranean and even Central-Africa. The French president had pushed the national oil giant ELF to finance the expedition. The ELF-engineers were skeptical but went along anyway. The president had insisted that "even if there is only one chance in a thousand that this works, we need to get in on it."

Bonassoli threatened to sell his system to the Americans in case the French cut off their funding. The fake professor sweetened the deal by confirming that his apparatus could also detect uranium deposits and even submerged nuclear vessels. This made the whole affair "top secret defense," a convenient state of affairs. Long story short, Bonassoli turned out to be a talented charlatan who had fooled both the believers and the skeptics into spending billions of francs. *Or so the official story goes.* Had

Bonassoli really been at the origin of the fraud or had his invention been used by the president's entourage as a pretense to bleed a few billions off the ELF state company? The question would remain unanswered. It was assumed that part of the money had found its way to the Vatican. Even Mitterrand, Giscard's opponent and 1981 successor, had initially kept silent about the giant scam, until some overzealous civil servant discovered the huge deficit in ELF's annual accounts. Mitterrand and his party had probably raked in part of the loot, as a pay-off for the Socialist Party's swing to the right, definitely cementing the SP's allegiance to the postwar Atlantic ruling class.

In Italy and Switzerland, the SASEA fraud topped both the Matesa and the Sniffer Planes scams. As the story broke in 1992 the fraudulent SASEA bankruptcy was the largest ever recorded in the Helvetic State. Thousands of investors had been duped by the seemingly infallible SASEA investment strategy. The Italian national oil company ENI was deeply involved. The SASEA tentacles stretched out all the way to the Vatican and the P2 Lodge. The SASEA company itself had been under Vatican control until its acquisition by Florio Fiorini, who had started his career in the ENI oil company, and his partner Giancarlo Parretti. The SASEA company was acquired via Parretti's Interpart holding. Oddly, Interpart had just recently bought an important stake in Thai Present Co., a company founded in Thailand by a Belgian citizen by the name of Antoine V. On paper, Thai Present produced tin trinkets for the tourist industry. In reality it was smuggling drugs. Interestingly, one of the stakeholders in SASEA was the Cortaillod Group, part of the French Alcatel-Alsthom concern, a recent spin-off of the old American-German-French cluster GE-AEG-CGE. Swiss top-politician Yann Richter, member of the board of Cortaillod, was one of the managers of SASEA. Richter was only small fry next to the billionaire stakeholders Paul Kahane, Baron [Hans Heinrich] Thyssen-Bornemisza, Fentener Van Vlissingen and Pehr Gyllenhammer.

The affair had more than one link to Belgium. Leon Deferm, involved in the Agusta bribery scam, was doing business with SASEA, in particular in a Bruges hotel real estate project that had turned sour. The project mirrored that of the Brussels "Black Tower" in which "the Insider" Michel Verdeyen wast involved. More about the Insider later. A series of straw companies had been founded by Deferm's attorney in order to mask the connection between the two projects.

Also involved here were Jewish "businessman" Abraham Shavit of the ASCO arms company and the Antwerp Red Maffiya's M&S International company. The link to the Maffiya cluster also became visible in the connection between the Belgian bank Caisse Privée and its Swiss affiliate Banque d'Investissements Privés (BIP). Both were involved in the Comuele bankruptcy that was briefly sketched in the ATLAS Report, involving the

Red Maffiya. Caisse Privée was sometimes dubbed the "private bank" of Belgian ex-premier Paul Vanden Boeynants, better known as "VDB," and his Brussels entourage. VDB, right-wing figurehead of the Christian PSC party, was suspected of importing drugs in frozen meat from Beirut, via Malta.

The director of BIP was the prestigious Swiss attorney Robert Turrettini of the Poncet & Turrettini law firm. Adnan Kashoggi and Saudi Prince Turki were two of his most prominent clients. Turrettini's associate Dominique Poncet, a brilliant lawyer, was one of the pillars of the modern Swiss judicial system. He had successfully defended Bernie Cornfeld in the mid-1970s, when Bernie lost control of his IOS investment fund to Robert Vesco. Another remarkable client of maître Poncet was the SASEA company itself. No surprise here. Charles Poncet, Dominique's brother, was one of the SASEA managers.

SASEA director Fiorini at one point had set his sights on the Belgian Group Brussels Lambert. He had the good fortune of being offered a big stake in GBL by Lefebvre d'Ovidio, who had bought the shares from his father-in-law, the Belgian baron Cardon de Lichtbuer. The baron was quite startled when he found out that his son-in-law had sold out behind his back to a less than respectable fund. It was quite embarrassing to see Fiorini move close to acquiring a majority stake in GBL, one of Belgium's crown jewels. Bank Lambert was represented on Wall Street by Drexel Burnham Lambert, who was making billions in the Jewish junk bond scam. Drexel & Co., was a late nineteenth-century offspring of the House of Morgan. The Belgian Rothschild-related Lambert family had entered the Drexel orbit when Drexel merged with Dean Witter in 1976. At that time Dean Witter was controlled by the Lamberts. It was Burnham who had convinced Lambert to invest 20-million dollars in Michael Milken's junk-bond venture, which proved to be very profitable while it lasted.

And then of course there was the link between the SASEA bonds swindle and Winnie Kollbrunner, mentioned in the ATLAS Report, and the role of Kredietbank, Almanij and Karfinco in the financing of the Socialist Parties of Italy, France, Luxemburg and Belgium, (Appendix 7). Winnie Kollbrunner reportedly was the mistress of both Leon Deferm and Felix's Przedborski, the "spider in the Nebula web."

After his arrest in the wake of the SASEA collapse, Karfinco boss Pacini Battaglia had stated that the Medellin gang, via the Madonia clan, was the main source of the money influx. So there you had it. In essence Battaglia admitted having bought off the Socialists and other parties with funds originating from grand scale Central-American drug money laundering operations. At the time, the Madonia family appeared to have acquired the "master franchise" for the distribution of Medellin cocaine in Europe. The involvement of Don Felix in the SASEA fraud seemed to suggest that he might also have been part of the cocaine operations in Europe. He was accused by Belgian MP Van Rossem of running drugs inside the cargo space of Central-American banana carriers.

According to Battaglia, the Medellin money was initially deposited in the Oficina de Cambio Internacional account at Edmond Safra's Swiss Trade Development Bank in Geneva. Safra was one of the characters named in the ATLAS Report. Battaglia was responsible for handing out the millions to the Italian political parties. Mostly in cash! This job was taken care of by the financial courier service company Finanziaria Mobiliare (Fimo), who worked for Safra as well. As Fimo became more and more involved in banking but was denied a banking license, it had forged an alliance with Albis Bank. Over time Fimo and Albis "had become like twins." Incidentally, Winnie Kollbrunner too had been doing business with Albi. Had she been on the Fimo-team of "spalloni" or top-notch smugglers?

Interestingly, the Fimo and Albis twins proved to be shareholders of Belgian companies Cofibel and PB Finance, both of the Empain-Schneider group. As the SASEA bubble burst, Fimo was subpoenaed in Belgium. In 1993 Cofibel-boss Didier Pineau-Valencienne, one of France's most revered captains of industry, even landed behind bars in Belgium for a few days, which caused an outrage in his home country. Pineau-Valencienne was yet another name mentioned in the ATLAS Report. A few years before the outbreak of the Fimo scandal, the Albis bank had already been under investigation by the Swiss authorities for its involvement in the Magharian brothers' giant money laundering scheme on behalf of the Colombian drug cartel. The 1988 Swiss Magharian dossier had left no doubt about the involvement of Edmond Safra's Trade Development Bank.

DANDOLO

In his 1991 report on organized crime in Belgium, state prosecutor [Jean-Francois] Godbille stated that there existed a major connection between the local criminal gangs, Italy and the Banco Ambrosiano, the biggest Italian private bank. After the Ambrosiano crash and the "suicide" of banker Roberto Calvi in London, a scandal of epic proportions had engulfed criminal Vatican actors like American bishop Paul Marcinkus and mafia banker Michele Sindona. The latter, a business partner of Continental Illinois of Chicago, was on the board of the Italian subsidiaries of several American companies. The Vatican, because of its freedom from national currency regulations, was seen as a key relay for the interests of the growing new-style money economy propagated by the Wall Street cartel. According to Kees Van Der Pijl in his book *The Making of an Atlantic Ruling Class*, Marcinkus was parachuted into the Vatican to get its financial operations aligned with those of the "Atlantic establishment" that had emerged after WWII. It is safe to say that this new "Ruling Class" coincides to a great extent with the "Absolute Power" structure sketched in the "ATLAS Report."

As the new Vatican structure and its new aggressive partners ventured into the realm of international financial speculation, they soon linked up with the powerful P2 Lodge, directed by Licio Gelli. This criminal alliance, according to Van Der Pijl, marked the start of the "Strategy of Tension" that aimed at forcing the Atlantic financial hegemony on Italy. That is just a polite way of saying that the Wall Street cartel was behind the bloodshed throughout Europe in the 1960s, 70s and 80s. Interestingly, Van Der Pijl does not cite anti-communism or any other ideological motivation behind the Strategy of Tension in Europe. In his view, its sole motivation was the imposition by all means of a new global financial hegemony. The struggle against the Soviet enemy provided the perfect cover as well as the pressing incentive to mobilize the fascist elements in society. In other words, citing General Smedley Butler, the Cold War, as any other war before or after, was just a racket.

In his report, Godbille accused a Swiss-Belgian citizen by the name of Gherardi Dandolo, a self declared descendant of the Venetian Doges, of having imported mafia practices in Belgium. His link with Banco Ambrosiano was obvious. His wife Dominique Gherardi was a shareholder of Pacini Battaglia's Karfinco bank. Dandolo was involved in the bankruptcy of the CCF bank, where documented mafiosi like Carmelo Bongiorno and Albert Faccenda had opened accounts. Black Baron [Benoît de] Bonvoisin was a CCF client as well. The CCF débâcle was directly connected to those of Caisse Privée and Comuele, named in the ATLAS Report. CCF was considered to be the conduit of Richard Van Wijck for the sponsoring of ultra-right action groups in Belgium. Van Wijck, who had been a millionaire shareholder of Unilever, ended up flat broke.

UNILEVER

If there was one company worth adding to the ATLAS-list of "Absolute Power" corporations, it was certainly Unilever. This multinational of Dutch-British origin was an early and avid subscriber to the concept of "Atlantic Unity" that was strongly promoted in Europe at the start of the 1950s. Nelson Rockefeller, for one, was a strong supporter of the Atlantic Unity project. It was Unilever, in association with the CIA, that sponsored the very first Bilderberg conference in Holland in May 1954. Its purpose was to reconcile opposing European and American standpoints on communism, the European defense community and the future economic policy. The initiative could count on the royal support of German-born Prince Bernhard of the

Netherlands, who had been an SS-officer and member of the NSDAP party. The conference was intended to be a testing ground for the plans and projects of the new Atlantic elites. It proved to be a huge success.

Oddly, the Van Wijck-Unilever connection suggested a link to a bizarre and secret episode of Belgian history: the vanishing of the Coetermans empire. By the end of the nineteenth century, Louis Coetermans, an Antwerp diamond tycoon, was considered one of the richest people in the world. He employed thousands of workers in the diamond cutting business. He had invested heavily in railroads and shipping lines from Rio de Janeiro to Shanghai. The Shah of Persia was a regular customer and visitor of the Coetermans residence in Antwerp. Coetermans, nicknamed "Prince Diamond" by the grateful citizens of Antwerp, was appointed Persian general consul to Belgium. When it came to trading African diamonds, Coetermans was the only real competitor of the early Rothschild-De Beers cartel. Around the turn of the century, the German Kaiser appointed the Coetermans company as the sole distributor of South-West African diamonds. At the time, Germany was still a colonial empire. Coetermans imperial Berlin channel entered into fierce competition with the Rothschild channel based in the City.

Coetermans was on excellent terms with the Persian government. This proved very helpful in pushing the Kaiser's negotiations with the Shah over the construction of the strategic Berlin-Baghdad railroad. This project was a thorn in the side of the London channel as it would allow direct German access to the rich Persian oilfields, bypassing the British-controlled Suez canal.

In 1918 Germany lost the war, and all of its colonies. Consequently, Coetermans lost his battle against De Beers. At the time of his death in 1925, Coetermans was still unmarried. After his passing away, two things happened. First, the entire Coetermans fortune "vanished." Second, the Coetermans name was meticulously removed from all national and local official documents, registers and archives. It was as if he had never existed. Thus history was re-written in order to obfuscate the largest theft in Belgian history. This could not have happened without the complicity of the Christian Democratic government, probably in association with some Anglo-American financial heavyweights. What does this have to do with the Unilever story?

The Unilever company was the result of the 1930 fusion of the Dutch Margarine Unie and the British Lever Brothers soap factory. Elisabeth Jürgens, heiress to one of the Dutch founders, had married Richard Stephan Van Wijck, the father of the less fortunate Richard. Coetermans' sister Adriana had married Edmond Michaux, who became one of Coetermans' trustees. Michaux may have been involved in the looting of the Coetermans empire. After his death in 1945, Adriana unexpectedly turned out to be the owner of a very large number of Unilever shares, that had never shown up in her husband's official legacy. Why had Michaux kept silent about the Unilever shares?

According to Adriana the shares had been just "a gift from her husband." Had Michaux secretly invested some of the stolen millions in the Unilever start-up? It certainly looked like it. Their Unilever investment linked Edmond and Adriana Michaux, both upright Catholics and loyal Kredietbank clients, to Van Wijck senior. Van Wijck senior and junior probably knew the truth about Michaux and the Coetermans scam. In 1948 Van Wijck first surfaced in the Bufa holding, a financial cluster linked to Kredietbank, Homberg-Lazard, City Bank of New York and Barclays Bank. Guy Mercier, legal heir to the Coetermans family fortune, entered the Bufa board of managers in February of 1978. Was that part of the deal to ensure Mercier kept silent about the whole matter?

Guy Mercier, a descendant of Louis Coetermans' sister Adriana, was one of the third generation heirs. Apparently, Guy Mercier was never short of cash. His nephew Vincent Mercier, who spent years of his life searching for the truth about Coetermans' death and legacy, suspected his uncle of having been bought by the same clique that had stolen the Coetermans fortune. Guy Mercier had always refused to talk to his nephew about what really happened back in 1925. It wasn't hard to imagine that Van Wijck and Mercier, by financing the ultra-right forces in Belgium in the 1970s, had furthered the agenda of the same "Atlantic financial order" that had stolen the Coetermans billions.

It looked like Bufa's and Van Wijck's sponsoring of the ultra-rightists was the continuation of Unilever's pro-Atlantic policy. It was Van Wijck who in 1969 had financed the start-up of the elite Atlanticist "Cercle des Nations" club, a kind of Bilderberg on the national level, where politicians, businessmen and high-ranking military gathered over a cup of tea.

Bufa was part of the Sodefina holding of Belgian Count Hervé d'Ursel, who had been a business partner of Don Felix since 1970. Bufa was accused of shipping truckloads of black cash out of the country. In 1980 count d'Ursel landed behind bars on account of money laundering and the financing of radical rightist groups. Upon which Bufa was acquired by Continental Food, a Unilever satellite!

Van Wijck's right hand in the CCF bank was Gherardi Dandolo, who would later be accused by judge Godbille of having "imported mafia practices" in Belgium. One of the banks that held a stake in CCF was the Banque Copine that proved to be involved in the preparations for a putsch in Belgium in 1973 and 1981. It's director, Leon Finné, was murdered in one of the Brabant Killers' raids.

Next to Bongiorno and Faccenda, French gangster boss and drug smuggler "Bruno" Farcy owned a bank account at CCF. Farcy was "special" in that he was obviously being protected at a very high level. His Dutch partner Henk Rommy, aka the Black Cobra, enjoyed a similar privilege in Holland. Both were working for a CIA/DEA-protected drug ring that also included a select group of Belgian policemen.

Albert Faccenda, who was employed by Dandolo, was involved in drug trafficking as well. In august of 1984, Faccenda was found suicided in his office at the Royal Belgian Boxing Union near Brussels. He was earmarked to be the next president of the European Boxing Union. His prospects were excellent. Then why the suicide? About a year earlier – in September of 1983 – a commando of Brabant Killers had raided the Wittock factory in Temse, stealing the prototypes of bulletproof Kevlar jackets. In an act of seemingly needless brutality, the raiders had killed the concierge. An insider of the Boxing Union became convinced that the concierge, a professional boxer, was killed because he had recognized some of the intruders, professional boxers themselves. Had Faccenda found out about the criminal escapade of his acolytes?

Very few people had known about the existence and the location of the prototype jackets. Only the Army and the Gendarmerie had been informed and had conducted some limited tests. Again, the Gendarmerie became suspected of having organized and led the deadly raid. Martial Lekeu, the ex-gendarme who, fearing for his life, fled to the USA in 1984, admitted to having been involved but insisted time and again that "he had no blood on his hands." Lekeu also confirmed that there had been plans for a coup in Belgium. Had the top-putschists given the order for the theft of the jackets that they hoped would save their lives when push came to shove? One could only speculate. As for the unfortunate concierge, he appeared to have been "in the wrong place at the wrong time."

As we will examine later on, Dandolo was also one of the key figures in the Unilabs success story that began after the Biorim laboratories had fallen into the hands of Jewish businessman Edgar Zwirn. The acquisition was preceded by the brutal 1983 murder of Baron Paul Cams in his Brussels villa. Cams was suspected of having made a fortune processing drugs. Swiss top-lawyer and Augusto Pinochet-sympathiser Pierre Schifferli, president of the WACL in Switzerland, was one of the Unilabs board members. Coincidently, Schifferli was the mentor of young Daniel Przedborski after he had concluded his law studies at the Brussels university. Obviously, Dandolo had been doing business right on the intersection of plain mafia criminality, drug-running and "Strategy of Tension" tactics; and of the high-level financial fraud that supplied the money to keep the European political class in line with the interests of the Atlantic financial cartel.

PICTET

The bank "Caisse Privée," as we have seen, was at the center of the CCF-Comuele bankruptcy that involved the Antwerp Connection of the Red Maffiya. According to the ATLAS Report it was real estate agent [Bruno] Goldberger who had introduced Red Maffiya boss Mike Brandwain to the Comuele company. Brandwain was a stakeholder in the Nayfeld brothers' M&S International company. Brandwain was on excellent terms with godfather Semion Mogilevitch. Goldberger had first been introduced to "the Russians" by Belgium-born millionaire Maurice Tempelsman, friend and advisor of President [Joseph] Mobutu of Congo.

Tempelsman had made a fortune in the African diamond trade. He was on excellent terms with the De Beers cartel as well as with the CIA. Tempelsman had met CIA station chief Larry Devlin in Congo as the country was in transit to independence from its Belgian colonizers in 1961. Devlin reportedly had refused to kill the newly elected "leftist" Patrice Lumumba, who, according to Washington, was going to turn the Congo into a "new Cuba." With the assistance of the Belgian military Lumumba was killed anyway, giving way to US backed Mobutu. Lumumba, dubbed the "Martin Luther King of Africa," was shot and his body dissolved in acid for fear that his grave would attract thousands of disgruntled black pilgrims. The murder was sanctioned by the Belgian king Baudouin. Lumumba, in his inauguration speech, had told the baffled king in no uncertain terms that he was not going to play the pseudo-independence game and sell out his country to the American corporations. Lumumba, instantly being labeled a Marxist, had signed his own death sentence. Devlin had later resigned his CIA post to join Tempelsman in the African diamond business.

The fact that Tempelsman was involved with Comuele came as no surprise. The roots of the company could be found in Belgium's colonial past. Its original name had been Société Commerciale et Minière de l'Uele. Uele being a rich province of the Congo. The company had been founded in 1919 in Brussels by the Lever brothers, who would later join forces with the Dutch Margarine Unie company, giving birth to Unilever. Tempelsman had a lot of experience in the African mining industry. He was no doubt familiar with the operations of Union Minère and Comuele in the Congo. By the time M&S International formed an alliance with the ex-colonial company, Comuele had shriveled to an empty shell owned by [Arthur] Fogel and Goldberger. M&S was working on a deal with the Russian Lada company for the development of a giant real estate project in Togliatti, Russia. Goldberger had started negotiations with the Russian Maffiya to get the project funded. He had been introduced to Maffiya bosses like Anton Malewski by his father-in-law, the Jewish diamond trader Itsu Kaszirer, who had excellent contacts with the Mogilevitch milieu in Prague.

In the 1970s, Caisse Privée was very close to defense minister VDB and to the right wing of his Christian Democrat party. The bank managed part of VDB's considerable fortune. The bank's founders, directors and clients were members of the Belgian financial elites, the noblesse and in some cases even of the Royal Court. VDB's legal problems had started after a house-search at the Caisse Privée in 1983. "The Crocodile," as VDB was called, would have to face 190 charges of fiscal fraud.

One of the founders and director of the bank was the esquire Jean Cruysmans, one of the Crocodile's intimate friends who had been involved in the latter's Brussels real estate ventures. Cruysmans and his son appeared to have a sexually inspired predilection for young male criminals, who they recruited as money couriers. This is how a violent gang, that would later be dubbed the "Haemers gang," first got involved in "banking operations." The youngsters were tasked with smuggling large amounts of cash to Andorra, Jersey and Switzerland. Some of that black cash came out of Baron Paul Cam's Biorim laboratory operations. The young criminals would soon find out that they were being protected at a very high level. Obviously, their boss was in a position to pull some strings on the Brussels upper class. And so they started a business of their own, blowing to bits armored money vans, including the security guards on board.

Whenever they were tasked with a money trip down to Switzerland, their destination was the Banque Pictet & Cie in Geneva. Cruysmans happened to be one of the directors of the Pictet bank. Pictet wasn't exactly what you would call the average private bank. It had been founded in 1805 in the Helvetic canton of Geneva, which at the time was occupied by Napoleon's troops. Pictet had been founded by De Candolle and Mallet.

Five years earlier, the same Jacques-Henry Mallet had been instrumental in the founding of the Banque de France that pulled Napoleon's strings. Albert and Jacques Mallet, two of his descendants, would be appointed vice-presidents of the Compagnie Générale des Eaux (CGE) around the turn of the 20th century. The Mallet dynasty had clearly gravitated toward the Rothschild banking cluster. By 1855 Pictet was advocating the founding of a Swiss central bank, funded with private capital. Around 1840 the bank's signboard was changed to Turrettini & Pictet. Charles and Alphonse Turrettini, who sat on the bank's board at the time, were the ancestors of Robert Turrettini, head of the Banque d'Investissements Prives (BIP), the Swiss subsidiary of Caisse Privée. Two of the most intriguing clients of the Turrettini cabinet were the Kashogi brothers and Saudi prince Turki. In the early 1980s Pictet was instrumental in the Guinness stock price manipulation that facilitated the takeover of the much larger Distillers Company. The bank called in the expertise of the Jewish Connection. Menashem Riklis, ex-associate of Bernie Cornfeld; Ivan Boesky, the junk-bond king; and the Bank Leu, had all joined the party.

FRIENDS FROM THE EAST

In the years before his death, André Cools had had several meetings with "friends from the East," among them ex-KGB agents. Was he looking for sponsors in Moscow to finance his projects in order to be able to by-pass the banking establishment? It surely looked like it. The liaison service between Liège and the East had been set up by the Uhoda clan of Liège. The Uhoda brothers had made a remarkable, meteoric ascent in the murky business milieu of Liège. After the meltdown of the Soviet Union they apparently had started acting as liaisons for the Russian tycoon Sergueï Mikhailov, who had left no doubt about his intentions to invest large amounts of money in the Liege area. He had big plans for a casino, which attracted a lot of attention. In Belgium casinos were illegal unless state-controlled. So far no one had succeeded in overcoming that law, be it by lobbying or bribing or both.

On top of that Mikhailov promised some "fat deals" for the renowned arms producer FN Herstal of Liège. FN representatives, escorted by the top dog of the Uhoda clan, showed up at Mikhailov's hotel only a few hours after he had set foot on Belgian soil. The Russian billionaire was acting on behalf of MAB International, a company registered in Antwerp. Interestingly, this company had originally been set up by Semion Mogilevitch, no less! Don Mogilevitch at the time was the godfather of the Red Maffiya. His name figured at the top of the international "most wanted" list. Yet he was traveling unhindered throughout Europe, courtesy of a Belgian diplomat in Paris by the name of Alfred Cahen. Throughout the Cold War, Cahen had been on the record as an outspoken anti-communist. Now he appeared to be pampering these ex-Soviets! Very odd. Or was it?

By the mid-90s, so it seemed, Belgium had become the favorite destination of the new rich from the former Eastern Bloc. For a better understanding of how that had come about, we need to take a closer look at the backgrounds of the leaked 1994 ATLAS police report. (Appendix 1).

Andre Cools

CHAPTER 3

"SIXTEEN TONS, AND WHAT DO YOU GET?"

Andre Cools had grown up in a time of growing social unrest over the decline of the coal mines and the blast furnaces of the dying steel giant Cockerill. These had long been the pride and riches of the Belgian coal belt in the Liege-Charleroi-Mons area.

As the Belgian heavy industry started to go under, the workers and their families were going through hard times. Many of them were sacked. The others had no choice but to accept lower wages that would barely feed their children. These were tough men who would not give in or give up easily. Their union leaders, leftists by definition, were even tougher. They organized the strikes that would drive the coal and steel barons to exasperation. The strikers soon found out which side the government was on. The crowds of workers were met by the Gendarmerie, armed to the teeth. Two people died. This, mind you, was not the nineteenth century. The year was 1961. As a consequence, the socialist workers unions gained the respect of the common people – the voters – to the dismay of the international establishment that would have preferred to do away with unions and strikes altogether.

Since the end of WWII the rise in popularity of the Marxist movements in Europe had angered Big Business, which was essentially American controlled. Europe had basically been annexed by the USA by way of the Marshall Plan. There could be no question of leftist governments in Europe, no matter what. The Pax Americana in Europe resulted in political corruption, false-flag terrorism, rigged elections, coups d'etat and black ops. And, of course, the Cold War offered the perfect excuse for the anti-Marxist operations.

Fascists and Nazi collaborators alike had become friends of America. Washington and Wall Street poured billions into hundreds of extreme right-wing political action groups. Journalists, authors, film-makers and artists of all kinds were recruited to win over the European hearts and minds for the American cause.

The socialist parties would soon face extinction, unless they severed the ties with Moscow, softened their standpoint and reverted to a more moderate form of Marxism. Clearly the way forward for the left was a move towards the center, abandoning their communist comrades who found themselves out in the cold. Short of that, they would never again be allowed to hold any political power. The murder of communist leader Julien Lahaut in 1950, as discussed earlier, left no doubt about the determination of the establishment to eradicate Marxism.

This shift to the right had begun during the war when Belgian socialist minister Paul-Henri Spaak had made a U-turn to please the bankers and top industrialists who literally ran the country while the government remained in exile in London. After the war Spaak had been instrumental in the exclusive sale of uranium from the Congo to the USA. Many old school socialists had felt betrayed by Spaak, who was ultimately rewarded with the position of Secretary General of NATO in 1957.

During the war Belgium was de facto run by a clique of bankers and industrialists who collaborated with the Nazi occupation force, with the blessing of Spaak and of King Leopold III. This non-political war government was headed by Alexandre Galopin who would be murdered in late 1944. Galopin allegedly had made a list of corporate war collaborators, which he had handed down to his grandson Baron Benoit de Bonvoisin, who was suspected of using it for blackmail. Bonvoisin was found to be a sponsor of the ultra-right action groups in Belgium in the 1970s and 80s. His name was all over the Brabant Killings files, but he was never convicted.

Interestingly, Bonvoisin acted as a representative of CGE. In this capacity he had even negotiated with Andre Cools. Bonvoisin felt at home at the CGE Paris headquarters salons, where he discussed important matters over a cup of coffee. One of his guests was Jean Violet, head of the influential Pinay Circle, named after the late Vichy minister and Cagoule member Antoine Pinay. In 1965 Antoine Pinay had been offered an enormous amount of money if he was willing to run for president against de Gaulle, who rejected NATO and the Americanization of Europe. The international Circle membership of high ranking politicians and intelligence agents clearly interlocked with that of the WACL, its Belgian off-spring IEPS, with CEDI, Western Goals and even the Israeli Jonathan Institute.

By the 1980s the tamed socialists were allowed into the power club, while the communist parties had all but vanished from the European political theatre. Andre Cools must not have liked this Faustian pact with the establishment. Still, he grabbed the opportunity to rise to power and to "do his thing."

The 1970s had seen the rise to power of the "new socialists" in Italy, France and Belgium. Cools had joined and supported this "Socialist Internationale." He was on excellent terms with Bettino Craxi, Italian premier and head of the Socialist Party, who indirectly controlled the Italian Agusta helicopter plant. Now that they were allowed to skim off their part of the government deals, it was only natural for the socialists to steer the Belgian military helicopter deal toward Agusta.

DOUBLE-FACED PRESIDENT

In France the socialist shift had not been limited to a mere selling out of the leftist ideals. They had volunteered to help stamp out communism. The case in point was the rise to the French presidency in 1981 of François Mitterrand. His standpoint was that the best firewall against the commies was a strong socialist party that would absorb any leftist sentiments that might yet flare up among the disappointed workers. This added a new twist to the ideological chicanery of the Socialist Internationale. Mitterrand's standpoint fitted the Cold War façade perfectly in that the socialists now turned on their former spiritual brethren. Insider Michel V, whose statements formed the basis for the ATLAS Report, repeatedly stressed the importance of Mitterrand's presidency in the context of the "Absolute Power" structure.

Mitterrand's maneuver was not totally new. In 1947 the French socialist minister Jules Moch had mobilized the Gendarmerie and even the army to crush the massive "communist" strikes in the Marseilles area. Moch had been under heavy pressure from Washington and Wall Street to use any means necessary to put an end to the uprising. The US intelligence services had dispatched American unionists Lovestone and Brown to France to undermine and split the French Marxist labor syndicate. They were successful. Lovestone could count on the full support of David Dubinsky and his Jewish Labor Committee. They had excellent contacts with many Jewish refugee centers across Europe.

Dubinsky was an American immigrant of Polish-Jewish descent who by 1935 was heading the largest workers union of the USA, that of the Jewish textile workers. "DD" Dubinsky had originally joined the Jewish Marxist community in Lower East Manhattan in 1911. As his influence grew, Dubinsky veered to the right to become "the most likable unionist in the USA." He was seen rubbing shoulders with high-flyers of various colors. DD must have made all the right moves. He was even granted membership in Rockefeller's exclusive Council on Foreign Relations! *Incidentally, Dubinsky was one of Felix Przedborski's contacts.*

On 9 December 1947 the Marseilles strikes were called off. The Corsican criminal Guerini clan, who had helped crush the strike, was given carte blanche in the port of Marseilles. It was the beginning of the French Connection that would funnel hundreds of tons of heroin from the Golden Triangle into Europe and the USA. At the time there was an important French military presence in Indochina. As Paris gradually lost its grip on Vietnam, the US would step in and set the country ablaze. With the arrival of the GIs the Golden Triangle opium trade expanded dramatically. "Air America," the CIA opium air cargo operation, had more aircraft in service than Pan Am. There were indications, as we will see later, that Felix was involved in the Golden Triangle Vietnam opium trafficking. (Appendix 2)

Let's return to the Mitterrand case. His offer to use the Socialist Party to get rid of the communists was "unusual," to say the least. But even weirder was the fact that "Tonton," as common Frenchmen used to call him, had a history of right-wing extremism! The French electorate at large hadn't been aware of that until a video recording surfaced showing Mitterrand and his wife at their home, having lunch with René Bousquet.

HOODED KILLERS

At this point the story gets very interesting. Mitterrand's hidden friendship with Bousquet went back a long way, to WWII and the collaborating Vichy regime. Bousquet was known to have been a member of the "Cagoule" – the French word for "hood" – a fascist terror group that was doing the dirty work for the cartel that sought to synergize the heavy industries of Northern France, Belgium and the German Ruhr area. This cartel had sold the country down the river long before the war. This was documented in minute detail by the French historian Annie Lacroix-Riz, who spent over thirty years researching primary sources in French, German and American archives. She proved that a group of bankers and industrialists, called the "Synarchs," had paved the way for Hitler's invasion in 1940. As Lacroix-Riz clearly demonstrates in her book *Le Choix de la Défaite (The Choice of Defeat)*, the Vichy government under Philippe Pétain had been in the making for a long time. General Pétain was the one who was giving the orders to the Cagoule. As a consequence of this treasonous collusion the German conquest of Northern France had been "a walk in the park."

After the war, the existence of the Synarchist movement and the Cagoule was strongly denied. The subject became the big taboo of French recent history. Not only because many of the Synarchs had risen to positions of power after WWII, but also because the evidence of French collaboration also substantiated the claims that the Vichy regime, put in place by the Synarchs, had actively assisted the Germans in decimating the Jewish population.

President de Gaulle, the last great statesman of Europe, who kicked NATO out of his country and fiercely opposed the "colonization" of Europe had known Mitterrand very well. He didn't think highly of him and nicknamed him "arsouille," which translates into "scum" or "arshole." On the subject of Mitterrand and Bousquet, de Gaulle said *"they represent the old ghost of anti-Gaullism, rising from the depths of the collaboration."*

The real story behind the ex-Cagoule president had long remained a carefully veiled mystery.

The only thing the Americans have never forgiven de Gaulle was not the French exit from NATO, but the fact that he had dared challenge the hegemony of the US Dollar.

As the bricks flew in the streets of Paris in the May 1968 student revolt, de Gaulle stood alone, surrounded by enemies. They were the same people who had supported the Vichy regime and its precursors. Daniel Cohn-Bendit, the Jewish figurehead of the student rebellion, was approached by the CIA and offered a huge amount of money, which he now claims he refused. The uncontrollable student violence in the Paris streets and squares was used by the Atlantic ruling class to discredit de Gaulle, who had correctly anticipated that their voracious Atlanticism would render the great French nation obsolete. "In fact," Cohn-Bendit once said, "what we were doing benefited Mitterrand." Forty years later the same Cohn-Bendit would state that "anyone opposing the EU-treaty was mentally ill."

In 1994 François de Grossouvre committed suicide in his office in the Elysée palace. He was said to be "the keeper of the Mitterrand family secrets." Although he had no official function in the government, Grossouvre had his own office inside the palace. After his death, his confidential correspondence with the president, the content of which might have destabilized the French Republic, was nowhere to be found. Many viewed his death as very suspicious.

Mitterrand considered himself the last great president of France. After him, he wrote, all presidents would be mere administrators of the EU. At the conclusion of his 14 years in office, he wrote *"France does not know it, but we are at war with America. It's a permanent war, an economic war. A war without casualties but a war to the death nonetheless. […] Yes the Americans are voracious. They want it all for themselves. They want to control the world."*

Today the history of the French Cagoule is well documented. The taboo has been lifted, the evidence being too strong to maintain it. This group of thugs and flat-out killers formed the lowest of four echelons within the Synarchist organization. At the upper level one found the "ideologues." The second echelon consisted of very wealthy businessmen who bribed their way into politics regardless of the plumage of the government in office. Below them, the technocrats, who qualified themselves as non-political "neutral" experts. Theirs was the task of rationalizing the actions taken by their superiors. On the lowest level, the Cagoule, eliminating opponents and carrying out false-flag attacks.

The Synarchist organization had infiltrated the military, the police, the justice department, the finance department and about all major state institutions. They had prepared a fascist coup in 1936, but the plan failed. The Nazis would finish the job for them in 1940. This type of rightist infiltration very much resembled that of the Italian P2 Lodge in the early 1970s in preparation of the failed Borghese coup. P2 had its own Cagoule that carried out deadly false flag attacks in Italy and even exported its terror tactics to Latin America in the mid-70s. The name of Stefano Delle Chiaie, a confessed P2 terrorist, springs to mind. One of his cronies,

Vincento Vinciguerra, serving a life sentence, explained to the world, on videotape, what the "Strategy of Tension" had been all about.

In Belgium too rumors about an impending coup surfaced at regular intervals in the 1970s and 80s. The investigation into the Brabant Killings in the mid-80s brought to light the far-right infiltration of the Gendarmerie, the military, the judicial institutions and even State Security. In many cases these infiltrators could be linked to the CIA, to various anti-communist cliques such as the WACL, to wartime collaborators and to Big Business.

Was it any wonder that the people of Belgium had started to ask questions about the involvement of the US and the NATO-Gladio in the terror that paralyzed the country in the 1980s? These horrible crimes remain unsolved to this day. That fact alone speaks for a massive cover-up at the highest levels.

As far as the Italian imbroglio was concerned, one name in particular caught the attention: that of Henry Kissinger. Kissinger was suspected of having resuscitated the P2 Freemasons Lodge as an instrument to destabilize Italy and keep the commies out of the government. The widow of Italian premier Aldo Moro, who was building a government of national unity including the CP, pointed her finger at Kissinger as the one responsible for the murder of her husband in 1978. Heinz "Henry" Kissinger, protégé of David Rockefeller, takes us right into the heart of the matter when it comes to "Absolute Power": the Council on Foreign Relations, the Trilateral and the Bilderberg group. They are the global equivalent of the top echelon of the Synarchist power structure.

President of the Bilderberg conferences for many years was Belgian viscount Etienne Davignon, director of Kissinger Associates, member of the CFR and the Trilateral. Davignon's grandfather Julien had been a minister in the Belgian government at the outbreak of the First World War. Etienne Davignon, a staunch catholic with ties to Opus Dei, was the prototype of the impeccable top notch businessman-politician. He had co-founded the European Round Table (ERT) of Industrialists, who feverishly proselytized for the cause of the EU single market and the Euro. The ERT became the most powerful lobby group steering the European commission. The ERT's figureheads, next to Davignon, were Wisse Dekker of Philips; Jean Monod of Lyonnaise des Eaux; and Pehr Gyllenhammer of Volvo.

CHAPTER 4

THE EMPEROR'S NEW BANK

"After 1981 I asked François Mitterrand the following question. 'Now that you have power, why don't you do what you had promised?' His answer was that he did not have the power to confront the World Bank, capitalism or neo-liberalism. That he had inherited a government but not the power. And so I learned that being a government, being a president, doesn't mean much in societies that are subjugated to capitalism."

– Danielle Mitterrand

"ABSOLUTE POWER"

Investigative journalist and Felix-watcher Walter De Bock had always been intrigued by the romance between big money and politics. When he debuted, back in the pre-computer era, he kept notes in his typical, small handwriting. Stacks of them have been archived at the Catholic University of Louvain, one of the oldest universities of Europe. He had shown quite some interest in the American multinationals that had "invaded" Europe, and Belgium in particular, after WWII. He had shown particular interest in General Electric, the mammoth of the energy industry, and its close pre-war links with German banks and with AEG, the German energy giant. (Appendix 3).

One of his charts reads *"Before 1902. MORGAN > General Electric° 1892 > Thomson Houston: International'* and, further down the page: *'SOFINA,' 'Banque de Bruxelles'* and, near the bottom of the chart, *'CIE FRANCAISE Thomson Houston > ALSTHOM.'* On another page, under the heading 'Empain,' he had jotted down: *'Control of the electro-business: Empain-Schneider, Lazard, Morgan, Rothschild, Mirabaud."* Mirabaud was the dominant Protestant bank of the inter-war period.

Why is this relevant? Because the chart shows the interconnection of American, German, French and Belgian interests in the GE energy monopoly before WWII and even before WWI. It also shows the close connection of the utility cartel to the oldest upper levels of financial hegemony, Rothschild and Lazard. The House of Morgan had financed the start-up of GE back in 1892. John Pierpont Morgan was the most successful Rothschild agent on the new continent. GE soon controlled the expanding electricity grid of the entire USA. GE's historical French affiliate, through Thomson Houston, was the Alsthom company that would later morph into the communications giant Alcatel.

This company was named in the ATLAS Report as one of the companies that make up the Absolute Power structure, dubbed "the Nebula." The report says

> Let's not forget that this Nebula controls most of the money transfers worldwide and also controls the highest political authorities. This Nebula could, if so desired, put pressure on most of the important cities worldwide and get control over almost everything (energy supply, water supply, environment), through corruption. This has been going on for several years. Let's not forget that this same Nebula provides the security forces, police and military to several countries, including their equipment (weapons, communications etc..).

The Belgian branch of GE was SOFINA. One of the most extravagant directors of this holding was Danie Heinemann, an engineer who used to work for German AEG, a GE partner. He was GE's man in Belgium for all of WWII. Another prominent SOFINA figure was Arthur Salomonssohn of Disconto Gesellschaft, the biggest German bank by far before it merged with Deutsche bank in 1929.

Disconto Gesellschaft was known to be the Rothschild subsidiary in Frankfurt. Both Heinemann and Salomonssohn were of Jewish descent. This goes to show the interlocking of German-Jewish capital and American big business going back to the start of the 20th century. This Jewish Connection would resurface for all to see in 2002, when Edgar Bronfman became co-director of CGE, that had just changed its name to Vivendi. As we will see, the Bronfman family played a big part in the history of the power cartel.

So there you have it. What the police investigators referred to in their report is a monopolistic corporate giant that controls money flows, energy and water supply and waste disposal. The connections with the Rothschild cartel – the only plausible candidate when it comes to "controlling half of the world economy" – are obvious. Rothschild agents on the American continent were known to be Belmont and Morgan, they in turn financed the Rockefeller oil empire, the Carnegies, the Guggenheims, the Harrimans. They realized from the very start that there was a lot of money to be made by controlling the supply and the price of the basic human needs: water and energy. Add to this the control of the money supply. *"Let's not forget that the Nebula controls most of the money transfers worldwide."* The foundation of the Federal Reserve in 1913 was without any doubt the top achievement of the cartel.

In more recent years the cartel added to its power structure a monopoly position in waste management and in the media-entertainment industry. Ever since the Rothschilds had acquired the Reuters, Wolf and Havas newswires and financed the rise of the New York Times, media control had been at the center of their attention. And, of course, a company capable of engineering the giant power generators that supply energy and light to entire cities can also build jet engines and weapons systems. *"Let's not forget that this same Nebula provides the security forces, police and military to several countries, including their equipment (weapons, communications etc...)"*

When it comes to water supply monopolies, one of the oldest documented cases is that of the French Compagnie Générale des Eaux (General Water Co.) and the Lyonnaise des Eaux (Lyons Water Co.). Both are mentioned in the ATLAS report. This is what Michel V said about them:

> ...this being said, a thorough investigation is required into the roots and the history of the Compagnie Générale des Eaux and all things related to Crédit Lyonnais. There you would find the leads to the absolute power structure and in particular to its instruments that can order assassinations, start wars and terror campaigns, or impose complete silence.

Credit Lyonnais, an early business partner of the banking moguls Lazard and Hottinguer, was heavily involved in the SASEA scandal.

WATER

So let's take a closer look at CGE and its history. The company was founded in 1853 to provide large French cities with drinking water. One of the key figures was Prosper Enfantin, who had co-financed the Suez canal and the French railroads, which were in Rothschild hands. Out of the Suez canal endeavor the GDF Suez company has grown, an energy giant in its own right. In the 1980s the Belgian businessman Etienne Davignon, member of the CFR and the Trilateral and EU-lobbyist, rose to the top of the GDF Suez management.

As an interlude, let's have a brief look at Davignon's career.

Davignon was one of the most powerful people in the European political machine. He was vice-president for the European Commission from 1977 to 1985, where he was in charge of industry, research and energy. In 1982, as Industry Commissioner, Davignon challenged Pehr Gyllenhammer to organize a group of top European businessmen to lobby the European Commission. The latter was the CEO of Volvo who had strong ties to Chase Manhattan, Kissinger Associates, and the Aspen Institute. Gyllenhammer later became managing director of Lazard, vice chairman of Rothschild Europe, and chairman of the Rothschild Pension Funds. Davignon was clearly well introduced in the very highest circles of global finance.

The Gyllenhammer group was to become the highly influential European Round Table of Industrialists (ERT), drawing up policies for Europe. ERT-member Etienne Davignon chaired the working group on Trade and Investment. In 1985, he left the European Commission and joined Société Générale de Belgique. After the French Suez Group took over SGB in 1988, Etienne Davignon became its chairman.

Next to Gyllenhammer and Davignon, Jean Monod of Lyonnaise des Eaux, and Wisse Dekker of the Philips company, were the architects of the early ERT successes. In a Telex message, Wisse Dekker, speaking for the ERT, had threatened the EU to put in place a single market and a single currency, failing which the industrialists' cartel would "take their business elsewhere." By 1990, the ERT had made itself indispensable. It had become an integral part of the EU institution, basically dictating "suitable" legislation to the European technocrats .

Davignon was named "European of the Year 2003" by European Voice, an Economist Group publication focusing on European affairs. Surprisingly, Etienne Davignon also sat on the Board of "Dialogues: Islamic World – U.S. – The West," together with Frank Wisner Jr, stepfather of Nicolas Sarkozy. "Dialogues" was sponsored by the Carnegie Corporation and the Rockefeller Brothers Fund.

CGE was not exactly a charity organization. In 1853 the company was granted, by Imperial Decree, the license to supply water to the city of Lyons. It was the very first water concession worldwide. The city of Lyons was charged seventeen francs per 1000 liters.

In 1854 the city of Nantes abandoned its own water supply project in favor of CGE. By 1860, Paris too had become a CGE client. Remember paragraph 17 of the ATLAS Report: *"This Nebula could, if so desired, put pressure on most of the important cities worldwide and get control over almost everything (energy supply, water supply, environment), through corruption."*

It came as no surprise that CGE could count on the support of the French heads of state. Two of the founders and later directors of the CGE were Mallet and Hottinguer, the famous banker families who had co-founded the Banque de France in the year 1800.

Both had ties to the Rothschilds. Hottinguer senior had been a leading figure in the credit negotiations between Rothschild and the cash-strapped Ottoman Empire. The Imperial Ottoman Bank, in essence the central bank of the Ottoman Empire, had been founded by Mallet, Hottinguer, and by the Rothschild-related banks Bisschoffsheim and A.J. Stern & Co. So Michel V's suggestion to study CGE's past leads us straight to the Rothschild cartel. Come to think of it, who else than the Rothschild cartel qualifies when it comes to "controlling half of the world economy"?

The five Jewish brothers from the Judengasse in Frankfurt initially derived their political and economic power from loans they granted to governments across Europe. They had learned all the tricks of the trade from the Bethmanns and the Hofjuden, the Court Jews. The simple trick that made them rich beyond imagination is called "compound interest." It used to be called "usury." Most religions had banned usury long ago, because it was a recurring cause of misery, unrest and wars. The effect of the rapidly snowballing debt under the weight of the compound interest was often underestimated by the debtor, leading to his ruin. Here is what Einstein said about it: *"Compound interest is the eighth wonder of the world. He who understands it, earns it ... he who doesn't ... pays it."*

In 1830, the new-born state of Belgium was added to the Rothschild target list. James Rothschild from the Paris house wrote to his brothers *"The Belgians are donkeys, we must use their hunger for money to grasp the control of the state finances."* By 1845 they had reached their goal.

The Jewish favorite "donkey"theme resurfaced in a 2010 statement by the late "wise man" Rabbi Ovadiah Yosef. *"Why are gentiles needed?,"* he asked himself. *"They will work, they will plow, they will reap. We will sit like an effendi and eat. That is why gentiles were created. [...] With gentiles, it will be like any person – they need to die, but [God] will give them longevity. Why? Imagine that one's donkey would die, they'd lose their money. This is his servant ... That's why he gets a long life, to work well for this Jew. Gentiles were born only to serve us. Without that, they have no place in the world – only to serve the People of Israel."*

ENTER FREEMASONRY

Having said this, the picture would be incomplete without placing the Rothschilds in the framework of Freemasonry. The Masonic aspect of the conquest of Belgium by the Rothschild clique as explained above is amply illustrated by the many Masonic symbols that can be found on the monuments, buildings and paintings of its capital Brussels. In Belgium, some say, nothing can be accomplished without the fiat of the Masons.

If Masonry was to be sketched in broad strokes, what we would get is the vague picture of a sect that is intent on 'bringing the light to the world'. This 'Enlightenment' is being presented as being 'liberating'. It is said to be liberating in particular from the superstitions of religion, especially from Catholicism, but also from the oppression of the ruthless monarchies. Masonry claims to lead its Brothers out of the darkness of blind superstition into the light of knowledge and truth. The Enlightened Man is his own God, Man is divine. No need for a bad deity that keeps the people in the dark. The source of the Masonic light is Lucifer, the Bearer of Light, the anti-Christ. As Head Mason Albert Pike explained in his writings, the high Masonic degrees above the 30th are engaged in Luciferianism.

The ideals of the French Revolution are transpiring here. Critics of Masonry tell us that the French Revolutionary 'Liberté. Égalité. Fraternité.' is in fact a Masonic slogan. Indeed, it is the motto of the 32nd Degree of the 33 Degree Scottish Rite. It can be explained as having a meaning that is much less 'democratic' than what we have been told. The Masonic meaning of the slogan would be that the Fraternity (Masonry), through the preaching of Equality would attain Liberty of action for its members.

It is clear that the French Revolution that brought Napoleon to power was not a popular, spontaneous uprising as we have been taught. It was a Masonic-Protestant undertaking that had been financed and planned well in advance, directed against the monarchy and the Church. What had followed was not the liberation of the people but a bloodbath.

The Masonic-Protestant constellation that ruled France after the Revolution saw the rise of Protestant banks to become some of the largest banks of the XXth century. It also allowed "Protestant" enterprises like the Lyonnaise des Eaux and Compagnie Générale des Eaux to flourish. The enormous success of the Lyonnaise des Eaux company led to the foundation of the Crédit Lyonnais, the French bank that became involved in several financial scandals of epic proportions.

As we have seen, Napoleon also had to deal with Jewish pressures, which he tried to appease. Masonry cannot be viewed as being free of Jewish influence. Quite the contrary. Masonry is full of Hebrew slogans and Kaballistic symbolism. It often refers to Hiram, Mizraïm, Solomon or Jewish Old Testamental rites. In reality, Freemasonry is a Judaïzing force, as Dr E. Michael Jones pointed out. Indeed, Masons and Jews alike are in combat against Christianity. As are the Protestants. History has shown strange alliances between Protestants and Jews, one example being the banking world and the tolerance of usury, the pernicious use of compound interest. As for Freemasonry itself, according to the official record it was founded by two protestants in England in 1717. This appears to be the origin of what is sometimes called 'speculative' Masonry, as opposed to the much older Guild of the Masons, skilled builders of the most magnificent cathedrals, who knew the secrets of geometry, architecture, Fibonacci and the Golden Ratio.

This new Freemasonry had soon spread its Lodges over England and the continent.

These Lodges initially pretended to be religious in order to avoid abolition. In reality they were atheïst from the start, engaging in esoterism and occultism, hidden behind a façade of charity and humanism. Initiates have to swear to keep the basic secret of the Masons, which, according to the critics, is that there is no secret, only rituals. For the members of the

Rotary and Lions clubs, affiliates of Freemasonry, as for the lower Degree Masons, the real goals of the sect remain hidden. These lower ranks are but the wide-eyed footsoldiers of the Masters who seek to rule the world. They enter Masonry on the prospect of economic gain and career furtherance. Over the years, Freemasonry had infiltrated and 'infested' the world of business and banking, and all the institutions of the state.

Nesta Webster in her 1921 book *World Revolution: The Plot against Civilization* proved the existence of the Masonic plot behind the French revolution and its 'sister revolutions' that followed in later years. The French Revolution was nothing but a coup d'état that had terrible consequences. Nesta Webster also revealed that Freemasonry and Illuminism had joined forces in July of 1782. The already influential Illuminists of Adam Weishaupt shared with the Masons the ambition to "enlighten the peoples of the world."

In his speech of November 5th, 1919, Winston Churchill acknowledged the existence of the "worldwide plot that started with the Illuminist Weishaupt and ended with Marx."

From the start, Freemasonry had been under the spell of Judaism. In London, where it originated, Sephardic Jews were in control of finances and banks even before the arrival of Rothschild. The parents of the City, financial nexus of the world in the heart of London, were Jewish and Protestant. The Sephardic Jews, Marrano's or 'false converts', having been expelled from Catholic Spain by Queen Isabella in 1492, had first settled in Amsterdam, that over time came to be known as the 'Jerusalem of the West'. The first ever Central Bank was founded in Amsterdam in 1609. After Cromwell had readmitted the expelled Jews to England, the Sephardic bankers had expanded their business in London, laying the groundwork for the City. In 1694, the central Bank of England was founded. This, of course, was the background against which the House of Rothschild, within the Masonic framework, had started its phenomenal rise to power. Rothschild was profoundly instrumental in the installation of the Jewish state in Palestine.

In his book *The Controversy of Zion*, that remained hidden for 22 years after its completion in 1956, ex-journalist Douglas Reed explains that the shocking *Protocols of the Elders of Zion*, which we are constantly told are a forgery, in reality corresponded to the greatest extent to the Illuminist 'means and methods' as laid out in the Weishaupt papers.

On the subject of the *Protocols*' origins and importance, Reed wrote :

> Comparative study of the Protocols and of the Weishaupt papers leads to the strong deduction that both derive from a common and much older source.[...]

Weishaupt's documents speak of Freemasonry as the best "cover" to be used by the agents of the conspiracy.[...]

They might equally well be the product of non-Jewish or of anti-Jewish revolutionaries, and that is of secondary importance. What they proved is that the organization first revealed by Weishaupt's documents was in existence 120 years later, and was still using the methods and pursuing the aim then exposed; and when they were published in English the Bolshevik revolution had given the proof. In my opinion the Protocols provide the essential handbook for students of the time and subject. If Lord Sydenham, in 1921, was arrested by the "uncanny knowledge" they displayed, on which prophecies now literally fulfilled are based, how much more would he be impressed today, in 1956, when much more of them has been as literally fulfilled. Through this book any man can see how the upheavals of the past 150 years were, and how those of the next fifty years will be brought about; he will know in advance just how "the deeds" of his elected representatives will differ from their "word."

Reed continues:

The resemblance to Weishaupt's documents is very strong in the passages which relate to the infiltration of public departments, professions and parties, for instance:

It is from us that the all-engulfing terror proceeds. We have in our service persons of all opinions, of all doctrines, restorating monarchists, demagogues, socialists, communists, and utopian dreamers of every kind. We have harnessed them all to the task: each one of them on his own account is boring away at the last remnants of authority, is striving to overthrow all established form of order. By these acts all States are in torture; they exhort to tranquillity, are ready to sacrifice everything for peace; but we will not give them peace until they openly acknowledge our international Super-Government, and with submissiveness.

Among the "upheavals" that had followed the 1789 Revolution, one of the most important was the Bolshevik Revolution of 1917, which was in essence a Jewish coup.

This implies that Jewish interests, including the Lodge B'Nai B'Rith, had succeeded in instrumentalising the Masonic-Illuminist network. Both Dr. E. Michael Jones and Douglas Reed see Judaism as a destructive, revolutionary force. This destruction is required to bring about the coming of the 'real', Talmudic Messiah, sweeping aside the myth of the imposter Jesus Christ.

Mr. Ben Hecht, one of the most extreme Zionist chauvinists in America, once published the following dictum:

> One of the finest things ever done by the mob was the crucifixion of Christ. Intellectually it was a splendid gesture. But trust the mob to bungle. If I'd had charge of executing Christ I'd have handled it differently. You see, what I'd have done was had him shipped to Rome and fed to the lions. They never could have made a saviour out of mincemeat.

Reed specifies:

> The end is that first revealed in Weishaupt's documents, and it is apparent that both spring from a much earlier source, although the Protocols, in time, stand to the Weishaupt papers as grandson to grandsire. When the Protocols appeared in English the minor point, who was the author of this particular document, was given a false semblance of major importance by the enraged Jewish attack on the document itself. The asseveration of Jewish leadership of the revolutionary conspiracy was not new at all; the reader has seen that Disraeli, Bakunin and many others earlier affirmed it.
>
> In many passages the Protocols appear, at first sight, to recommend destruction as a thing virtuous in itself, and consequently justifying all the methods explicitly recommended to promote it (bribery, blackmail, corruption, subversion, sedition, mob-incitement, terror and violence), which thus become virtuous too. But careful scrutiny shows that this is not the case. In fact the argument presented begins at the end, world power, and goes backward through the means, which are advocated simply as the best ones to that end. [...] The final aim is the destruction of all religion and nationhood and the establishment of the super State, ruling the world by ruthless terror.

Reed continues:

> The attack on the Protocols in the 1920's proved above all else the truth of their contention; it showed that the standing organization for suppressing public discussion of the conspiracy had been perfected in the intervening 120 years. Probably so much money and energy were never before in history expended on the effort to suppress a single document. It was brought to England by one of the two leading British correspondents of that day in Moscow, Victor Marsden of the *Morning Post* [...] The campaign against the Protocols has never ceased since then. In communized Russia all copies discoverable had been destroyed at the revolution and possession

of the book became a capital crime under the law against 'anti-sem-itism'. In the direct sequence to that, though twenty-five years later, the American and British authorities in occupied Germany after the Second World War constrained the Western German government to enact laws against 'anti-semitism' on the Bolshevik model...

Reed, who resigned as a journalist due to "external pressures," explains:

> In one point I am able from my own experience to test Lord Syden-ham's dictum about fulfilled prophecies. The *Protocols*, speaking of control of published information, say: "Not a single announcement will reach the public without our control. Even now this is already being attained by us inasmuch as all news items are received by a few agencies, in whose offices they are focused from all parts of the world. These agencies will then be entirely ours and will give pub-licity only to what we dictate to them." That was not the situation in 1905, or in Lord Sydenham's day, or in 1926, when I became a journalist, but it was developing and today is the situation.The subjugation of the press has been accomplished as the Protocols foretold, and by the accident of my generation and calling I saw it come about.

As to the "Liberté" that revolutions were to bring about, Reed quoted the *Protocols*:

> Ever since that time (the French Revolution), we have been lead-ing the peoples from one disenchantment to another.[...] The word 'freedom' brings out the communities of men to fight against ev-ery kind of force, against every kind of authority, even against God and the laws of nature. For this reason we, when we come into our kingdom, shall have to erase this word from the lexicon of life as implying a principle of brute force which turns mobs into blood-thirsty beasts.... But even freedom might be harmless and have its place in the State economy without injury to the wellbeing of the peoples if it rested upon the foundation of faith in God.... This is the reason why it is indispensable for us to undermine all faith, to tear out of the minds of the masses the very principle of Godhead and the spirit, and to put in its place arithmetical calculations and material need...

The Vatican has not always acknowldged the seriousness of the Jew-ish-Masonic threat. Pope Leo XIII around the turn of the 20th century had warned of a Masonic infiltration of the Holy See. For some time it was forbidden for clerics to become member of the Brotherhood. In 1903, after the death of Leo XIII, Cardinal Rompolla del Tindaro had been chosen to become the new Pope. Only the strict veto of Austrian Emperor Franz Joseph I, who had gathered intelligence on Rompolla, had prevented a Mason from acceding to the position of Pontifex Maximus. The Cardinal was a Freemason and 8th and 9th degree member of the Cult of Lucifer, which was linked to the infamous Ordo Templi Orientis, headed by Aleister Crowley, the most infamous Satanist of his time. This was not the end of the story.

The Second Vatican Concilium of 1965 had profoundly transformed the Church. Many were of the opinion that the Vatican had turned Masonic. Rome was now preaching tolerance of Judaism. Rome now openly stated that "the Jews were not waiting for their Messiah in vain," which amounted to the rejection of Jesus as the sole Messiah, one of the essential Christian dogmas. It was discovered that Cardinal Béa, in preparation of Vatican II, had been consulting with some top Rabbis. Also, Vatican II failed to formally condemn Communism as the enemy of the Church and of humanity, in total disregard of the instructions given by the Holy Mother herself in Fatima. This infuriated many virulent anti-Communist movements that had sprung up at the start of the Cold War. Vatican II, it was said, had turned the Church of Rome into a 'Synagogue of Satan'.

World History, re-written in the light of Jewish-Masonic actions would result in a totally different book from the one we have been taught in school. That is no coïncidence. Jewish Masonry had a grip on world politics long before Vatican II. In the USA the Lodge of B'Nai B'Rith had significantly influenced the course of history through some of its high-level members: Jacob and Mortimer Schiff, Edgar Bronfman, Otto Kahn, Max Breitung and Henry Kissinger. Justice Brandeis, Morgenthau, Warburg, Marshall, Freud and even British Prime Minister Arthur Balfour were members of B'Nai B'Rith. Adolf Hitler was initiated in the secret Order of Thulé by his mentor Karl Haushofer, an Illuminist who was a member of the Golden Dawn. Haushofer was the 'Lebensraum' geostrategist who visited Hitler in Landsberg prison in 1924 and inspired him to write *Mein Kampf*.

Heinz 'Henry' Kissinger, as we now know, although never elected, has had a profound influence on world events in the last six decades. Kissinger was intimately linked to the Rockefellers Council on Foreign Relations, Bilderberg and the Trilateral Commission. The UN, a Rockefeller pet, appears to be a Masonic project, furthering the abolition of nation states. The Lucis Trust, an official "Good Will" appendix of UNESCO, used to be called the Lucifer Trust.

The super-elitist Bohemian Grove as well as Skull and Bones are linked to Masonry.

Among their adherents we find Theodore Roosevelt, Harry Truman, Nixon, Ford, Bush, Helmut Schmidt, Forbes, Greenspan, Cheney, Powell...The slogan 'Ordo ab Chao', often used in connection with the New World Order, is in essence a Jewish-Masonic slogan. It hints at the destruction of the established order, some cataclysmic event, resulting in the chaos that will bring the New World Order to power. At the same time it hints at the total chaos that is required for the coming of the Jewish Messiah, as Dr E. M. Jones explains, which will usher in a New Order where the elected sacerdotal Jewish people will reign over the ignorant masses of the earth as the sole interlocutors between humanity and God.

By bringing about this chaos in total contempt of the Goy, the elected people is expediting the sequence of events that leads to this great event. Here, as laid out in the Weishaupt papers, the end justifies the means: usury, blackmail, corruption, sedition, terror, violence and perversion. Which brings us back to the many cases of child abuse, human traficking and even Satanic child sacrifice. These too often involve high-level politicians, magistrates and clericals, which explains why they have remained hidden for so long.

The link with the Nebula as portrayed in the ATLAS report is not hard to establish.

Felix Przedborski himself was a Grand Master of the Lodge. The Italian Lodge P2 was connected to the branches of the old Lansky-Vesco-Cohn network. P2 Master Licio Gelli also was a Knight of Malta, connected to the Vatican and its Ambrosio banking scandal. Everything is connected.

Remember the words of the Przedborski milieu insider Michel V about

> ...a structure that is well organized, well equipped and well trained. Its existence is justified by the paramount interests of the nation states. For a number of reasons, this structure is accountable to no-one. This structure had its origins in history and it is so well established that nobody really directs it any longer, while nobody knows all the intricacies of it any more. The more so because anyone in the know keeps silent *or lies about it.*

In the light of what we have learned our conclusion must be that this structure is international Freemasonry, that has financed capitalism and communism, that has caused and financed conflicts and wars. As Michel V had pointed out, he who thinks in terms of 'left' and 'right' is missing the whole point. *"Below a certain depth, all fish have the same color."*

On the subject of the Nebula controlling half of the world economy, consider this.

In his 2012 book *La Faillite du Monde Moderne* (*The Downfall of the Modern World*), Salim Laïbbi cites two witnesses who had publicly spoken out about Freemasonry and its enormous power in France. The first witness, Khaled Amalou, who used to be a chef in some of the most prestigous, exclusive restaurants in France in an hourlong interview explained that the ports on the Côte d'Azur were all controlled by the Masonic Brotherhood. The second witness, Marie Laforet, had worked together with the Swiss intelligence service for two years. She had discovered a mass of compromising data on the computer of her ex-husband, Eric de Levandeyra, who was a high level Master of the Grande Loge Nationale de France. Laforet stated in an interview in front of the camera that *'there exists a criminal organisation that controls a budget 250 times the Gross National Product of France'*, which, according to Laïbbi, amounted at the time to about 87,000 billion Euro. Laforet is said to have survived five attempts on her life. Among the figures she named was Anatoly Chubais, a Russian Jew who worked as a minister under Boris Yeltsin, the vodka-president who sold out his country. Chubais also worked for J.P. Morgan, helping to privatize the Russian economy. Chubais attended the 1998 Bilderberg conference.

Laforet also pointed out that the Order of the Solar Temple (OTS) massacre was linked to Gladio, the intelligence agencies and the mafia. In October 1994 OTS had been involved in the ritual murder of a three-month old baby in Quebec, Canada. A few days later the Swiss nation was shocked by the mass suicides and murders of dozens of OTS members in Cheiry and Salvan, two villages in Western Switzerland. Laforet had sent the evidence she had found to the FBI and the CIA. Nothing happened. Only the Swiss, who had to deal with the massacre, took her seriously. The media remained completely silent.

After she was invited by TV station Canal+, her computer, containing the incriminating evidence, which was to be 'double-checked' by the TV station's bosses in order to avoid legal problems, was never returned to her. Fortunately, Laforet, a courageous ex-singer and actress, had made copies. Incidently, Canal+ is one of the names that is cited in the ATLAS Report. The connections between Freemasonry and NATO-Gladio were clearly not limited to those of the Italian Lodge P2 and the secret Stay-Behind network.

French rightist military elements, attached to Gladio stay-behind units in France designed to carry out attacks against Warsaw Pact forces after a Soviet invasion, included La Rose des Vents, Arc-en-ciel ("Rainbow"), the Western Union Clandestine Committee working closely with the French Intelligence service SDECE, and the 11th Choc Parachutist Regiment of the French Army. In 1961, many of these units formed the infamous OAS, the Organisation de l'Armée Secrète, which was trying to stop Algerian independence and to assassinate French President Charles de Gaulle.

US General Andrew Goodpaster reported: *"Army officers - those stationed in Algeria as well as those stationed in the south of France - involved with right-wing Algerian activists, constitute a sort of secret society that is very well hidden."*

The Grande Loge Nationale de France or GLNF was founded in November 1913 by eight members of the Grand Orient of France. Two weeks later this Lodge was officially certified by the United Grand Lodge of England, the global Masonic mother-lodge. In 1958 the GLNF merged with the Grande Loge du Rite Rectifié. In 1964, this powerful French Lodge laid the first stone of its new temple in Neuilly. Surprisingly, this Masonic ceremony was attended by US General Lyman Lemnitzer, who at the time was the Commander of Nato Forces in Europe.

Lyman Lemnitzer had been stationed in Algiers, Algeria, during the North African Campaign toward the end of WWII. According to his biography Lyman Lemnitzer was a 32 Degree Mason of the Ancient and Accepted Scottish Rite, who in 1956 had attended the 'communication of the Grand Lodge of Japan' in Tokyo. He was a member of the Nile Shrine Temple of Seattle and of St Paul's Lodge of Newport.

Lemnitzer was a 'Hawk' whom President John Kennedy had banished to Europe for his involvement in the Cuban affair surrounding the failed Bay of Pigs invasion. It was Lyman Lemnitzer who had proposed a series of false-flag attacks designed to discredit Cuba. He was behind the plans for Operation Northwoods, staging a false-flag attack on a fake American airliner, that he hoped would trigger an all-out war against Cuba. In the wake of the Cuba-related shenanigans, Kennedy had sacked CIA boss Allen Dulles and exiled Lemnitzer. Back in Europe, hardliner Lemnitzer had forged ties with ultra-right anti-Communist forces, including ex-Nazi collaborators from France and Belgium, to serve as his Gladio warriors.

THE EMPEROR'S NEW BANK

By what mechanism the Rothschilds and their central banks controlled the policies of the nations is extremely well documented by the historian Lacroix-Riz. In her pursuit of the truth about the collaboration of the French elites with the fascist regimes of Mussolini, Franco and Hitler, she uncovered the Synarchist plot.

Since the mid-1920s three major banks and the powerful industrialists Humbert De Wendel and Adolphe Schneider had conspired to transform the République into a dictatorial corporate state run by businessmen, military and technocrats. The banks involved were the Banque de France, Banque Worms and Banque de l'Indochine.

The Banque de France was de facto the central bank of France. It had been founded back in 1800 by Napoleon and fifteen protestant bankers, all linked to Jewish interests, who had basically financed the Revolution that had brought Napoleon to power in the first place. Initially the Emperor had been a major shareholder together with the famous "seventy Israelites," among whom were many Jewish-Swiss bankers. Napoleon had consulted with the Great Jewish Sanhedrin in 1806, resulting in the founding of a Central Consistory of Israelites. Once again a minority Jewish community had succeeded in carving out a privileged niche for themselves.

In 1811 the house of Rothschild was established in Paris. By 1830, barely fifteen years after the defeat of Napoleon and Nathan Rothschild's magnificent London stock market bamboozle, the Rothschilds and their associates Laffitte, Fould, Hottinguer and Mallet had acquired a majority stake in the Banque.

Count Nicolas François de Mollien, Treasury minister from 1814 to 1818, expressed his bitter disappointment with Napoleon in his memoirs. The Emperor, product of the "Liberté, Egalité, Fraternité" revolution turned out to be just another monarch who sought to please the banks. De Mollien complained *"The Corsican had even entrusted the Banque de France with the supply of the paper money. The private company Pergot Mallet has been granted the privilege to produce paper money. At no cost, since no gold, silver nor any metal was involved."* De Mollien continued his rant: *"Napoleon crawls at the feet of the bank, as he always will."*

In February of the year 1800 Perregaux had informed Napoleon that the new Banque, which the bankers had insisted on erecting, was to be a private bank but that it would be called Banque *de France* nonetheless. And that it demanded a state guarantee from the Emperor. Perregaux, one of the first directors of the bank, was a business partner of the Bethmann brothers who had pioneered the floating of international bonds. By the end of February of that year, Napoleon had agreed to provide the state guarantee and to entrust the bank with the circulation of paper money. Also, by law, money counterfeiters would henceforth face the death penalty.

And so it was that the Banque de France acquired power over French politics. Each and every newly elected government, no matter its color, needed to present before the Banque's council and pledge an oath of loyalty to it. The Banque basically dictated the conditions for the extension of credit, without which the new government simply could not function. Whenever the Banque imposed a regime of "austerity" on the government, that meant that top-bracket taxes needed to be lowered and workers' wages crushed.

Next to the Banque de France the Banque Worms was the second most powerful bank of the République. It held majority stakes in every field of economic activity: steel, coal, real estate and insurance. One of the companies in its portfolio was Lyonnaise des Eaux. Banque Worms had Jewish origins and was known to control half of the French economy. The roots of the Worms family lay in the Frankfurter Judengasse. Benedict Moses Worms had married Jeanette Rothschild on 18 October 1795. By 1840 Hyppolite Worms had been appointed Rothschild's agent in Saint Petersburg. His wife Séphora Goudchaux was related to the Lazard bankers family, who were in business with Otto Kahn, Jacob Schiff and the Warburgs. These were the moneymen that planted the seeds for the US Federal Reserve.

A communiqué to President F. Roosevelt dated 7 January 1942, by US ambassador Anthony J. Drexel Biddle made it perfectly clear that the Synarchist Banque Worms dominated the Vichy government. On the subject of the Synarchy Biddle wrote:

> This group should be regarded not as Frenchmen, any more than their corresponding members in Germany should be regarded as Germans, for the interests of both groups are so intermingled as to be indistinguishable; their whole interest is focused upon furtherance of their industrial and financial stakes.

This "natural" convergence of interests of the German and French industry barons that started in the early 1920s proved to be the earliest groundwork for the European Union.

Since Napoleon's days the power of the bankers over French politics had gradually been strengthened. After Mitterrand's death, his widow Danielle stated :

> After 1981 I asked François Mitterrand the following question. "Now that you have power, why don't you do what you had promised?" His answer was that he did not have the power to confront the World Bank, capitalism or neo-liberalism. That he had inherited a government but not the power. And so I learned that being a government, being a president, doesn't mean much in societies that are subjugated to capitalism. I have lived through that experience for fourteen years. In France there are elections and the elected impose laws that they themselves never proposed and that we never wanted. Is France a democracy? A world power? As a French citizen, I say that means nothing.

FASCIST SYNERGY

The EU wasn't born after WWII as they would have us believe, historian Lacroix-Riz insists. It was conceived in the 1920s as part of a fascist project, that would later be overtly supported by the USA. In the post-war years the USA would secure its European bridgehead with the help of fascist elements and a flood of Marshall Plan dollars. The EU project also found a lot of supporters among the European Roman Catholic "old money" elites orbiting the Hapsburg dynasty, a vestige of the Austrian-Hungarian empire.

The Vatican had sided with the Hapsburgs during their days of glory at the helm of the Austrian-Hungarian Roman Catholic Empire. Ever since the Empire's demise in 1918, the Vatican had been on the look-out for new strategic partners. In the 1930s the Vatican, while still supporting Hapsburg, committed itself without restriction to the Nazi cause, especially after Hitler's plans for the annexation of Austria had transpired. For the Vatican as well as for the Hapsburgs the fascist movement promised to be the catalyst for a new European Catholic Empire. This convenient convergence of interests of US capital, the Reich and the Holy See would result, among other things, in the "Nazi ratlines" to Latin America via the Vatican.

In 1922 the Synarchist cartel consisted of twelve French "captains" of the coal and steel industry who sought to implement radical political reforms in order to silence the parliament and the unions and freeze workers' wages. They spent enormous amounts of money recruiting journalists, authors and "malleable unionists" for their cause. That same year Mussolini started his fascist conquest of Italy, supported by the House of Morgan.

When the Spanish throne came under severe pressure in 1930, the Banque de France bluntly refused to return the Spanish gold reserves, stacked in its underground vaults, to the legitimate government. Instead it transferred the gold into the hands of the fascist General Franco. He had promised to repay the Spanish debt to Germany, whose finances were in very dire straits at the time. In turn, this move allowed Germany to honor its own debt payback schedule to the banking cartel.

John J. McCloy

CHAPTER 5

NAZISM TO GLADIO

"Sound Thinking insists that wars will not be abolished until its roots are cut;
and one of its main roots is a false money system and the high priests thereof."

Henry Ford.

GERMAN DEBT

Due to the economic downturn following the Wall Street crash of 1929, Germany found itself on the brink of ruin in 1931, threatening to default on its debt. There had been a massive influx of investments into the country, starting in the early 1920s. Since 1919, Germany had been discretely rearming. Its industry had grown at a remarkable pace. Within a few years it had taken a dominant position in the world, especially in the chemicals branch. DuPont, IBM and General Motors were heavily invested in IG Farben, the largest chemical company in the world by far.

IG Farben's initial success was based on the production of a synthetic blue dye as a substitute for the expensive biological pigment. Hence the "Farben" i.e. "Colors" in the company name. The toxic by-product of the chemical process proved to have interesting applications: it killed bugs and small animals. Insecticides such as DDT and Zyklon would prove to be a huge success. They made it possible to quickly decontaminate entire ships, factories and buildings with great efficiency. Zyklon was in high demand in the USA too. IG Farben opened a branch on the new continent. One of its American counselors was John J. McCloy, who would rise to a position of great power. By the end of WWII McCloy was dispatched to Germany as the US High Commissioner. He was one of the very few unelected key figures that had a profound but hidden impact on American and world history.

McCloy had completed Harvard Law School where he befriended the Rockefellers. In 1924 he had been hired by Cravath, Henderson & de Gersdorff. His boss Paul Cravath was vice-president of the CFR. McCloy had co-engineered for his client J.P. Morgan a 110 million dollar loan to Hitler. He had attended the 1936 Berlin Olympic Games as one of Hitler's personal guests. Here's how McCloy had become a friend of the Nazi top.

As a Cravath lawyer McCloy had managed to defuse the tricky "Black Tom" case. On 30 July 1916 a very powerful explosion had rocked Ellis Island. It caused an earth tremor that was registered as far away as Lower Manhattan. A trainload of ammo for the British and French armies had gone up in smoke. Bethlehem Steel ordered an investigation into this "act of German sabotage." McCloy found out that Franz von Papen and Ernest "Putzi" Hanfstängl were behind the attack. Von Papen would rise to the position of vice-chancellor under Hitler, while Hanfstängl became Hitler's close friend and foreign press director. Incidentally, Putzi Hanfstängl had completed Harvard, where he befriended F.D. Roosevelt.

McCloy had diligently hammered out a deal between the Kaiser and Bethlehem Steel. In the process he made some interesting new friends and clients. One of whom was Paul Warburg of the Federal Reserve, whose banker brothers were counselors to the German Kaiser. McCloy became involved in negotiations over the financing of Mussolini, after which he would spend most of his time on the European continent.

After the German defeat in 1945 McCloy intervened in the Nuremberg War Trials to keep his industrialist friends out of jail. Incidentally, McCloy was related by marriage to Konrad Adenauer, the first post-war Chancellor of Germany. Both McCloy and Adenauer had married a Zinsser, of the American Zinsser & Co chemical company that had supplied mustard gas to the US troops in 1918. Allen Dulles of the Sullivan & Cromwell law firm and McCloy of Cravath & Co., played similar roles in the run-up to WWII. Both were tasked with safeguarding the massive US investments in Germany. This put them in an ambiguous position as mediators between Hitler's Nazi party and Wall Street.

The crippling German reparation payments to the victorious allies of the Great War of 1914-18, imposed by the Treaty of Versailles, had already been suspended, yet, by 1931, Germany was exhausted. A German default would have brought on disaster. The reschedule of its debt payback led to the Dawes Plan, the Young Plan and the installation in Switzerland of the Bank for International Settlements (BIS). What Germany needed was an Italian-style fascist regime that would eliminate the parliament and force austerity upon its workers and civil servants. Hitler was found to be willing to do the job. By march of 1933, the German parliament lay in ashes, thousands of communists had been shot or jailed and Hitler had grabbed dictatorial power. He vouched to repay the debt to the banks in gold, which he did up until 1945.

The Bank for International Settlements was instrumental in Hitler's gold scheme with the banks. The BIS was in essence a "central bank of central banks," directed by top Nazi banker Hjalmar Schacht. Hitler profoundly disliked bankers, but Schacht, he once said, was an exceptionally talented swindler. And so Schacht, being very well connected internationally, ended up heading the Reichsbank and the BIS.

As Hitler annexed Austria and consequently invaded Czechoslovakia, Belgium and France, the international gathering of bankers at
the BIS simply agreed on transferring these nations' gold reserves into
the Nazi vaults, thus making sure that Herr Hitler was never in short
supply. The case of the Czech gold was particularly enlightening. After
his occupation of the Czech nation, Hitler insisted on having the Czech
gold confiscated. However, that gold was sitting in the underground
vaults of the Bank of England, a Rothschild bank. Montagu Norman,
president of the BoE, was a close friend of Schacht. After some hesi-
tation Norman agreed to hand the Czech gold over to Schacht and so
the British people had to put up with the fact that their bank had just
financed the murderers of their sons. Obviously the nation's bankers,
peacefully arranging affairs over a cup of tea, were fighting a very different war from the soldiers out on the frontlines. Governments and
wars came and went, but bankers just carried on their business as usual,
financing them. Soon there would be more money to be made rebuild-
ing old Europe. *Ordo ab Chao.*

CGE-FELIX

While investigating the GE-CGE-SOFINA power structure the late
journalist Walter De Bock made the following intriguing note:

> "CGE-Alsthom has been using Deferm for years; the role of Felix: Pompi-
> dou > Rothschild and >Mitterrand via Merli. Wartime past." (Annex 4).

This needs some explanation. "Deferm" is Leon Deferm, the Jewish
Connection businessman who made off to Costa Rica with part of the
socialists' Agusta bribes. What De Bock had discovered was that Deferm
obviously was part of the CGE-network, a branch of the larger Nebula.
Don Felix was found to serve the same masters. He had apparently been
in contact with George Pompidou, successor to de Gaulle as president
of the French Republic in 1969. Before his term in office, Pompidou had
been a Rothschild banker. The links to the Rothschild-Banque de France
cartel that dominated French politics were obvious.

"*Mitterrand via Merli. Wartime past*" proved to be quite revealing too.
Pierre Merli was the mayor of the French city of Antibes, on the Mediterranean coast, where Don Felix had acquired the Villa Campanelle. They
had become friends. On one of the very few pictures ever published of
Przedborski senior he could be seen in the company of André Cools, Baron Édouard-Jean Empain and Pierre Merli. The picture, taken at a garden
party in Antibes, was used to illustrate a 1995 *Le Soir* article about the life
and death of Andre Cools. (Appendix 5).

As we now know, Mitterrand had been a fascist member of the Cagoule in WWII. He and Merli had been close childhood friends. Was Don Felix tasked to lobby Mitterrand via Merli on behalf of CGE? Quite possibly so. Mitterrand had been of the opinion that "what is good for CGE, is good for France," thus justifying his interventionist economic policy. Mitterrand had taken the decision to nationalize CGE. In reality, what that meant, critics said, was that CGE was taken in protection by the Republique, so as to facilitate its international expansion into the communications and media industries. Exactly what role Deferm and Don Felix had played in all of this remains unknown. What can be said with certainty is that Mitterrand has divorced French socialism from Moscow-inspired communism. In doing so he rendered a big service to the Nebula – the modern day Synarchs – as he had done during his time in the Cagoule, forty years earlier.

"WINNIE" KOLLBRUNNER

According to the ATLAS Report, Deferm and Don Felix shared a mistress by the name of "Winnie" Kollbrunner. She was quite a character. Winifred Hélène was born in Zürich in 1955. She grew up on the up-scale right bank of the Zürich Lake, dubbed "the Gold Coast" by the locals. Her father was a well reputed building contractor who had done very well in the booming 1960s, on either side of the Swiss-Italian border. Yet "Winnie" had decided to go in business for herself. Pretty soon she was seen in high circles. Some qualified her as the "financial secretary" of Italian socialist premier Craxi. In August of 1992, as mentioned in the ATLAS Report, she was arrested in Geneva while trying to cash some stolen bonds. She was not on her first trip.

Pretty Winnie confessed having traveled regularly from Italy into Switzerland, carrying bonds. That was what her bosses had hired her for and she was good at it. In fact she had special underwear made to conceal the documents she was smuggling. Winnie liked to brag about never being checked – let alone caught – when crossing the border.

Winnie Ellen Kollbrunner was not just a small-time courier. She had very high-level political connections in Italy. One of her close friends was minister Claudio Martelli, the right hand of premier Craxi. From her correspondence with Martelli – "Caro Claudio" – one could take it that she had shared her bed with him too. One of Winnie's associates was Vito Rallo, who had been involved in the sale of 450 tons of gold from an "unspecified central bank." The pivotal agents in the whitewash of stolen or false titles turned out to be Cabinet Pinto, Cabinet Strehli and the AIM Group of Zürich.

The network that Winnie was working for was being investigated by the Italian Parliament, that produced a 200+ page report. The investigation had been triggered by the "Tangentopoli" – or "Bribesville" – scandal involving illegal kickbacks for Craxi and his Socialist Party. In early 1993 a young lady by the name of Pia Vecchia was arrested in Ponto Chiasso carrying 294 bonds that had been stolen from the Banco Di Santo Espirito in Rome on 2 November 1990. Vecchia was close with magistrate Ugo Ziletti, who had just been arrested for his share in the bankruptcy of the Compagnia Générale Finanziaria, which managed the funds of Licio Gelli and other P2 members. Craxi was quick to deny the accusations but fled to North Africa when the larger anti-corruption operation Mani Puliti or "Clean Hands" kicked off.

Many other VIPs and companies were named in the Italian report. Alcatel, for one, was the communications spin-off of CGE-Alsthom. Prudential Bache was another. On page 12 of their report the Parliamentarian investigators even hinted at the fact that the same type of Prudential Bache bonds had surfaced in the cabinet of Belgian socialist minister Van der Biest, whose cabinet was infested with Italian mafiosi.

Most importantly, the report revealed the network's links to the top Christian-Democrat Giulio Andreotti, the 41st Prime Minister of Italy. He had been in and out of office in various governments since the late 1950s. He was obviously very well connected. He was often seen in Washington. Many considered him to be the hidden hand behind the P2 Lodge, directed by Licio Gelli. Henry Kissinger was suspected of having revived the P2 Lodge with the aim of destabilizing Italy. It was Andreotti who in 1991 first officially acknowledged the existence of the secret NATO underground network Gladio in Italy. His revelations triggered an official Gladio investigation in Belgium. Many suspected NATO to be involved in the destabilizing attacks in Italy in the 1970s and in Belgium in the 1980s. These suspicions were not without grounds. The Italian police protocol 509/62 of 23 July 1996 titled "Psychological and low intensity warfare in Italy via Aginter Press (1969-74)" laid bare the connections between NATO and Aginter Press (AP).

AP was a façade for the Nazi underground network that had been activated in 1945. This "Paladin Group" had been established by SS colonel Otto Skorzeny, one of Hitler's favorite war heroes. It had set up headquarters in Madrid and Buenos Aires. In Madrid the Skorzeny network was protected by General Franco, whose staff consisted mainly of Opus Dei members. Franco, it should be remembered, had risen to power with the help of the Nazis: witness the 1936 bombing of the Spanish town of Guernica by the Luftwaffe.

In and around Madrid, the said "convergence of interests" united fascists, Roman Catholics, anti-communists and Europeanists under the aegis of Generalissimo Franco. Incidentally, out of these ultra-Catholic circles rose the future queen of Belgium, Fabiola de Mora y Aragon. With the blessings of Franco, she would marry the young Belgian King Baudouin in December of 1961. The media were all over the royal wedding. The Holy See was jubilant. Over the years, the couple would continue to display their sympathy for Franco, while Queen Fabiola was said to have introduced the Opus Dei mantras in Belgian high circles.

Aginter Press was in fact the Portuguese branch of the Paladin Group. AP was involved in black operations in Angola, a former Portuguese colony, Central Africa and Latin America. It had joined forces with the Italian P2 terrorists and the OAS – the French Secret Army Organization. This alliance had led to the cooperation between ex-Nazi Klaus Barbie and the Italian P2-terrorist Delle Chiaie, who was involved in Italy in the covert operation Piano Chaos, together with Aginter Press.

Barbie was heading a major cocaine smuggling operation in Colombia. He had become a powerful figure to be reckoned with, even on the political scene. He was behind the Cocaine Coup in Bolivia in 1980. The Italian protocol provided yet more evidence of a NATO-Gladio involvement in the bloody "Strategy of Tension" in Italy and Belgium. The document named the Belgian attorney Mario Spandre as the middleman between AP and NATO. Incidentally it also made mention of a "Belgian weapons pipeline" in the context of a coup d'état in 1974. (Annex 6). In Italy Gladio turned out to have become an instrument of covert, "deep state" operations.

GREY WOLVES

Before his return to Italy to direct the P2 Lodge, Licio Gelli had been hiding in Argentina for 20 years. His accomplice Stefano Delle Chiaie was involved in all terrorist attacks in Italy between 1969 and 1980. He was a key figure in the implementation of the "Strategy of Tension" in Italy, yet he was protected by the Italian intelligence services. Even after his complicity in the Bologna bombing in 1981 had been established, Delle Chiaie was still traveling freely to South America. The Craxi government concluded that he was covered by the CIA as well.

On 9 September 1982, Stefano Delle Chiaie landed in Miami. He was accompanied by Abdullah Catli, head of the Turkish Grey Wolves. US Customs were informed of their arrival but did not interfere. Catli was a close friend of Mehmet Ali Agca, who had attempted to kill Pope John Paul II the previous year. The investigation into the assassination attempt uncovered the connections between the Grey Wolves, the Bulgarian Connection, and the P2 Lodge. The international press fingered the Bulgarian secret service and the KGB as the instigators of the attack. The incident proved to be a great opportunity to heighten anti-Soviet sentiments in the West. Catli had been called in to make sure that his friend Agca would say the right things to make the KGB involvement plausible. Both were offered money by the German police to change their stories. Francesco Pazienza, an Italian secret service agent, admitted to having supported the Moscow-linked core of the Italian communist party in an attempt to compromise it. Pazienza turned out to be an adviser to the Center for Strategic and International Studies (CSIS), a pro-NATO propaganda and lobby group. The investigation clearly showed the connection between Italian official instances, Bulgaria, NATO, and some criminal figures.

The Bulgarian Connection was part of a centuries-old smuggling ring for heroin and rare and exotic Oriental products. Pakistani morphine and heroin, processed by the Afghan Pathan tribe, was transported to Persia by the Baluchi nomads. From there, Kurdish smugglers carried it into Turkey. From Turkey the stuff either founds its way into Bulgaria or into Lebanon, via Syria. The Bulgarian network had tentacles to Yugoslavia, Trieste, Munich, and Palermo, the transshipping point for the USA. Since the 1970s the Bulgarian state had been participating in the traffic of drugs and weapons, via the Kintex company. Turkish traffickers, who used to do their wheeling and dealing in the Vitosha Hotel or in Café Berlin in Sofia, now found themselves covered by the Bulgarian "apparatchiks."

Due to their Grey Wolves contacts, two of the main Turkish drug barons, Abuzer Ugurlu and Bekir Celenk, to their dismay, saw their names appear in the headlines. Both ended up on the "most wanted" list. Diplomatic relations between Italy and Bulgaria were temporarily suspended.

Celenk had made a fortune selling drugs via the Grey Wolves HQ and the Turkish expat community in Munich. Via his off-shore companies, Celenk had started up his own shipping line, which was found to be subcontracted regularly by the Milanese Stibam International Transport company. Surprisingly, the Stibam headquarter was established in offices belonging to the infamous Banco Ambrosiano, linked to the Vatican. The company director was "baba" Hanafi Arslayan, a Turkish underworld godfather.

Stibam's reach had been underestimated. It was found to have sold hundreds of tanks to Taiwan; aircraft, helicopters and missiles to the Philippines and Somalia. Stibam even had the feared Exocet anti-ship missiles in the offering. It was a missile of this type that sank the British HMS Sheffield during the Falkland War of the early 1980s. The Argentinian Air Force had probably acquired the Exocets with the help of Italian premier Bettino Craxi.

After the crash of the Banco Ambrosiano, investigators linked the Stibam affair to the P2 Lodge and to Licio Gelli. Dozens of P2 members were indicted. Pazienza admitted having armed the Italian Red Brigades in order to make the communist threat more tangible. The Mossad too had supported the Red Brigades. Supposedly the logic behind this was that whenever Italy proved to be an unreliable ally, the USA would turn to Israel for control over the Mediterranean region.

Arslayan was never tried. He was found to be on the payroll of the DEA. Arslayan suddenly died of a heart attack. As for Catli, he quickly and quietly returned to business as usual. He managed to stay out of the headlines until the Süsürlük incident of 1996, which caused quite a stir in Turkey.

THE SÜSÜRLÜK INCIDENT

On 3rd November 1996 a speeding armoured Mercedes crashed into a tractor near the village of Süsürlük, in the Turkish province of Balikisir. Among the car passengers were Abdullah Catli and Turkish MP Sedat Bucak. They survived. Huseyin Kocadag, a high-level police officer, and beauty queen Gonca Us, Abdullah Catli's concubine, died in the crash.

The press was all over Süsürlük. Why was a mafia criminal traveling on board an official government limo, in the company of Turkish government officials? At the time of the crash Catli was carrying six different passports and a handgun. The investigation revealed embarrassing connections between the Turkish regime; the secret service; the Turkish branch of Gladio, called Ergenekon; and the Turkish mafia.

Apparently, the Turkish armed forces were using their Gladio contacts to force their way to political power. And then there was this puzzling Grey Wolves-NATO alliance and their meeting, ahead of the 9/11 attacks, with Zawahiri, second in command of Al Qaeda,. It was revealed that Ergenekon and the parallel Turkish political power structure had hired Catli to wreak havoc and destabilize the country. In exchange, Catli was allowed to continue his drug business unhindered.

Sibel Edmonds, a Turkish-born interpreter married to an American, was given a job at the FBI only a few months before 9/11. She was the only translator available to translate Turkish and Farsi into English. This is why several secret messages ended up on her desk. She soon discovered that some weird things were going on. She found out about the bribery of high US officials by the Turkish-American Council. Also, she found evidence of the sale of scientific and military information, including nuclear secrets, to Turkey and Israel. Sibel had stumbled upon a spy network that hinged around the AIPAC, the American Israel Public Affairs Committee, and involved some Turkish-American producers of nuclear bomb components. The trail led not only to Catli and Ergenekon, but also to Fethullah Gulen, Al Zawahiri and Al Qaeda.

On the subject of Gulen, Sibel explained that "he was their boy," meaning he was the protégé of the American neo-conservative elites. Gulen boasted about his excellent relationship with B'Nai B'Rith and with Turkish female president Tansu Ciller, who was indicted in Germany for drug trafficking. After Sibel Edmonds had alerted her superiors, nothing happened except that she lost her job. Yet, Sibel remained determined to spread the word about the Süsürlük group, Saudi prince Bandar, and some US agents having met with Al Zawahiri ahead of the 9/11 attacks. Congressman Tom Lantos and neo-con Douglas Feith, who had never made a secret of his sympathy for Israel and Turkey, were allegedly involved in the scam.

At first Ergenekon had contracted Turkish babas to do the dirty work, but in the 1990s, after the successful Mujahideen operations against the Soviets, Muslim extremists had taken over that role. Sibel labeled this new "edition" of the stay-behind network "Gladio B." Gladio B did not restrict itself to Turkish inland operations. It spread out to destabilize the entire Caucasian region, the Caspian basin and the countries bordering on Russia. In this oil-rich area of operation, the "moderate Turkish Islam" built 350 new mosques. The 20-billion dollar tab was almost certainly picked up by the US. This strategy suggested that the West and NATO were using Muslim extremism to complete the military encirclement of Russia and the conquest of the region's oil reserves. Next on the list was no doubt the destabilization, from the Muslim Turkic territory of East-Turkestan, of the Chinese province Xinjiang.

After 9/11, the heroin traficking from US-controlled Afghanistan had continued as before, via Iran, Iraq and Turkey to Belgium and on to the UK and the USA. The FBI, Sibel added, was eavesdropping on all embassies in the US, except on those of the UK, Turkey, Azarbaijan…and Belgium.

NAZISM LIVES

In retrospect, the connection between the post-war Nazi Continuum and NATO should not have come as a surprise. After all it was Nazi General Gehlen who had co-founded the German, American and NATO intelligence services. Reinhard Gehlen, code names Utility and Zipper, had been recruited by the allied powers on account of his experience in fighting the Bolsheviks.

In post-war Germany, Gehlen was fighting the "internal enemy" as well. In the early 1950s he was of the opinion that the West German Socialist Party (SPD) would support Moscow in the case of a Soviet attack. And so he kept "kill lists" of SPD people to be liquidated as soon as the Soviet tanks crossed the German border. Gehlens motto was "Early blood prevents a bloodbath."

The ex-Nazi general could call on two anti-communist components in West Germany, the "Stay-Behind" that would become a division of NATO-Gladio, and an extensive network of Nazi sympathizers in all German official institutions. Christian-Democrat chancellor Adenauer knew about this but kept silent. SPD members who had started legal action after the existence of the kill lists had been revealed were boycotted by the USA. According to German law, what Gehlen had done amounted to nothing less than high treason. But he was never bothered.

The anti-Soviet "Stay-Behind" in Germany had already been in full swing by 1952. With the help of the CIA the Bund Deutscher Jugend, and in particular its section "Technische Dienst," had recruited hundreds of ex-Nazi's for the defense of Germany in case of a Soviet invasion. A "Brotherhood" of about 2000 ex-Nazi officers had been set up illegally for the same purpose. These underground partisans were all in permanent contact with Gehlen and with SS-colonel Otto Skorzeny, who had found refuge in Spain.

The de-nazification of Germany after WWII had obviously been a farce. Of 924 judges and prosecutors in public service in Bavaria in 1949, 80 percent had been member of the NSDAP. According to German investigative journalist Jürgen Roth the authoritarian "Nazi mentality" remained dominant in Germany in all core state institutions – especially Justice and Security – until very late in the 1980s.

HOW MUCH IS SOCIALISM?

The Mani Puliti operation had revealed that not only Craxi's socialists but also Andreotti's Christian Democrats and even Umberto Bossi's Lega Nord had been showered with money. Operation Mani Puliti and the many arrests that ensued in the early 1990s left no doubt about the capitalist nature of the "new socialism" in Italy. It was Craxi who had been cooperating closely with André Cools in founding a "Socialist Internationale" in Europe. Mitterrand must have been involved too. The large corruption scandals around the socialist parties in Italy, France and Belgium seemed to indicate that the banking cartel had elected to buy the leftist parties rather than to keep them on their kill list. In the SASEA case that involved Kollbrunner and the P2 Lodge, the bribe money had been funneled via Karfinco, Pacini Battaglia – Craxi's right hand – to ENI and on to the Socialist Parties in Italy, France, Belgium and Luxembourg. Almany NV, at the apex of the system, was the holding company of Belgian catholic Kredietbank, known to be close to the Banco Ambrosiano and the Vatican. (Appendix 7).

Some of Kollbrunner's accomplices when arrested declared that they had been acting on orders of the military secret services. Winnie had been recruited, they said, because of her experience in smuggling documents and paper money across borders. She was very pretty, and that helped. Her boyfriend at the time had been the liberal minister Renato Altissimo, who had introduced her to the top politicians of the country.

According to Belgian MP Van Rossem, Winnie had been instrumental in switching the Prudential Bache bonds that Craxi had dispatched to

André Cools after the Agusta deal. Cools, upon discovering the forgery, had threatened to spill the beans. According to Van Rossem, Kollbrunner had acted on behalf of Felix Przedborski. The MP pointed the finger at Don Felix as murder suspect number one. On 7 April 1995 Van Rossem took the stand to explain to the members of parliament who and what he thought was behind the Cools murder. However, the moment he mentioned the name Przedborski, whom he called a "dangerous individual," his microphone and all cameras were switched off. He was not allowed to speak. The angered MP faxed the text of his aborted speech to various newspapers, but none published it. (Appendix 8).

Van Rossem himself was not a choir boy by any stretch of the imagination. He had been the founder of the infamous "infallible" Moneytron investment system that had raked in and laundered billions of black money. Some accused him of having set up a tax-avoidance structure for Don Felix's banana imports. As it was, Don Felix had successfully mediated between the European and Central American authorities for the import of Latin American bananas into the EU. To this end he had welcomed the Central American heads of state and top EU technocrat Jacques Delors at his villa in Tervuren. Delors was a close friend of Etienne Davignon and his European Round Table club of industrialists.

In retaliation, Van Rossem accused Don Felix of smuggling cocaine into Europe in banana shipments. This "banana theme" leads us right back to three important issues: operation Yellow Fruit in Santa Elena, Costa Rica, which was a sub-operation of Iran-Contra; the well documented cocaine trafficking in banana carriers by United Brands, which was linked to the Barbie drug operations; and the exile of drug baron Robert Vesco to Costa Rica. All three can be linked to Felix Przedborski.

PART II

Deep State

OLIVER L NORTH
DOB 10 7 43

CHAPTER 6

SHIPS, TRAINS AND PLANES

MONEY, LOTS OF IT

In the mid-70s Don Felix all of a sudden seemed to have hit the jackpot. He bought a house in the exclusive "Impasse des Milliardaires," one of the very few private streets in Belgium. The Impasse was a refuge for the super-rich, a gated dead-end street, an appendix of the Avenue Louise, the "Champs Elysées of Brussels." He had quickly become the "biggest taxpayer" of Tervuren, where he lived most of the year. Not that he was a big fan of paying taxes. He skilfully used his Tradin company in Vaduz to "optimize" his taxes. Still, by 1980 he would run into trouble with the Belgian fiscal authorities over the profits he had made in the Lufthansa and SABENA deals.

The taxman had found out about Felix's companies Serdan and Tradin. Obviously Felix had made a complete mess by mixing the companies' and his private financial transactions. Some of the Serdan invoices to Lufthansa were paid to Tradin and vice-versa. Other invoices had been settled in cash, which had been picked up in suitcases by Felix.

As he started getting nasty letters from the taxman, Felix had nearly pulled off the perfect scam. He simultaneously filed for bankruptcy of Serdan, Tradin and himself personally. Had he succeeded, as he very nearly did, he would have remained unbothered by the fiscal authorities for the rest of his days. Just in time the judicial system realized what was at stake in back taxes and rejected the request. Some time later, in February of 1991, the attorney Philippe Pauly, who was initially appointed to handle Felix's bankruptcy filing, was sentenced to 3 years in prison for fraud. One of Pauly's aides was Luc de B., a good friend and co-student of Daniel Przedborski. Judging by the list of Daniel's 2016 Facebook friends, their friendship still stands.

Anyway, the fiscal matter would be settled in 1982 after Felix had agreed to pay the equivalent of 3 million dollar. But where was all this money coming from in the first place?

FLYING HIGH

In 1962 Felix had hired Mr. Gilissen as his private secretary. Gilissen's son-in-law was an employee of SABENA's marketing department. Felix was a close friend of Giovanni Dieu, a WWII pilot and war hero whose brother Gaston was the big boss of SABENA in the 1950s and 60s. Felix had probably used these contacts to hammer out a deal with the airline. He started selling cheap gadgets that the airline would use as promotional gifts to the passengers. After a while Felix was producing hundreds of small blue textile travel bags. His business was now being recommended by his banker to other airlines like Pan Am and Lufthansa. Then the nature of the deal somehow changed.

Lufthansa was grossly overcharged for the gadgets Felix had supplied. At first no one at Lufthansa seemed to notice. Felix's invoices were paid out of an "unofficial" parallel fund dubbed "K2." Several million mark had been spent and thousands of cheap gadgets stocked in extra warehouses before the proverbial muck hit the fan. Why had Lufthansa boss Herbert Culmann been overpaying for these worthless gadgets for so long?

Culmann, who had become honorary consul of Costa Rica, thanks to Felix, never offered a reasonable explanation other than that "the investment was necessary to open the markets for Lufthansa." The whole affair was stinking to high heaven. All of a sudden, the German press was all over Felix Przedborski. It was assumed that Lufthansa and SABENA, via Don Felix, had bought their way into the monopolistic IATA machinery. Questioned by Belgian authorities, Don Felix stated that he "could never reveal the whole truth." He advised the investigators to go and talk to the CEO of SABENA, who, according to Felix, "had complete knowledge." SABENA being a state-owned airline at the time, it is very doubtful that its CEO was ever bothered.

IATA was founded in 1945 in Cuba as a private company aiming at streamlining the chaotic, rapidly growing airfare business. In reality IATA, headquartered in Geneva, operated like a cartel, dictating the price of airline tickets. In the early days of air travel, nearly all of the airlines were state-owned and thus were supervised by civil servants in some ministerial cabinet. Most of them had no experience whatsoever in aviation or air travel. They happily gave their fiat to whatever the "experts" of IATA put forward. Over the years this had inflated the status of IATA to that of a quasi-official institution. IATA had succeeded in making itself indispensable. Any well-reputed airline just had to join IATA.

Many had hoped that modern air travel would be a new mode of transport available to all. Obviously, IATA had another vision. Only the well-off could afford their tickets. This caused many airlines to operate at a loss year after year. Not to worry, the taxpayer would pick up the tab every time. Any airline bypassing IATA, offering cheap tickets, was targeted as an "unfair competitor" and stopped cold. As air traffic grew denser, IATA made itself indispensable yet again as a broker of airport landing slots. Being banned from landing at important airports like New York or London was out of the question for big airlines. IATA would cater to their needs if enough money was passed under the table. For Lufthansa the deals with Felix had obviously left a lot to be desired. The airline spent 18 million dollars hiring Wilmer, Cutler, Pickering and Lloyd as their legal counselors in judicial hearings and procedures in the US on the subject of "airport landing rights."

IRAN-CONTRA

Don Felix loved to travel. He had always shown great interest in tourism, travel and transportation by air or sea. By the time he had the Lufthansa scheme going, he had opened his own chain of Primus and EuroLloyd travel agencies. Felix was using his new riches quite wisely. He had spent some of the Lufthansa millions to buy a major stake in Global Bank. This bank then granted a five-million dollar credit line to his Serdan company.

The Primus office in Vienna, where Felix himself spent much of his professional life, was run by Günther Arlow from 1981 to 1999. Arlow declared in 1999 that the Primus agencies were in fact subsidiaries of the Kühne & Nagel company, originally a sea freight company founded in 1890 in Bremen, Germany. K&N had expanded its business to include airfreight. By the 1990s, K&N was one of the top three airfreighters operating at Brussels National airport. Over time, Felix would practically take over K&N through Tradin, with the assistance of Global Bank.

Arlow had made some friends in the East. Anatoli Katric, aka Ketridge, for one. Katric was taking care of business in Austria and France on behalf of top-maffiyoso Semion Mogilevitch. With the help of his friend Shabtai Kalmanovitch, honorary consul of Costa Rica in Saint Petersburg, Mogilevitch had obtained an Israeli passport. Shabtai Kalmanovitch was part of the Mikhailov network, as was Don Felix, according to the 2001 Belgian police report PV18367. (Appendix 2).

K&N was growing rapidly into a top multinational logistics company. In 1981 the company set up shop in Switzerland. At the top of the list of shareholders of the Swiss branch was Roland "Tiny" Rowland, the boss of the giant Lonrho conglomerate. Lonrho stood for London-Rhodesia, referring to the former British colonial empire and its ties with the Rothschild-Rhodes endeavors in Africa. Lonrho owned African mines, the Harare oil pipeline and a fleet of aircraft. Rowland, not surprisingly, had been involved in illegally supplying goods to embargoed South Africa. Rowland later admitted having been involved in the logistics of the Iran-Contra operations too. He had been doing business with Ollie North, John Poindexter, Kashoggi, Amiram Nir and Manucher Ghorbanifar. "With the blessings of the White House," as he would add.

In mid January of the year 1983 the Swiss paper *Die Wochenzeitung* published an article titled "Dick im Waffengeschäft," accusing K&N of having supplied weapons to Tehran, via Dubai. The initial negotiations had taken place in 1981 in London under the supervision of Michael Aspin, whose brother Leslie was a close friend of CIA boss Bill Casey. The Aspin brothers were quite well-reputed in mercenary circles. They had smuggled arms into Beirut on behalf of the Christian Falanx. K&N also appeared to have delivered at least 31 arms shipments to South Africa. The affair had political implications in the UK, since Thatcher, the British customs service and even the Swiss government had turned a blind eye.

All this seemed to indicate that Felix was a friend of South-Africa and a staunch opponent of communism. The former should come as no surprise. South Africa was in a nuclear weapons development program with Israel. Both nations allegedly felt equally threatened – Israel by its "bellicose" Arab neighbors; the South African Apartheid regime by its own black population. Both countries had purchased Gerald Bull's extended range howitzers that could fire nuclear charges at targets 25 miles away. Bull was a brilliant Canadian engineer who dreamed of firing satellites into orbit with a specially designed supergun. He had ties with the Canadian-Jewish Bronfman family, with the international Powder Cartel and with the Belgian arms producer PRB. In March of 1990 Bull was shot in the head as he entered his Brussels apartment. Don Felix, being an insider of the International Atomic Energy Agency (IAEA) in Vienna, must have been of great use to the Israeli nuclear program.

THE ROCKET BOY

It was a middle-aged German lady, visiting him in Montreal in 1956, that had thrown the life of Gerald Bull onto the tracks towards his final destiny. At the time, Bull was an employee of the Space Research Institute of McGill University. Her father, the lady explained, had been on the team of German engineers that had designed and built the Top Secret "Paris Kanone" during the First World War. And she was in possession of the blueprints, which, she hoped, would interest the bright young engineer. Oh boy, would they ever! Bull was jubilant. To him, the Rausenberger papers were truly a gift from heaven.

Bull was in his late twenties at the time, but he had been a brilliant student. He was by far the youngest doctor of the university of Toronto. He was born in 1928 in North Bay, Ontario. His mother died when he was three, and he was raised by his aunt and uncle. His youth had been no bed of roses. He had always felt abandoned and betrayed. He couldn't stand being rejected. Failure was never an option for young Gerald. Maybe that's why he was such a brilliant student.

Bull became a gifted designer of military hardware. At age 32, he was the star of a Pentagon ballistics lab. The weaponry he designed included a highly accurate long-range howitzer and a gigantic supergun, a mortar with a barrel over 120 feet long. He was the Canadian "Boy Rocket Scientist" whom *McCleans* magazine dedicated an article to in 1953. He was a typical hands-on scientist – "earmarked for stardom" – who disliked sterile discussions and bureaucracy.

The giant Paris gun was a 140-ton howitzer with a barrel length of 37 meters. It was capable of firing huge 23 centimeter shells over a distance of 130 kilometers. At the time, the range of conventional artillery was limited to about 20 kilometers. At the top of their trajectory, the shells reached an altitude of 40 kilometers. The time of flight of the projectiles was close to three minutes. The key scientist behind the German project was Fritz Rausenberger of the Krupp steel company. Three of these mammoth guns had been deployed to France during the spring offensive of 1918. On Good Friday of that year, a shell "out of nowhere" hit the Saint-Gervais church in the heart of Paris, killing 91 and wounding 100 people. After the war, these steel monsters were dismantled and hidden, to keep them out of enemy hands. As long-range artillery was gradually replaced by aircraft in the following decades, the concept of the supergun had slowly faded – until 1956 – when Bull decided to revive the technology that, he hoped, was capable of firing satellites into orbit.

Bull left government work in 1968, when he was hired by the Space Research Corporation (SRC) then being founded by the Bronfman group, of Seagram's Whiskey fame.

In reality, the firm was an arms smuggling operation, sanctioned by the U.S. and British intelligence services. Bull developed one of the world's best 155mm howitzers, capable of firing a tactical nuclear warhead at targets 40 miles away. The howitzers were illegally sold to Israel, South Africa, and Iran. As the representative for their Middle-East operations the Bronfmans recruited Israeli agent Shaul Eisenberg.

SRC was shipping weapons to Iran with the assistance of the Jewish Zim Shipping company. This continued even after the fall of the Shah in 1979. The Bronfmans sold SRC to Pakistani businessman Saad Gabr, a protégé of Agha Hasan Abedi, chairman of the infamous BCCI bank. For his involvement in the delivery of weapons to embargoed South Africa, Bull landed in jail for a while, after which he continued his arms deals as before.

In March 1988 Gerald Bull was contracted by Iraq to build three superguns, one of them a smaller prototype, capable of launching a 2-ton rocket-propelled projectile into orbit.

Saddam Hussein's "Project Babylon" was largely financed by Belgian Société Générale, with the consent of British intelligence. An unauthorized four billion dollar loan to Iraq, granted by the Atlanta branch of the Italian Banca Nazionale del Lavoro (BNL), was uncovered in the press. BNL was Italy's largest bank, headquartered in Rome, across the street from the US Embassy. It was the start of the Iraq-Gate scandal. An Italian Senate report stated that BNL Rome had been running the Iraqi weapons program, while BNL Atlanta had been launched by "some circles in the American political-military-industrial complex."

Kissinger Associates was BNL's legal adviser. Belgian viscount Etienne Davignon was a one-time director of the Kissinger law firm. Part of the Iraq-Gate money had been used to buy weaponry from Gerald Bull and his SRC. BCCI helped Bull smuggle propellant for his super guns from Belgium to Iraq. The bank granted a $72 million loan, via Bank of America, to Space Research financier Banca Nazionale de Lavaro (BNL). Next to Kissinger, Belgian Baron Lambert and Edmond de Rothschild were sitting on the BNL advisory board.

Bull's supergun propellant was provided by the Poudreries Réunies de Belgique (PRB). The European SRC subsidiary, Space Research Corporation International, had been co-founded and financed by PRB, that owned 45 percent of its shares. PRB was part of the Société Générale holding that was headed by Etienne Davignon at the time. Like the Swedish Bofors group, PRB was a prominent member of the international "Powder Cartel," that was suspected of being behind the Olof Palme murder. Both Société Générale and PRB would later end up in the hands of the Albert Frère-Paul Desmarais empire GBL, that also controlled GDF Suez and Bertelsman, the former Nazi media conglomerate.

In the 1980s, the Powder Cartel was also doing business with Oliver North and the Iran-Contra crowd. In Austria, arms dealer Walter Schön was involved with the Powder Cartel. He was the representative of arms producers Oerlikon and Dynamit-Nobel. Schön, a friend of Felix Przedborski, had been appointed honorary consul of Costa Rica in 1974.

In March of 1990 Gerald Bull was killed when entering his apartment in Uccle, a rich suburb of Brussels. The murder was never solved. There were claims that Belgian minister Andre Cools, shot dead 16 months later, had been investigating the Bull murder and was ready to blow the whistle.

According to Belgian police report PV18367, one of Felix's contacts was Marc Rich. Rich, born in Antwerp as Marc "Reich," is a wealthy Jewish commodity trader and key figure in the illegal shipments of oil to South Africa. Jewish billionaire businessman Baruch "Bruce" Rappaport was involved in these shady deals. Rappaport was a banker as well as a shipping magnate. His Bank of New York, aka BONY, was the favorite bank of the Russian-Jewish Maffiya of Little Odessa in Brighton Beach, New York. Little Odessa had stretched its criminal tentacles all the way to Antwerp, Belgium, resulting in the Comuele debacle mentioned in the

ATLAS Report. Rappaport was involved in the maritime logistic operations of Iran-Contra, together with CIA-agent Ed Wilson, who knew his way around shipping operations from his days in the US Navy Task Force 157 operation. Wilson was one of the old CIA "China Cowboys" who had joined the Enterprise.

Felix claimed to have excellent contacts with the CIA. These may have come about in several ways. Felix might have been recruited by the CIC or the OSS at a very early stage. That would explain his many trips behind the Iron Curtain. Or he might have been in touch with US intelligence via the Vatican, where CIA agent James Jesus Angleton was cooperating with the papal Pro Deo intelligence service, set up by the Belgian Dominican father Felix Morlion. Angleton, incidentally, was a big supporter of the Zionist cause and co-founder of the Mossad. Or maybe Felix had become involved in David Dubinsky's and Irving Brown's CIA-backed anti-communist operations in France in 1947. Whichever may have been the case, Felix was obviously siding with the financial establishment in the fight against the Red Menace.

ALL ROADS LEAD TO GENEVA

Felix's sons Daniel and Serge, some insiders claimed, were not equally talented. Serge studied medicine and specialized in Alzheimer's disease. The less gifted Daniel became a lawyer. He was earmarked to succeed his father "in business." As young Daniel was drafted into the military in 1979, his father made sure he would have an interesting time serving his country. Przedborski junior was parachuted into the staff of socialist figurehead José Desmarets, defense minister and vice-premier.

Desmarets had warned repeatedly of the new versions of communist subversion: pacifism and the green movement. These were clearly inspired by leftist sentiments, he said, and sponsored by Moscow. Coming from a "leftie," Desmarets' warnings were quite surprising. They even earned him some sympathy from the ultra-right. As we have seen, the "new left" had veered to the right quite significantly in the previous decades.

Desmarets even joined the World Anti-Communist League (WACL), the Washington-sponsored action group that had declared war on the commies wherever they could be found. The WACL was headed by ex-US general Jack Singlaub, one of the old "China Cowboys" who had been in the thick of things in China, Korea and Vietnam. He had witnessed first-hand how a well-organized opium ring could finance an entire army. A few years later Desmarets would succeed Singlaub as the head of the WACL, that held yearly conferences in Europe, Asia and the USA.

After his apprenticeship in Demarets' defense cabinet, young Przedborski moved to Texas for a while, probably as a guest of billionaire Fred

Tramell Crow. According to *Forbes* magazine, real estate magnate Crow was "the country's largest landlord" in 1971. In late 1984 Przedborski junior moved from Texas to Geneva, Switzerland, where he was to be submerged in the wonderful world of silent money. He landed a job in the cabinet of Python, Schifferli, Peter & Partners, who over the years had proved their absolute loyalty to even the highest of the financial elites.

Piere Schifferli was obviously a multi-talented person. He was in national politics and he was the director of marine logistics companies like Masshipco and Massmariner. Shipping and freight insurance is big business in Switzerland. At the same time he was head of the WACL in Switzerland. He must have known Belgian minister Desmarets. Incidentally, one of Daniel Przedborski's clients was Bruce Rappaport. This leads us back to the Iran-Contra affair.

Colonel North was employing Rappaport and Wilson for his weapons shipments by sea. In the mid-1980s he and Richard Secord had bought the rusty Danish freighter *Erria*, to do some business for themselves on the side. They tasked the Swiss-American lawyer Willard Zucker in Geneva with setting up facade companies in Panama. Willard and Schifferli were both involved in the Santa Elena project in the north of Costa Rica, where a Panama company was to construct an airfield. The man behind this construction company was none other than drug-lord Manuel Noriega.

Zucker, North and Secord were also doing business with Edmond Safra, one of the key Nebula figures according to the ATLAS Report. Zucker often joined forces with the Geneva lawfirm Magnin, Dunand & Co, counselors of "the Enterprise." Baudouin Dunand was on excellent terms with the Swiss Nazi banker François Genoud, who had been financing Muslim Brotherhood and Arab extremists ever since the end of WWII. Dunand was co-director of the Saudi Investment Company in which the bin Laden family held a big stake. Ernest Backes, author of the book *Revelations* about the Clearstream fraud, wrote that "he wouldn't be surprised at all if the 9-11 evidence would lead directly to the Swiss bank accounts operated by Genoud." Indeed, there appeared to exist a continuum from Genoud's sponsoring of the Muslim Brotherhood to the Saudi Wahabites, the Mujahideen and Al Qaeda.

The unexcelled investigative journalist Lucy Komisar commented:

> Following the September 11 attacks on the World Trade Center and the Pentagon, the United States started focusing its investigation on the financial trail of Osama bin Laden and the al-Qaeda network. Like any other large, global operation, international terrorists need to move large sums of money across borders clandestinely. In November, U.S. authorities named some banks that had bin Laden accounts, and it put them on a blacklist. One was Al Taqwa – "Fear of God" – registered in the Bahamas with offices

in Lugano, Switzerland. Al Taqwa had access to the Clearstream system through its correspondent account with the Banca del Gottardo in Lugano, which has a published Clearstream account (No. 74381). Furthermore, one of SICO's administrators, Geneva attorney Baudoin Dunand, is a partner in a law firm, Magnin Dunand & Partners, that set up the Swiss financial services company SBA – a subsidiary of the SBA Bank in Paris, which is controlled by Khaled bin Mahfouz. Mahfouz's younger sister is married to Osama bin Laden. SICO is associated with Dar Al-Maal-Al-Islami (DMI), an Islamic financial institution also based in Geneva and presided over by Prince Muhammed Al Faisal Al Saoud, a cousin of Saudi King Fahd, that directs millions a year to fundamentalist movements.

Back to the talented mister Schifferli. By 1989 he was on the board of the Unilabs company, a chain of highly specialized medical laboratories. The company had some of its roots in Belgium. Its history was quite intriguing. Schifferli's boss at Unilabs was the Belgian-Jewish businessman Edgar Zwirn, who had acquired the company after the mysterious murder of self-made millionaire businessman Baron Paul Cams. On 17 November 1983 the silver-haired baron was shot in the face with a .38 handgun while watching TV in his villa in Ganshoren, near Brussels. He had started his career as a hairspray salesman but had diversified into medical lab services in the early 70s. His labs were found to be involved in a mega-fraud to the prejudice of the Belgian national health service. Baron Cams was also linked to the Kirschen affair, a gold and diamonds scam in the Jewish milieu of Antwerp that involved high-level liberal party politicians. According to the ATLAS Report the liberal party minister Willy De Clercq was "eating out of the hand of Felix Przedborski."

Cams was also suspected of being involved in the processing of opium for the Madonia mafia clan. His murder would forever remain unsolved. His widow moved to Marbella, on the sunny Spanish coast, were she enjoyed life on a monthly allowance of 50,000 Euro. Incidentally, the Cams residence soon became the home of "underworld debt collector" Sergio Ferrari, suspected of smuggling drugs for the mafia. By 1987 Edgar Zwirn and Unilabs had joined forces with "Count" Gherardi Dandolo, a shady Swiss-Belgian businessman whom many considered to be the financier of the ultra-right action groups behind the Brabant Killings. Dandolo's network stretched all the way to SASEA, the P2 Lodge an the WACL.

Patokh Chodiev

CHAPTER 7

SKINNING THE BEAR

SKINNING THE BEAR

Don Felix had no doubt turned anti-communist at a very young age. He may even have recruited pro-Western agents on his many journeys to the Eastern Bloc. Hence his contacts within the WACL and his involvement in the Iran-Contra operation. By the late 1980s, though, he was in touch with some of the most important figures of the Eastern Bloc underground. One can only assume that these millionaires, many of them Jews, were more than willing to help topple the Soviet regime and embrace capitalism. This is where US operative Leo "Lee" Wanta comes in.

Leo Wanta portrayed himself as "the 27 Trillion Dollar Man" who helped sink the Russian Ruble back in the 1980s, as part of president Reagan's economic war against the USSR. Wanta, aka Rick Reynolds, aka Frank Ingram, operating from Austria and Switzerland, claimed to have used several straw companies for his Ruble transactions. One of which was New Republic/Financial USA who, according to the ATLAS Report, was involved in a two-billion dollar transfer from the Belgian Bank CGER. Farouk Khan, an employee of CGER, confirmed the transfer but denied he had authorized it without the consent of the account holder Leo Wanta. Khan declared that the large Ruble transactions were handled directly by the bank's Brussels headquarters. That sounded quite plausible.

Another company used by Wanta was M&S International of Antwerp. The acronym M&S stood for Mike Brandwain and his brother-in-law Sasha Krivorushko. The company was managed by Brandwain and Riccardo Fanchini, who had opened accounts at the CGER and Kredietbank. They had set up branches in Moscow, New York, Tel Aviv, Warsaw, Berlin and Vilnius. Brandwain had clear links with the Balagula clan in Little Odessa. In July 1998, four 9mm bullets killed Rachmiel "Mike" Brandwain in the center of Antwerp, a few steps away from the secluded Jewish diamond quarter, where he had set up shop. Marat Balagula was said to have started up this Antwerp Connection with Boris Nayfeld in order to start recycling blood diamonds from Sierra Leone.

Balagula and Shabtai Kalmanovitch, sponsored by Marc Rich, had rapidly gained political influence in the West African state. They had president Joseph Saidu Momoh on a leash. Kalmanovitch – honorary consul of Costa Rica, thanks to Don Felix – was being protected by Mossad agent David Kimche. Part of the blood diamonds were shipped to Vietnam, where they were traded for heroin. Felix Przedborski was suspected of being involved in the Vietnam drug trade. Leo Wanta denied having done business with Don Felix. Wanta "had heard his name mentioned" but had not known him personally.

Why were Don Felix and his diplomat friend Alfred Cahen, both anti-communists, accolading prominent Red Maffiyosi like Mogilevitch, Mikhailov, Chodiev and others?

They had most probably been instrumental in skinning the Russian Bear. Felix's long-time friend ambassador Alfred Cahen had been cultivating friendships in Eastern Europe as far back as the early 1970s, at the height of the Cold War. He and many others hoped to undermine the Soviet authority from within by sowing the capitalist seeds and creating pro-Western cells within the USSR. Obviously the prospect of business expansion into Western Europe, where hard currencies were to be had instead of the ruble, must have incited some Eastern Bloc businessmen to help bring down the Soviets. Presidents Gorbachov and Yeltsin, both flush with US dollars, had given the final push. As the Bear went down, the vultures landed to feast on its cadaver.

After the fall of the Berlin Wall, the Eastern Bloc oligarchs swarmed to Belgium, France, Germany and the UK. By the early 2000s the richest Belgian citizen next to Albert Frère of GBL was Patokh Chodiev. Chodiev, Alexander Machkevitsh and Alijan Ibragimov – the infamous "Kazach Trio" – had the Belgian politicians' dream of a bonanza and even of a "new Congo" in Kazachstan. But all was not well. The deeply politicized Belgian Tractebel company, part of the GBL holding, lost 55 million euro in the Kazach venture.

The Kazach Trio were doing business with the Seabeco company of Boris Birshtein, who had helped Boris Yeltsin funnel cash and gold into his Swiss bank accounts. As Eric Van de Weghe had testified in PV18367, they were also doing business with the Mikhailov network, including Felix Przedborski. Young Eric should know. He had been recruited by Anatoli Katric on behalf of Mikhailov. Eric had been Mikhailov's proxy in all matters pertaining to his naturalization request in Belgium. He and the Uhoda brothers had been catering to all the needs of the Maffiyosi. Eric Van de Weghe was close friends with Maxo Cahen, son of the ambassador who had helped out Mogilevitch. Eric's tutor was Jewish millionaire Pierre Perlmutter, a friend of Edmond Safra. Eric was deeply involved in the Tractebel debacle, as were the Uhoda brothers of Liège. They were all somehow linked to André Cools.

COTE D' AZUR

By the late 1990s the French government started to voice concerns over the unusually large influx of Russian billionaires, especially in the Monaco area. An investigation revealed that the names of top European businessmen were surfacing in the financial constructs built with Russian funds. One of these was Belgian baron Edouard Jean Empain, aged 61, of the once great Empain dynasty. At the start of the 20th century Empain was a household name in the field of urban electrification and the construction of tramway and subway systems. This placed the company in an orbit close to the water-power-banking cartel.

In 1905, at the height of his glory, Empain senior had built the city of Heliopolis, in the north of Egypt. The Empain Palace still stands on Salah Salem street in what has now become a suburb of Cairo. By 1969 Ed Empain had succeeded in merging his company with the French industrial behemoth Schneider, much to the dislike of the French Elysee. Schneider, as we have seen, had been a major player, together with De Wendel, in the fascist Synarchist clique in the run-up to WWII. The merger would catapult Empain, who had close ties with GE-Westinghouse, to the very top of the French nuclear industry. That would cost him dearly.

In January 1978 he was kidnapped in Paris and held for ransom for two months. After his release, he and his company appeared to have undergone drastic changes. Empain accused the French authorities of having engineered the kidnapping that cost him his left ring finger. And worse, in his absence his close associates had pulled some levers that put him completely off to the side. Disgusted, the embittered baron turned his back on his associates and resigned. This put the control levers of the French nuclear industry back into French hands.

The same baron Ed Empain was seen rubbing shoulders with Felix Przedborski and Pierre Merli at an Antibes garden party in the early 1990s. The baron must have liked the area. The French report stated that he owned 98 percent of the shares of Azur Trading Company, importing and exporting oil and other goods. ATCO was run by an ex-OAS hit squad figure by the name of Jean-Paul Cullet, codename "BlondBlond," who was close to ultra-rightist Le Pen. This was another strange case of an ultra-right figure rolling out the red carpet for Eastern Bloc cronies.

ATCO had attracted the attention of French intelligence when it was doing business with Baghdad in the 1980s, when the Iran-Iraq war was still raging. In particular, the company had deals going with a group of companies controlled by two Russians residing in Monaco: Vladimir Ponomarenko, born in Baku, Azerbaijan; and Leonid Minin, born in Odessa, Ukraine. Minin, a citizen of Israel, was persona non grata in France. He was among 18 Russians considered a danger to France's national security. Ponomarenko and Minin were entangled in a web of companies centered on Griffon holding, registered in Panama. Empain was dealing with the Russians via the Swiss firm Flomer, in which he held a 20 percent stake alongside Griffon Finance. Flomer had created a stir by trying to buy the renowned Victorine cinema studio in Nice and by offering 21 million francs for the luxurious Croix de Gardes property in Cannes. Nordex, a multinational company based in Vienna was also involved. The latter had been set up by KGB operatives. The Red Maffiya, conspiring to "use France as an aircraft carrier for the conquest of Europe," was showing a clear preference for the Monaco-Antibes-Nice triangle. Don Felix's estate was sitting right in the middle of it.

CHAPTER 8

POLITICS FOR PROFITS

*"If the Jews succeed in erecting their own state, which they will call Israel,
then let me predict what will happen.*

*The Jews will not emigrate there but they will stay in their host countries and
continue their crimes as long as they possibly can. Only then will they seek
shelter in their country, that will never extradite them."*

Adolf Hitler, ca 1924

THE LIQUORMAN

"Four and twenty Yankees, feeling very dry,
Went across the border to get a drink of rye.
When the rye was opened, the Yanks began to sing,
'God bless America, but God save the King!'"
Popular Prohibition song (1920-1933)

In 1843, Henry Jones and eleven other Jewish immigrants gathered at
Sinsheimers Café in Lower East Manhattan to confront the deplor-
able condition of Jews in their newly adopted country. Under the im-
pulse of Isaac Rosenbourg, the twelve -one for each of the tribes of Judea
– founded B'Nai B'Rith, the Children of the Covenant – committed to
provide for the Jewish widows and their children. Over time, and with
the funding of Jewish tycoon Jacob Schiff, B'Nai B'Rith would evolve into
the biggest Lodge of the 33rd Degree Scottish Rite. The Rothschild cabal,
siding with the British Crown and the City against the abolition of slav-
ery, were heavily invested in the Southern cotton industry. B'Nai B'Rith
would prove to be an excellent tool to further their agenda. This Jewish
group, intent on helping poor Jewish families, soon started recruiting Jewish youngsters who were out of work. Some would join the Jewish Lower Eastside criminal syndicate, where they would learn all the tricks of
the trade. Soon they were involved with prostitution, alcohol smuggling,
gambling and extortion.

The Lower Eastside became the scene of violent clashes between the
Jewish and the Italian and Irish gangs. This milieu would produce a new

type of criminals that would rise to respectability thanks to their fortune and the bribing of political figures. They proved very useful when it came to breaking strikes and eliminating "troublemakers."

This Jewish biotope produced top criminals like Maier Suchowljansky and Benjamin Siegelbaum, better known as Meyer Lansky and Bugsy Siegel. The latter had started his career as "schlammer," a strike breaker and a hitman. Via the Yiddish Connection of Arnie Rothstein they teamed up with the notorious Abe Zwillman, Dutch Schultz and Charles "Lucky" Luciano. Rothstein had risen to the top under the wings of the ruthless killer Edward Osterman, aka Monk Eastman, who by 1900 controlled a gang of about 75 men. They regularly clashed with the Italian Five Point Gang in the streets of the Lower Eastside.

Arnie Rothstein, son of a rich Jewish immigrant from Bessarabia, was a gambler and bookmaker who had made it big. He succeeded in imposing a Pax Mafiosa on the gangs of Lower Eastside. Instead of competing by the bullet, the Jewish and Italian gangs joined forces. By 1920 Arnie Rothstein had upgraded himself from a street criminal to a respectable businessman. He was running his own luxury casino, where he met high fliers like the oil baron Harry Sinclair and the Canadian bootlegger Joseph Seagram, the future business partner of the Canadian Jewish Bronfman family. Thanks to Rothstein's Pax Mafiosa the illegal whiskey convoys were guaranteed safe passage to the many popular "speakeasies." This state of affairs resulted in a de facto Prohibition syndicate involving Rothstein, Bugsy Siegel, Meyer Lansky, Lucky Luciano, Frank Costello, Lepke Buchalter, Dutch Schultz, Gurrah Shapiro and Jack "Legs" Diamond. In Detroit, near the Canadian border, the Jewish Purple Gang was escorting the whiskey convoys of Samuel and Harry Bronfman. The Bronfman family had fled czarist Russia in 1889 and settled in Quebec. By the mid-1920s they were making a fortune selling booze to the speakeasies of New York, Boston, and Chicago. Like Rothstein, the Bronfmans would soon become respectable businessmen.

Over time the family of bootleggers would join forces with Sir William Keswick, a successful opium smuggler linked to British Petroleum, Jardine Matheson Co., and the Hong Kong and Shanghai Bank. The Bronfman network proved very useful in smuggling opium into the USA. And so the bootleg family turned into servants of the British Crown, for which they would be rewarded in 1969 with the Knighthood of the Most Venerable Order of Saint John of Jerusalem. Keswick introduced the family to the exclusive clique of the Hofjuden, the Montefiores, the Hirsches and the Rothschilds. They coached the Bronfmans into star positions within the Canadian and global Zionist movement. In May of 1949 Phyllis Bronfman married Jean Lambert of the Belgian Banque Lambert, a Rothschild subsidiary.

DUBINSKY's FRENCH CONNECTION

The Bronfmans were not the only Jewish family that had fled Czarist pogroms in Russia. By the turn of the century, thousands of Jews had flocked to Manhattan. Many of them were eager to return to Russia to support the Bolshevik revolution. Trotsky himself resided in New York, where he enjoyed a lavish lifestyle until his departure for Saint Petersburg in 1917. The first Bolshevik coup of 1905, financed by Wall Street and the City, had failed.

In 1917 things were different. The Bolsheviks grabbed power and murdered the Czar and his family. The Russian revolution was in essence a Jewish undertaking that would soon affect Germany. A state of affairs that worried Adolf Hitler a great deal. He had survived the carnage of WWI only to discover, upon his return to Germany, that München had been taken over by Bolsheviks. They had wrecked the government at the worst possible time with the war still raging on the Western Front. The Kaiser had abdicated and, fearing for his life, had fled the country. These events had profoundly changed young Hitler's views on the Jewish Question.

In the USA communism was still viewed as a respectable ideology at the time. The Jewish successes in Russia motivated many American Jews to embrace Trotskyism and communism. Not surprisingly, the first communist party and union of America originated in the Jewish milieu of Manhattan. By the mid-1920s the biggest communist newspaper in the USA was the New York *Morgen Freiheit*, published in Yiddish.

Jay Liebstein "Lovestone," editor of *The Communist* magazine became president of the Communist Party in 1927. Thousands of Jewish workers in the New York area joined the communist unions, the biggest one of which was David Dubinsky's International Ladies' Garment Workers union. "Dubinsky" was born in 1892 in Brest-Litovsk as David Isaac Dobnievski. He was raised in Lodz, where his father had a bakery. As a young unionist he was arrested and deported to Siberia. He had fled the Russian internment camps and managed to reach the New Continent. He set foot on American soil in Lower East Manhattan in 1911. However, both Lovestone and Dubinsky would soon turn their backs on communism. They were both recruited by the CIA to undermine the leftist unions in France that had organized the great Marseilles strike of 1947. The Corsican Guérini gang had been more than helpful in decimating the ranks of the leftist strikers. Their reward was a carte blanche for their Golden Triangle opium and heroïn trafficking via the Marseilles port. It was the start of the successful "French Connection."

Dubinsky's number was in Don Felix's notebook. One of the Guérini contacts was Charles Pasqua, who would later become a minister in the French government. He made a fortune selling the famous French liquor Pernod-Ricard. He had married a daughter of the Canadian Joly bootleggers family, who was in business with the Bronfmans. Pasqua mentored young Sarkozy whose stepfather was Frank Wisner Jr, son of "Whiz" Wisner of CIA-fame.

Nicolas Sarkozy completed lawschool in the USA. He was very close to the Canadian Desmarais family, the energy barons who control PowerCo. The Desmarais in turn are stakeholders in the listed Belgian holding GBL, Group Bruxelles Lambert. "Lambert" refers not only to the late baron Lambert and his Rothschild bank but also to Drexel Burnham Lambert, deeply involved in the Jewish junk bond scam of Carl Lindner, Ivan Boesky and Milken. Two of the companies in GBL's portfolio are Pernod-Ricard and the utilities giant GDF Suez, whose director for many years was the Belgian pipe-smoking captain of industry Etienne Davignon. (Annex 9). He was a prominent CFR member, president of the Bilderberg conferences and a close friend of Kissinger. Needless to say, Davignon was on excellent terms with the Desmarais family, who practically owned the Canadian government. At this point it is important to note that Canada is still part of the Queen's Commonwealth. Unsurprisingly, Paul Desmarais is a fierce opponent of the independence of the francophone Quebec province, one of the Queen's worst nightmares.

In July of 1967, President de Gaulle, visiting the World Fair in Montreal, had shocked the establishment by concluding his speech to a large crowd with the historical words "Vive le Québec libre!," which translates as "Long live free Quebec!." That put him on the Queen's black list. De Gaulle survived several attempts on his life.

EU INCORPORATED

The Bronfman picture wouldn't be complete without the figure of Jean Monnet, one of the mythical "fathers of the EU," if we are to believe conventional history. Monnet, to a great extent, was "Made in USA." French president de Gaulle had called him a US agent.

Monnet had started out as a cognac salesman. In 1904 J.G. Monnet & Co., set up shop in London. Young Monnet often sailed to North America, in search of new export markets for his excellent French brandy. He went into business with the bank Lazard Frères and with the Hudson Bay Company (HBC), a well established British colonial enterprise. Soon Monnet's company United Vineyard Propietors shipped huge quantities of French brandy to Canada. Just like the Scottish whiskey, the French brandy flowed to hundreds of American speakeasies through the Bronfman channels.

Monnet then succeeded in hammering out a $200 million contract for the HBC. This deal propelled Monnet's career to a whole new level. He became friends with HBC director Lord Robert Kindersley, member of Rhodes' Pilgrim Society, ex-director of the Bank of England and ex-president of bank Lazard Frères. Lazard was deeply involved in the foundation of the Federal Reserve in 1913. The bank's origins went back all the way to the Frankfurter Judengasse. In 1916, opium-lord Keswick became involved in the HBC. Around the same time Arnie Rothstein went in business with Bronfman's Pure Drug Distribution Co., who was making big money during the Canadian prohibition of 1915.

In the USA, prohibition had been promoted by the John D. Rockefeller, who sponsored the Anti-Saloon League movement. At the time there was a fierce competition between alcohol and gasoline for use in combustion engines. Rockefeller boycotted the use of alcohol by all means. Also, the existing electrical car public transportation system, that stood in the way of Henry Ford's gasoline-consuming motorcar, was basically destroyed by the Rockefeller-Ford cartel.

The Bronfmans went in business with Monnet and the Hudson Bay Co. This is how Bronfman became involved in the Keswick-Jardine Matheson opium trade. In the early 1920s Rothstein and Meyer Lansky started prospecting the Hong Kong opium market. In Latin America the Jewish mob would later strike deals with the Colombian cocaine cartel that saw it's business flourish after Klaus Barbie had entered the scene. The involvement of Lansky in drug running takes us one step closer to Robert Vesco, who was Lansky's successor. Felix Przedborski, who appeared to be involved in both the Central American cocaine and the Vietnam opium trafficking, was a Vesco business partner.

By the end of the 1970s Ed Bronfman had bought his way to the top position of the World Jewish Congress (WJC), where he succeeded in extracting a few billions of reparation money from the Swiss banks. The WJC was intricately linked to other Jewish lobby groups such as the notorious Anti-Defamation League (ADL) and B'Nai B'Rith. The ADL was known for bullying critics of Israel into compliance and for turning worldwide Holocaust compassion into a billion dollar money source.

Being a Grand Master of B'Nai B'Rith, Przedborski must have known Bronfman, but their relationship could not be documented. His expertise in maritime transport between France and the New Continent served Monnet well. He became an advisor to the French government during WWI. Under his supervision and with the assistance of Arthur Salter the Inter-Allied Maritime Transport Council was founded in 1917. Salter was an Oxford alumnus who claimed to be a member of a secret committee that counseled several European heads of state. He was the author of the 1931 book, *The United States of Europe*, that would inspire Monnet.

In 1925 Monnet settled in the USA. He was a partner of New York Blair & Co, whose legal advisor was the high-flying lawyer Cravath. This was how Monnet got to meet John J. McCloy, who was employed by Cravath.

In 1932 Monnet was invited to travel to China to assist Chiang Kai Shek. After his Chinese adventures, Monnet and his associate George Murnane founded a company in 1935. Monnet, Murnane & Co was financed with the help of J.F. Dulles of the Sullivan & Cromwell lawfirm. Murnane was very well connected with the Swedish Wallenbergs, the German Bosch and with the Belgian Solvay and Boël families. The duo's company was on excellent terms with Rockefeller, the Dulles brothers and Douglas Dillon. Murnane was also vice-president of the New York Trust Co., which was part of the Speyer group, an old branch of the Rothschild cartel.

Monnet and Murnane ran into trouble in the US for having done business with the Nazi's but the affair was quickly covered up. By 1939 Monnet was in London, helping the British government prepare for war. He was sent to the US, where he negotiated with Harry Hopkins, President Roosevelt's "shadow." Hopkins, as it turned out later, was one of the most effective Soviet spies in America. According to Major Jordan's diaries, Hopkins was responsible for the deliveries by air of high-tech matériel, military aircraft and even nuclear blueprints and plutonium to Russia at the end of WWII. There is no reason why we shouldn't believe Jordan's reports. He was a US Army Major of the Lend-Lease Division, stationed at Newark Airfield, who kept meticulous records of what was airlifted out of his base. He also reported that he had witnessed a disgruntled Soviet officer, supervising the airlift, calling Hopkins directly on the phone.

By the end of the war, Monnet was brainstorming about the construction of a New Europe without the old national borders. His plans coincided in most aspects with the blueprints of Hitler's advisor Walter Hallstein. Together with George Kennan and Dean Acheson he lobbied Marshall for the establishment of a US bridgehead on the Old Continent. The Marshall Plan was the launching pad for the fascist-inspired post-war United Europe. Fascist? Well, what else could one call it with the very first president of the European Commission being Walter Hallstein himself?

MELLOW YELLOW

Next to the WJC, the ADL was an important instrument of Jewish power. In fact the League was a 1913 spin-off of B'Nai B'Rith. It specialized in bullying critics of Israel by portraying them as anti-Semites, revisionists or even Holocaust deniers. As Norman Finkelstein explained in his book "The Holocaust Industry," the persecution and genocide of the European Jews was shamelessly being exploited for a giant extortion racket. The ADL also excelled in buying the votes of some US Congressmen and pressuring others into pro-Israel standpoints. One of the main sponsors of the ADL was Carl Lindner, who belonged to the Meyer Lansky drug syndicate.

After the defenestration of Eli Black, Lindner had been placed at the helm of the United Fruit Company. Coincidently, Allen and John F. Dulles were major stakeholders in that company. United Fruit, who operated a fleet of banana carriers, was known to be the biggest importer of Latin American cocaine into the USA.

United Fruit had been exploiting the rich soil of Latin American countries for its successful banana business for decades. In Guatemala the company had basically taken over the country. It owned ports, railroads and large stretches of land. When in 1954 the local Arbenz government started to put pressure on the dictatorial United Fruit Company, the CIA mounted a coup and installed a military junta in the country. As for drugs and bananas, we now know that Felix Przedborski was involved in both.

Large amounts of money were poured into the ADL via the Roundtable PAC and the tax shelter company Integrated Resources in Manhattan. Integrated was in essence a laundering operation for the drug money that went into the junk bond scam of Michael Milken, Ivan Boesky and Drexel Burnham Lambert. Yes, that is the Lambert of the Belgian Rothschild bank. One of the directors of Integrated was Steven Weinroth, CEO of Drexel. The connections couldn't be any clearer. In the early 1980s one of the biggest donors to Roundtable PAC was Lindner's United Brands.

At this point in time Robert Vesco had already amassed a fortune by taking over Bernie Cornfeld's IOS company that had been founded in Switzerland, with Rothschild money, by Tibor Rosenbaum. Cornfeld was one of the "founding fathers" of Israel who had helped finance and arm the Stern Gang, the Haganah and the Mossad. Rosenbaum, of Hungarian descent, stood at the helm of the Swiss Banque de Crédit International, that laundered Meyer Lansky's drug money. By the 1970s most of the Jewish cartel's business interests seemed to be converging in Geneva, Switzerland.

SAFRA

Edmond Safra, whose name figured in the ATLAS Report, was a Syrian Jew, born in Aleppo. After the collapse of the Ottoman Empire, many Aleppo Jews, called Halabi, had fled Syria. The Safra, Dweck, Tawil, Shammah, Sasson and De Picciotto families had flocked to Beirut. Some had crossed the Mediterranean to settle in Geneva. Dweck, De Picciotto and Safra would turn Geneva into the most prominent Sefardic banking center in the world.

Safra's successful Trade Development Bank employed many of his fellow Halabi. Safra, Bronfman and Max Fisher co-presided over the board of the World Jewish Congress. Safra was on excellent terms with Richard Secord and Albert Hakim, two of the key figures of the Iran-Contra operation. On the subject of the Belgian financial scandals Michel V once said: "Edmond Safra was much bigger than this! The ASCO, Boas en VDB affaires in comparison are small, small, small! Even before Republic National, Safra had his Trade Development Bank. Did I hear you say "Iran-Contra"? Yeah, sure! Michel V was referring to the deals of the Belgian arms producer ASCO who was involved in arms shipments to Tehran in the early 1980s. Iran-Contra indeed. One of the leading figures inside ASCO was the Israeli agent Avraham Shavit, a friend of the Iranian-American lobbyist Houshang Lavi who had illegally shipped F-14 spare parts to Iran. VDB stood for Vanden Boeynants, the Christian Democratic ex-defense minister and notorious, convicted swindler. Felix Przedborski was on excellent terms with VDB, being "a longtime friend of Israel" himself.

In Geneva, the banking trio was joined by Nessim Gaon, the president of the World Sefardic Congress. Gaon was one of the names listed in the ATLAS Report. He was born in Egypt and had amassed a fortune by exploiting local peasants and workers in the Sudan, a British protectorate. Since 1969 Gaon had been a business associate of the Jewish private banker Nicolas Bär from Zürich. Gaon was vice-president of Bronfman's World Jewish Congress. In 1984 he had singlehandedly saved the Likud government by buying the dissident Tami party. Above all, Gaon was a "member" of the Magbit society, a gathering of rich businessmen who had engaged in "politics for profits" and who had financed the arduous start of the state of Israel.

MAGBIT

One of the earliest Magbit sponsors of the Zionist project was Samuel Bronfman. In 1953 Bronfman's contribution was deemed below par by Moshe Sharet who wrote:

> He has made a fortune smuggling alcohol. He throws his money around left and right in Canada and the USA, donates millions to McGill and to Columbia University. [...] Compared to his fortune, his gift to Israel is but an alms.

Although there is no direct evidence of Felix's involvement in the Zionist politics for profit, his proximity to people like Nessim Gaon, cited in the ATLAS Report, suggests that he was personally involved. Reportedly Gaon held a stake in the Costa Rican Santa Elena project. He and Felix were both close friends and sponsors of Menachim Begin. Felix's neighbors in Miami, where he liked to retreat on occasion, turned out to be the super rich Jewish Arison family. The widow of legendary Ted Arison, of the famous Cunard and Carnival Cruises companies, had her residence at 9999 Collins Avenue, Bal Harbor, Florida. Felix shared the same address.

As we know, he loved travel, tourism, airfare and seafare. Ted Arison was one of the early heroes of Israel. He was the first to launch a freighter under the Israeli flag. It was the humble start of the badly needed Israeli merchant fleet. Everything the young nation needed had to be imported by sea, mostly via the port of Haïfa. Aliya Bet, the clandestine immigration of thousands of Ashkenazi Jews from Russia and Poland, was one of the motives for the development of a merchant fleet. Arison had been one of its pioneers.

By the 1980s, the prevalent Jewish shipping companies were Zim, Dizengoff, El Yam, and the Maritime Fruit Carriers Co. These four catered to all the needs of the Israeli citizens, from petroleum to bananas. Maritime Fruit Carriers had evolved out of Mila Brener's humble 1961 Atlantic Fishing Co, that operated three rusty fishing trawlers. One of them was equipped with a refrigerated cargo space, which proved to be ideally suited for the transport of fruits and meat. Soon a new cargo ship was launched for the import of bananas. It was the first of 42 Maritime Fruit Carriers' cooled cargo ships. When the company went bust in 1976, part of its fleet was taken over by the Cunard shipping line.

One of the Israeli maritime supply lines passed via Nicaragua, not only to stock up on of bananas but also for the supply of weapons. Israel has been doing business with Central America since the early 1950s. At the time, the United Fruit Company dominated the Caribbean fruit market. UFC had been founded by Samuel Zemurray, in association with some friendly financiers from Boston and New York. Many well-known Jewish and Italian mob members popped up on the board of directors of the company. Zemurray was succeeded by Eli "Black" Schwarz, whose untimely death allowed Max Fisher and Carl Lindner to move in and take over the company. United Fruit was now in the business of smuggling drugs into the USA, via Miami. One of Max Fisher's main business partners in the Caribbean was Robert Vesco. This criminal network would later team up with the French Connection's American heroin branch.

Another Magbit star and Begin supporter was Samy Flatto-Sharon, a self-made billionaire who was born in Lodz in January of 1930. As a young boy he had started selling cigarettes on university campuses in France. He diversified into scrap metals, rags, toilet paper and Paris real estate. He partnered with Edmond de Rothschild for the launch of the successful Silhouette fitness center chain in France. His company Nemed obtained a license to export weapons to Nicaragua. By 1977 he had bought his way into the Knesset, which kept him out of jail in France where he was sentenced to a 10 year prison sentence.

Samy knew his way around Africa too. In the Congo, his support for Jean Tsjombé was rewarded with a diamond mine concession. It was Samy who had introduced Shabtai Kalmanovitch, who was said to be a

KGB agent, to the Likud Party. With the help of Don Felix, Kalmanovitch had made an inroad into Costa Rican diplomacy. He was the Tico honorary consul in Saint Petersburg. With Kalmanovitch we enter the realm of the Red Maffiya that would find refuge in Belgium in the 1990s.

Over time, the Magbit and the Politics for Profits tradition in Israel would gradually concentrate corporate power into five groups. The most important by far was the Israeli Discount Bank (IDB), who controlled the Elbit company. IDB was owned by the Recanati and Carasso families, by Goldman Sachs and by William Davidson. The second group was the Ofer family of the Zim shipping lines. Third was the Koor group and their companies ECI Telecom and Tadiran, where the Bronfmans were pulling the strings. The Arison and the Dankner groups completed the top-five list.

RED MAFFIYA

Shabtai Kalmanovitch, born in Latvia, had emigrated to Israel, where he joined the Labor party and became Golda Meir's political liaison man in the Eastern Bloc countries. When hardliner Menachem Begin's star was rising, Shabtai decided to join the Likud party. He was introduced to the party chiefs by Flatto-Sharon. By the early 1980s Kalmanovitch, sponsored by Marc Rich, was making headlines in Bophutswana and Sierra Leone. His African operations were covered by top Mossad agent David Kimche, one of the key Israeli figures in the Iran-Contra operations. Thanks to his diplomatic status, Shabtaï could travel freely to the communist satellite countries behind the Iron Curtain. He became involved with Marat Balagula, the Red Maffiya godfather in New York, who was working together with the Genovese clan. They controlled the oil smuggling operations along the American East Coast. The African nation of Sierra Leone proved to be an excellent transshipping point for oil deliveries to the embargoed South African Apartheid regime. At the time Tel Aviv and Pretoria were working closely together on a nuclear weapons project. Marc Rich was instrumental in providing South Africa with the much needed oil.

In the early 1980s Marat Balagula joined Kalmanovitch in Sierra Leone. President Momoh welcomed him in. It didn't take long for the combine of Mossad and Red Maffiya to take over control of the country. The Momoh government now served as a conduit for the transfer of weapons and high tech electronics to Abu Nidal and to some Eastern Bloc intelligence services. Balagula installed his headquarters in Freetown, from where he directed the trafficking of blood diamonds to Thailand, where they were swapped for heroin. Some of the diamonds eventually found their way to Antwerp. M & S International, the Brighton Beach subsidiary of Boris Nayfeld and Mike Brandwain in Antwerp became involved in the deal.

In 1994 Kalmanovitch traveled to Costa Rica and Miami in the company of godfathers Mogilevitch and Mikhailov. After Mikhailov was arrested in Geneva, Shabtaï often visited him in prison. He took care of business with the help of Anatoli Katric, honorary consul of Costa Rica and Mogilevitch's trustee in France and in the Czech Republic. Katric, Przedborski's agent in Budapest, was one of the names mentioned in the ATLAS Report. He was in contact with Günther Arlow, who was running Felix's Primus travel agency in Vienna.

Katric had attempted to have Mogilevitch, aka Serguei Schneider, nationalized in Belgium with the help of Philippe Rosenberg, a Brussels politician. Semion Mogilevitch, nicknamed "Seva," was one of the most wanted criminals. When the bribery was exposed, Rosenberg jumped on a flight to Pattaya, Thailand. Belgian ambassador Alfred Cahen came to Mogilevitch's rescue and handed him a travel visa for the European countries.

According to investigative journalist De Bock, Felix met with Semion Mogilevitch in May of 1998, probably in Bulgaria, where they were joined by ambassador Alfred Cahen. The meeting was part of the "Moscow Link" project that had been started by Cahen decades earlier. Cahen had been in close contact with the CIA since 1962, the Congo independence year, when he had met Larry Devlin and Maurice Tempelsman. All these years his "Atlantic contact" had been the charming millionaire "socialite" Pamela Harriman, one of Tempelsman's discrete flirts. She would end up US Ambassador in Paris in the early 1990s. Over time, the trio Mogilevitch-Cahen-Przedborski had built a privileged relationship with the Kremlin. Long before the fall of the Berlin Wall, the ambassador's contacts at the Moscow end had been Adomichin and Petrovski. The meeting was most probably set up in Bulgaria to please Nicolai, who had personally financed a NATO conference, attended by 700 people, in Bulgaria in 1997.

THE CAMPANELLE STAKEOUT

On September 21, 1999 the French police had a surveillance team watching Don Felix's Villa Campanelle in Antibes, France. Its report went, in part, as follows:

> At 08.15hrs: arrival of maître Schreinmacher and maître Niklaus. Business partner of Daniel Przedborski.
>
> At 08.45hrs: departures of mrs Przedborski and her aid (Jaguar).
>
> At 09.15hrs: departure of maître Schreinmacher and Daniel Przedborski (Bentley).
>
> At 10.30hrs: return of Schreinmacher and Daniel Przedborski, ac-

companied by Nicolai Astunas (identified as being the owner of the Lokomotiv Sofia soccer club, residing at the Eden Rock Hotel).

At 11.10hrs: arrival of Anatoli Katric and Igor Fisherman in the company of 2 individials, vehicle Renault Espace.

At 12.03hrs : departure of the Bentley with driver (Julio).

At 12.30hrs: arrival of Frans Roelants in the Bentley.

At 13.15hrs: arrival of general Saure in an official service vehicle.

At 15.45hrs: departure of general Saure in his vehicle

At 21.04hrs: departure of F. Przedborski, Frans Roelants, Anatoli Katric, Igor Fisherman and Nicolai Astunas in the Bentley and Mercedes

At 22.12hrs: return of F. Przedborski and Frans Roelants, accompanied by maître Jean Paul Carteron and Pierre Yves Olivier. Vehicle Swiss license plates.

At 23.04hrs : departure of maître Jean Paul Carteron and Pierre Yves Ollivier.

Quite a strange mix of visitors, indeed. Frans Roelants was a Belgian official and close friend of ambassador Alfred Cahen. He had been secretary-general of the Belgian Foreign Affairs cabinet for 15 years. Jean Saure, the general, was one of the top figures of the French secret service DGSE. He was on excellent terms with Pamela Harriman, heiress to the fabulous Harriman fortune and US Ambassador in Paris. One of Pam's close friends was her colleague ambassador Alfred Cahen, an intimate of the Przedborski family.

Pierre Yves Ollivier, nicknamed Monsieur Jacques, had been Jacques Chirac's long-time advisor for African affairs. He had been in the trade of raw materials with African countries for many years. Ollivier was involved in French "parallel diplomacy" in Africa. He had been instrumental in the liberation of Nelson Mandela.

Jean-Paul Carteron, of French and Swiss nationality, was another skewed character. He had studied law at the Sorbonne. As a young man he had ambitions for a political career in France. When that didn't work out he tried another shortcut to big money. In 1981 he emigrated to Haïti and became advisor and fund manager of the brutal dictator "Papa Doc" Duvalier. Carteron set up some real estate deals on the Côte d'Azur for Baby Doc, the dictator's son and successor. In 1985 he popped up in the UN as Haiti's ambassador. He forged strong links with Eastern Bloc countries and used these contacts as a basis to create the Crans Montana Forum in Switzerland in 1989. He now portrayed himself as a "humanitarian" benefactor. The Forum provided an aura of respectability to some of the most ruthless and corrupt African regimes.

In 1996, the Swiss authorities pressured Carteron to move his circus abroad. The Forum reappeared in the Principality of Monaco. To the embarrassment of prince Rainier, Carteron renamed his forum the Monaco World Summit, which suggested that the event was endorsed by the Principality, which it was not. Carteron now specialized in brokering honorary titles from Eastern European and Balkan countries. This put him in the same league as "ambassador" Felix Przedborski.

1 del 2 luglio 1990

Richard Brenneke

CHAPTER 9

DUCK AND COVER

THE BIG URANIUM SCARE

After his Paris adventures, Felix's associate Mauricio had focused on the skills he learned from his father and grandfather: diamond cutting and the antiques trade. In 1860, his grandfather had been a supplier of diamonds to the Austrian Crown. In the mid-1950s Mauricio sold uncut diamonds to the personnel of the Chinese embassy in Bonn, which was illegal. The German police had questioned him about that. According to Mauricio, the Chinese rewarded him with a visit to Mao Tse Tung in person.

In that same period, Felix Przedborski was arrested for selling uranium to the Chinese. At least that's what the ATLAS Report says. According to the report, German chancellor Adenauer had intervened in 1956 to get Felix off the hook. This part of the Felix story seems quite unbelievable at first sight. Yet, at the time, the industrial world was buzzing with plans and prospects for cheap nuclear energy worldwide. The "Atoms for Peace" initiative projected a utopian vision of prosperity for everyone. Despite the nuclear Hiroshima and Nagasaki catastrophes only a decade earlier, uranium wasn't viewed by the public as a lethal, toxic substance that could annihilate whole cities. For a while, the peaceful application of the new atomic energy technology outshone its destructive potential. Obviously, the prospects of cheap or free energy did not please everyone. If uranium was to replace coal and oil, the traditional establishment had to step in and take control of the new technology. General Electric's alliance with Westinghouse achieved just that. Additionally, the public was gradually indoctrinated with a fear of radiation.

Hollywood added to the general distrust of nuclear energy by releasing *The China Syndrome* in 1979. The movie suggested that an uncontrolled nuclear reaction would cause the white hot reactor core to eat its way right through the earth's crust. The Three Mile Island nuclear incident of that same year definitely changed the public's perception of nuclear energy for the worst. Atomic energy wasn't free or even cheap any longer. The required security measures and the unnecessarily high cost of nuclear waste disposal had seen to that.

Retired nuclear engineer Winsor Galen explained to audiences throughout the USA that the price of electrical power could and should be reduced by a factor of ten. He recalled having manipulated plutonium lumps with his bare hands in the early years. It was standard practice. As long as you don't bring together a near-critical mass of the stuff, it is harmless. You can play chess with it. Carry it in your hip pocket.

In his 1980s conferences, Galen correctly pointed out that normal life had resumed a long time ago in the cities of Hiroshima and Nagasaki, where "no grass would grow for a thousand years." To prove his point, Galen used to swallow some plutonium or uranium powder right before the eyes of the startled audience. "As long as it does not burn you, radiation is harmless, just like the sun," Galen explained. Then the industry big shots decided to tighten the security limits to absurdly high levels. Additionally, nuclear power plants were kept off-line without reason for long stretches of time, "for security reasons." The Three Mile Island incident had been a hoax. Galen had protested against the nuclear-scare hype by drinking nuclear cooling water daily and by taking a swim in the nuclear reactor cooling water reservoir on a regular basis. The GE-Westinghouse bosses didn't seem to like that at all. Why, Galen asked, couldn't large cities go off the grid and have their own, autonomous nuclear reactor, just like the US Navy aircraft carriers? It was the aim of the industry, Galen posited, to bury the "Atoms for Peace" and "cheap energy" dreams once and for all.

GERMAN NUCLEAR DREAMS

What interest could Adenauer have had in uranium? Germany had lost the war and was officially denied access to nuclear technology for military applications. Yet, Adenauer and his entourage had the secret ambition to develop a German nuclear weapon. In 1956, Washington had announced a US troop reduction in Europe. This was to be compensated by a "demonstrable superiority in retaliatory means." In practice, this amounted to a stepping up of nuclear capabilities, including those of the European nations. In May of 1957 Great Britain detonated its first atomic bomb in the Pacific.

That same month German defense minister Franz Joseph Strauss secured political support for nuclear armament of the Federal Republic. Bavarian ultra-rightist Strauss, nicknamed "the Bulldozer," was an outspoken Atlanticist and member of the Cercle Pinay. Apparently the German government had already agreed with France to share their nuclear weaponry. The power grab of de Gaulle in June of 1958 had abruptly ended this nuclear synergy. Strauss then hopped on a plane to the US to discuss Polaris nuclear missiles with defense Secretary Thomas Gates. Strauss made it clear that Germany would go it alone if the NATO nuclear force proposals were to be rejected.

In 2010, more than half a century after the fact, it was discovered that German experts had teamed up with Israeli nuclear researchers. The sale of

German nuclear-capable Dolphin class submarines to Tel Aviv in 2010 was seen by insiders as a quid pro quo for the German post-war sponsoring of the Israeli Dimona project. The Dolphin submarine story incited German Nobel laureate Günther Grass to write a critical poem "with what ink remained." In "What needs to be said," Grass condemned German hypocrisy for having assisted Tel Aviv in developing the weapon that could annihilate Tehran. The poem, published in all the main newspapers around the world, instantly earned Grass the label "Anti-Semite." (Appendix 10)

Some German press investigators linked the German nuclear ambitions to the bizarre 1970s OTRAG project of engineer Lutz Kayser. OTRAG stood for Orbital Transport and Rockets AG. It was Kayser's intention to build a cheap, flexible, modular rocket system that could launch satellites into orbit. The concept was quite simple: several identical standard tubular modules filled with rocket propellant were to be assembled into a single rocket system. Its performance, from short range to intercontinental, depended on the number of tubes being bundled. Kayser was serious about the project. He could count on the support of NASA boss Werner von Braun. OTRAG had hired von Braun's assistant Kurt Heinrich Debus, who had operated the Nazi V-2 rockets launch pad in Peenemunde in WWII. President Mobutu of Congo had agreed to lease a large testing area in the Shaba province, near the equator, to Kayser. There, dozens of rockets of various sizes were launched successfully.

Officially, the German government denied any involvement in the "commercial" project that obviously sought to compete with the Space Shuttle and Ariane projects. But some suspected that Kayser's rockets could be used for a German long-range nuclear weapon system. Some evidence seemed to point in this direction. As it turned out the German government had agreed to make private investments in the OTRAG project tax-deductible. In other words, the government and the German taxpayers were sponsoring it. As political pressure from Paris and Moscow mounted, the OTRAG circus was forced to leave Central Africa. By 1980 the OTRAG launch pad was operational yet again, this time in the Libyan desert near Sebha, about 500 miles south of Tripoli.

Some suspected a deal with Muammar Gadhafi that involved the German expertise in building and operating a biological weapons laboratory. There had been some speculation earlier about OTRAG's involvement in biological experiments involving the Ebola virus in the Congo, where it had absolute control over an area of 100,000 square kilometers. The German space adventure ended when Gadhafi, hoping to use the technology to his own benefit, simply confiscated the OTRAG infrastructure. As it turned out, Gadhafi's engineers lacked the know-how to operate OTRAG's machinery with any degree of efficiency. And so Kayser's project died in the Libyan desert sand.

IRAN-CONTRA FALL-OUT

In 1980 ex-CIA agent Ed Wilson resided in Tripoli. According to the official story, Wilson had gone rogue and was now working for Gadhafi, whom he had allegedly sold tons of C-4 high grade military explosives and a C-130 Lockheed cargo aircraft. To many it was clear that this was just a cover and that Wilson was still acting on orders of the CIA.

In 1980 Wilson was approached in Tripoli by the Belgian arms dealer Armand Donnay, who offered to sell stolen nuclear technology to Gadhafi via his Armaco company. Armaco had opened an account with the Brussels Geoffrey's Bank, owned by the Jewish Nejman family. Arno Nejman "Newman" was a close friend of Felix Przedborski, of jeans producer Pierre Salik and international arms dealer Jacques Monsieur. Wilson reported Donnay's offer to the CIA, but obviously the matter was of no interest to Langley.

That Donnay had contacted Wilson was no coincidence. Wilson had been involved in nuclear matters for some time. He had been part of the famous Navy Task Force 157, a secret team that was tasked with sniffing out nuclear cargo on board Russian freighters. Wilson's maritime experience had made him an associate of Bruce Rappaport, a client of Daniel Przedborski. Both Wilson and Rappaport were deeply involved in Marc Rich's oil smuggling operations to South Africa. Rappaport's Bank of New York was the favorite launderette of Balagula's Brighton Beach Maffiya. Rappaport was also doing business with Edmond Safra. Everything was connected. A great many of these connections intersected in Geneva, Switzerland.

Wilson and Rappaport were key players in the Iran-Contra affair. Ex-CIA agent Gene "Chip" Tatum claimed that the most secret aspect of the Iran-Contra scandal had never been revealed: the smuggling of nuclear material to Iran. Tatum's claim was justified. As early as 1974 the Shah had expressed his intentions to provide the Persian nation with cheap nuclear power. It would be a sin, the Shah once said, to just burn the precious oil. And so Iran embarked on a nuclear program that was initially supported by the USA and its allies. In 1979, however, after the Shah was exiled and Khomeini had taken over, an international nuclear embargo aborted the project. This led to a conflict between Tehran and Paris. Iran had invested a billion dollars in the Eurodif consortium, a joint stock company founded in 1973 by France, Belgium, Italy, Spain and Sweden. After some negotiations with the French, the Swedish part was taken over by Iran, which now owned 10 percent of Eurodif. In 1986, Eurodif manager George Besse was murdered, allegedly in an Iranian act of revenge for the boycott of Iranian access to Eurodif's enriched uranium.

The nuclear deal with Iran was not the only hidden part of the operation.

Fara Mansoor, an Iranian who was in the thick of things at the Iranian end in the run-up to the 1979 revolution, found evidence that proves that the revolution, including the US hostage taking in Tehran, was staged by George Bush and his parallel CIA. According to Fara Mansoor, Bush, who became CIA director in 1976, had learned about the health condition of the Shah via Richard Helms, US ambassador to Iran. Helms had befriended the Shah, who in 1974 had told him that he had cancer. At the time, President Jimmy Carter was not informed of this. The Shah had been in power in Iran since the CIA-backed coup against Mohammad Mossadeq in 1953. Interestingly enough, in the interim period Mossadeq had been replaced by Fazlollah Zahedi, a former Nazi intelligence officer, who would later be appointed head of the SAVAK, the brutal Iranian secret service. His son Ardeshir Zahedi married the Shah's daughter and became Iran's ambassador to the United States.

Bush, realizing that the Shah didn't have much longer to live, wanted to make sure Iran would remain an anti-Soviet ally. The plan was to oust the Shah and put Khomeini, who was living in exile in Iraq, on the throne. The aim of Bush was twofold: to ensure the continuity of the anti-Soviet policy of Iran; and to totally discredit the Carter presidency, thus paving the way to the White House for Ronald Reagan and himself.

According to Mansoor's "Deep October Surprise" testimony, Bush, Reagan and Thatcher, in preparation of the secret coup, had been in contact with Khomeini as early as 1977. In the final stages of the plan, Khomeini moved from Iraq to Paris, France, where he made it very clear in front of the press that he would not call on Moscow for his return to power in Iran. This was to signal that he could be trusted as an ally of the West.

Richard Brenneke, a US real estate business man with excellent contacts in Iran, claimed to have been involved in the preparatory October Surprise talks between Bush, Casey and the Iranians. Brenneke testified that he had been working for the CIA ever since the days of the Air America drug trafficking out of Vietnam. After the Iran-Contra scandal had broken in November of 1986, Brenneke was listed by the *Philadelphia Inquirer* as one of the personae involved in the attempt to sell 39 F-4E Phantom jets to Iran. However, V-P Bush qualified Brenneke's testimony as "slanderous." The Senate Committee came to the conclusion that Brenneke had never been on the CIA payroll. Consequently, Brenneke was indicted for perjury. However, no mention was ever made of the possibility that he had been working for "the Enterprise."

In 1990 Brenneke provided documents to Italian journalists regarding Licio Gelli and P2, documenting CIA support for their activities. He stated before the Italian TV Rai Uno cameras that he had been involved in monthly CIA payments to P2 of millions of dollars to finance terrorism and drug trafficking. Brenneke also provided details of an important meeting with the Dutch businessman Afman in the Rotterdam Hilton. Financial aspects of the weapons and drug deals with P2, Brenneke explained, were handled by the Dutch subsidiary of Credit Lyonnais. Frans J. Afman was a staff member of the bank's Entertainment Business section. Brenneke documented his claim with a detailed AT&T phone bill, proving that he had indeed called Gelli and Afman many times within the reported timeframe. The involvement of Credit Lyonnais didn't come as a surprise. The same Afman had been involved in the unorthodox financing of the failed MGM take-over attempt by the Italian criminal duo Fiorini and Parretti. The Credit Lyonnais involvement constituted a link between the giant SASEA bankruptcy, the secret financing of European socialist parties on the one hand; and the Bush-Casey Iran conspiracy on the other. These seemingly separate operations were all connected.

The involvement of P2 suggested that Gladio could have been involved as well. Indeed, Brenneke provided some details about the Belgian P2-branch, code-named P7. He also suggested that Dutch banker Afman was involved in the financing of the Dutch section of Gladio, started up in association with Dutch intelligence service O&I (Operations and Intelligence). In the early post-war years, O&I had been supported by the Phillips, Shell and Unilever multinationals, who, for obvious reasons, endorsed the "Atlantic Unity" concept.

Brenneke's information, if correct, provided yet more evidence of a connection between Gladio and the SASEA-affair, in which Don Felix's mistress Winnie Kollbrunner was involved. Brenneke also confirmed that Gladio had been under OSS/CIA control from the outset. In 1947-48 the US intelligence services, fearing a surprise Soviet blitz into Western Europe, had been recruiting stay-behind agents in Belgium. One of these early recruiters must have been Ted Shackley, who spoke fluent Polish.

It was Shackley who introduced Licio Gelli to Alexander Haig in 1969. This meeting led to the activation of P2 as an instrument of the Rockefeller-Kissinger clique to destabilize Italy in favor of the Atlantic ruling class. Had young Felix been one of Shackley's early Gladio-CIA recruits? One can only speculate.

One of the P7 names cited by Brenneke was the Hungarian-born lawyer Ernst Töttösy, who had been jailed by the Soviet regime in Budapest, back in 1952. The turmoil of the 1956 revolution allowed him and his family to flee to the West. In the early 1960s he was recruited into the ranks of the rightist Catholic milieu of VDB, headquartered in Brussels. In the Mid-1960s Töttösy, who was close to the Pinay Circle and NEM Club, was appointed president of the Hungarian branch of the WACL. His "Committee Hungary 56" was considered to be an antenna of the CIA, who loved to use disgruntled emigrés, be they Catholic or Muslim, in the covert war against the Soviets.

The second Hungarian émigré on Brenneke's P7 list of names was De Stankovitch, who was recruited by the secret society Académie Européenne de Sciences Politiques (AESP), where he was introduced to people like Otto von Hapsburg, VDB, Giulio Andreotti, "Black Baron" Bonvoisin and French lawyer Jean Violet. The latter being the right hand of the ex-Vichy minister Antoine Pinay, a former member of the fascist Synarchist movement.

THE ISLAMIC BOMB

While all of this was playing out in the late 1970s, the Belgian Nuclear Research Center (NRC) was engaged in helping Pakistan develop its own nuclear weapon. The official story reads like a cheap spy novel.

Pakistani engineer Qadeer Khan, studying in Belgium and working in the Dutch Urenco uranium enrichment plant, had stolen the blueprints of the high-tech uranium centrifuges. Back in his country, Khan was feted as the "father of the Pakistani nuclear program." Khan's unusual activities in Europe had not gone unnoticed. Dutch premier Lubbers reported them to the CIA. To his amazement, the Agency showed no interest. Around this time the CIA was financing bin Laden's Afghan Mujahideen via the BCCI and the Pakistani intelligence service. It was reported that a big part of the Mujahideen money was diverted into the Pakistani nuclear project. Obviously the USA did not object at all to the development of a Pakistani nuclear weapon.

Sarkis Soghanalian, a high-level weapons dealer of Armenian descent, had found himself entangled in the Safari Club, Enterprise and Mujahideen operations. He was doing business with prince Turki. Sarkis stated that the Pakistani bomb project had been under permanent control of the Saudis, not the Americans. He confirmed that three-quarters of the Mujahideen money had ended up in Pakistani hands. Sarkis could prove that George Bush, head of the CIA, had been perfectly aware of this. He openly questioned the relationship of the Bush clan with the Saudi Princes Turki and Bandar; and with the bin Laden family. Sarkis also spilled the beans on arms dealer Mark Thatcher, son of Maggie, and his role in the Iraq-Gate scandal. This caused a stir in London. A Parliamentary investigation was ordered. The sale of military helicopters and night vision goggles to Iraq appeared to have been connected to the 1990 murder of British journalist Jonathan Moyle in the Carrera hotel in Santiago, Chile.

As to the Khan story, the Belgian NRC had in reality been in contact with the Pakistani government several times over the supply of uranium and plutonium. It has to be remembered that the NRC had always been under close control of the CIA since its start-up. The story of Khan being the lone hero who stole the secret blueprints, didn't hold water. The Bhutto government had reportedly detached up to 36 Pakistani "students" to the research center. Khan's contact man inside the NRC was nuclear engineer Norbert Van De Voorde (VDV), who at the time was heading the High Temp Waste Incinerator project.

The affair escalated into an international scandal after the German press uncovered deals made by the German company Transnuklear and NRC for the sale of fissile material to Pakistan and Libya. Both these countries, Saudi-Arabia, Iran and Iraq were part of the Saudi-founded BCCI consortium that sought to finance the "Islamic Bomb" project. As a consequence of the Transnuclear scandal, Norbert VDV was sacked by the NRC. Part of the VDV story was particularly interesting.

CHAPTER 10

RUBLES, TOXINS AND MURDER

THE MISSISSIPPI CONNECTION

Norbert VDV's brother Etienne had been building a small waste-recycling empire for himself in Belgium. His companies were engaged in illegally mixing toxic fly ashes in cement, concrete and asphalt used in the construction and repair of roads and highways. His company made international headlines for having supplied "toxic waste for the construction of the Chunnel." Inspired by his brother's know-how in nuclear waste disposal, he became involved in talks about the construction of a nuclear waste recycling plant in the Liège area. Inevitably, socialist minister Cools and his acolyte Mathot were involved too. Interestingly enough, one of VDV's business partners was a real estate businessman by the name of Jacques Fourez. He and his female companion were brutally murdered by the Brabant Killers in 1983. Had the couple been in the wrong place at the wrong time, or was this yet another case of "elimination of witnesses"?

In a 1997 book titled *Waste Criminality in Europe*, Dutch journalist Charles Van Der Leeuw explained that:

> "[...] Much less is known about the Cools and Fourez cases in relation to illegal toxic waste dumping, simply because the key figures were eliminated at an early stage.[...] In 1983 Fourez had attempted to buy a site near Engis that he planned to turn into a nuclear graveyard. Shortly thereafter, he was trapped and killed." Van Der Leeuw further stated that he had discovered links between the VDV and the Ambrosini-Mississippi networks. Gianfranco Ambrosini was the alleged godfather of the waste-mafia in Genoa, Italy. He was allegedly doing business with the American Harrison gang.

The Mississippi gang can be defined as the international network of Dutch conman Dirk De Groot, who had set-up a giant stock market Ponzi scheme. His criminal network consisted of dozens of subsidiaries in Liechtenstein, UK, Holland, Belgium, Switzerland, Germany and the Antilles. Some of the money De Groot collected from gullible investors he had poured into the "waste recycling" business. De Groot was one of the business relations of Etienne VDV. In Belgium, Mississippi had attempted to break into the market via the Hody waste storage and transportation company, headquartered near Liège. Andre Hody was well introduced in the Cools milieu, but he was convicted for having illegally stored toxic waste, and the deal fell through.

OPERATION STILLPOINT/HAMMER

Another intriguing aspect of the Mississippi affair was that it was linked to the shady operations of Leo Wanta. One of the many documents Leo Wanta has produced to prove his involvement in President Reagan's attack on the Ruble was a handwritten fax-page that mentioned "De Groot in Belgium" as one of Wanta's contacts. (Appendix 11) The author of the message, addressed to Dick Cheney and Leo Wanta, was unknown. Dirk De Groot, via his Dove Trading company, was involved in what Wanta called the Anti-Soviet Operation Stillpoint/Hammer in at least two ways: Ruble speculation, and nuclear material smuggling.

Wanta and De Groot were both actors in a "compensated barter" agreement with Russian president Boris Yeltsin, whereby 140 billion rubles were deposited in an escrow account. The Ruble exchange and the barter deals were coordinated from Zürich, Switzerland, with the assistance of Marc Rich. Remember, Rich was one of Don Felix's contacts.

As part of the deal, massive quantities of Western consumer goods were shipped to Russia. But that wasn't all. The "compensated barter" also included nuclear material, red mercury, weapons, gold and heroin. One of De Groot's business partners was Gregory Elias, "the richest man of Curaçao," who was suspected of having smuggled nuclear substances into Cuba via the Antilles Islands.

Wanta himself provided copies of faxed documents providing clear evidence of "Red Mercury" deals, at a price of about 350 dollar per gram, with Israeli companies.(Appendix 12). Investigative journalist De Bock noted:

> Wanta arrested 20.7.93 in Geneva-fraud at the Charleston bank. Wanta group in connection with New Republic/USA activities. In Vicenza, courier arrested carrying Cesium 133. Repeatedly confiscated. Very dangerous radioactive waste substance. This leads to international traffic in weapons and nuclear material. New Republic/USA supplied nuclear material. Trail to Tremonti. 25 million dollar on account at Himbank in Moscow and Rochester (N.Y.). Wanta in Austria credit card fraud July 1990. Turns out to be a money laundering operation by Russian + USA mafia with Tremonti, according to Russian and Italian sources. [...] Gulevitch accomplice of Tremonti.[...] Connection with Biondo family and co, Sicily.

And, on the subject of Jack Tremonti:

> Italo-American from Detroit. Convicted in 1976 in Michigan for theft and dealing in stolen goods. Director of Global Technical Ser-

vices, Oklahoma. Gulevitch connection. Laundering narco-dollars via Ruble transactions?" (Appendix 13)

One of the companies used by Wanta was the New Republic GmbH, incorporated in Austria. Leo Wanta had resided in Vienna for some time, but he denied ever having been involved directly with Felix Przedborski. Which is strange, given the fact that Wanta's New Republic company was mentioned in the ATLAS Report. Additionally, Wanta had listed M & S International of Antwerp as one of his correspondent companies. This left no doubt about the Mikhailov-Mogilevitch network's key role in the skinning of the Russian bear. Boris Yeltsin, the "vodka president" who sold out his country, had demonstrably been on the payroll of the Red Maffiya.

As we now know, Felix Przedborski was a major actor of the Mikhailov cluster. Don Felix must have been involved in the economic warfare of the 1980s against the Soviet Union. In a 1999 fax reply to Jürgen Roth, journalist Franco of the Italian magazine *Avvenimenti* stated that he had stumbled upon the Przedborski name during his research into the backgrounds of a nuclear smuggling operation between Europe and Russia. (Appendix 14).

From all this we can safely take it that the Red Maffiya and the mafia not only had supported the Western effort to bring down the Soviet Union but also that they had grabbed the opportunity to launder shiploads of drug money.

"THERE WAS MORE. MUCH MORE!"

The waste recycling business in Belgium had remained largely unregulated until the beginning of the 1980s. This state of affairs had attracted some criminal figures who regarded this country as one giant, "free" waste dump. There was some easy money to be made. The citizenry, who didn't want to see their children poisoned, sounded the alarm. The press picked up the stories, which put pressure on the politicians to do something about it. One of the expert investigative journalists tracking the waste-mafia in Belgium was Mister X, working for a Francophone magazine. Mister X does not want to be named, nor does he want his 1996 handwritten notes to be published here.

Mister X had developed a particular interest in the Mississippi connections that all of a sudden seemed to pop up everywhere. He succeeded in charting the many tentacles of the Europe-wide criminal network. In Belgium, things seemed to revolve around the Cools-Mathot-Hody trio. The name of political insider José Happart wasn't on any of the charts but it did show up in the journalist's handwritten notes inside the Mississippi file. José Happart, one of Cools' colleagues and competitors within the Socialist Party, when interrogated by the police, had stated:

> Cools wasn't murdered over the Agusta helicopter millions. There was more. Much more!

Happart claimed to possess a secret file that revealed the real backgrounds of the Cools murder. Shortly after his bold statement Happart received death threats. The waste mafia had put a price on his head. As a consequence, Happart's secret file never surfaced. Happart lived and prospered. His political career got an unexpected boost.

Mister X's forbidden notes had been jotted down quickly during his interview with Happart. The handwritten French language text reveals some of Happart's secrets. It reads:

> Meeting with Happart, his brother and an engineer, 29 August 1996.

And, further down:

> Happart talks about pedophilia and the involvement of certain magistrates; Jose starts talking about money laundering and Cools being involved in it. At Cools' place they discovered a fortune, up to 2 billion Belgian francs.

Mister X continues

> The money had to be recovered via Switzerland and Germany. Happart holds the details of the accounts and of the money transfers. The laundering was done using financial securities. The money went to the USA and back via Switzerland. Mathot commissioned it. Cover being provided by the UNO. One million dollar payed to Andre Cools for services rendered. The money was provided by a minister of Agriculture of Great Britain ... close to the UNO.

On the third page, where the subjects of the conversation obviously were the Hody connection, drums filled with toxic waste and Locray, the prospective dumping site, he goes on:

> Deferm shows up close to Mathot [...] in Liege in the waste-laundering affair 8 people dead [...] Di Gregorio, very close to Hody, finances a mafia club > close to Mathot.

On the next pages the journalist noted,

> Etienne Van De Voorde had acquired the Sodipar company and
> was in contact with Mississippi [...] Cools and Mathot met with
> Eibrink and Merks on several occasions.

The latter two were agents of De Groot's network.

In a kind of "to do" list following his conversation with Happart, Mister X noted,

> The Nice casino affair; Jacques Médecin allegedly invested capital
> in Mississippi > Atlantis company.

Jacques Médecin was the long-term mayor of the city of Nice. He had come to be known as "the Godfather of the French Riviera." The Bay of Angels in Nice became one of the favorite spots of the Red Maffiya. Médecin was suspected of having been involved in the legendary "Great Riviera Bank Robbery" in the Societe Generale in Nice during the long July 14 holiday weekend of 1976. Médecin was a Freemason, a prominent member of the Grande Loge Nationale de France. He was one of the key figures of the ultra-rightist group "Le Cube." At the time the mayors of Toulon, Cannes, Antibes and Nice "controlled" the French Riviera. The mayor of Antibes was Pierre Merli, a close friend of Don Felix. Médecin was a great admirer and personal friend of Argentinian dictator Carlos Menem. In 1990, as his sordid past was catching up on him, Médecin fled to Brazil.

Whichever way you look at it, Happart seemed to know a lot about minister Cools' involvement in the toxic waste and money laundering affairs surrounding the Mississippi constellation. Mister X's notes go a long way in explaining what Happart had in mind when he said that "the Cools murder wasn't about the Agusta millions. There was more. Much more."

Much more indeed. The 2 billion francs – 60 million of 1980 dollars – found in Cools' possession were the equivalent of about 100 times the reported Agusta bribe. Some linked Cools' 2 billion to the 1991 SMAP-affair. SMAP was a Socialist-run company offering insurance services to registered civil servants at exceptionally low rates. Cools had been appointed president of SMAP just prior to his death. The director of the company, Leon Lewalle, admitted having taken stacks of cash money to Switzerland on a regular basis. According to Lewalle the Swiss account was meant to be SMAP's "financial buffer" for a rainy day. He ended up in jail. Had Cools found him out? For a while Lewalle was suspected of being behind the Cools murder. "The money was mine," Lewalle now claimed, "I have earned it in commissions, paid by the Swiss Re reinsurance company." There must have been some scam going on with the Swiss reinsurance company. Swiss Banker Leon Genoud – no relation with François Genoud – was arrested and convicted in Belgium. Part of the money, it was found, had flowed back to Belgian politicians, but the biggest chunk of the loot had reportedly gone missing.

CHAPTER 11

AFRICAN BLESSINGS

DIMONA DREAMS

Had Felix been involved in Israel's search for uranium as early as 1956? Don Felix had a definite interest in all matters nuclear, witness his Tico representation at the International Atomic Energy Agency in Vienna. The IAEA was a new UN initiative that was to supervise the safe and peaceful use of fissile material. In reality the agency was used to put pressure on dissident countries like China and to consolidate the position of the GE-Westinghouse cartel. If Felix was working for the 1952-founded Israeli Atomic Energy Commission, his presence at the IAEA, supposedly countering nuclear proliferation, must have proved quite useful. Incidentally, Israel was one of the very few countries that would never ratify the international non-proliferation treaty.

In 1955, Israel signed a contract with the USA for the sale of a small nuclear reactor as part of the "Atoms for Peace" project. But at the time premier David Ben-Gurion and defense minister Shimon Peres had other priorities. In secret they had called upon the French government for its assistance in the development of a nuclear weapon. Some sources say that France and Germany built the Dimona nuclear plant in exchange for US nuclear technology, stolen by the Israeli's. Possibly this is what Don Felix had been involved in the mid-1950s. In 1951 a secret agreement was signed over the collaboration of the CIA and Mossad. J.J. Angleton, the CIA representative in the Vatican in the late 1940s, was a co-founder of Mossad. Angleton was known to have used the Mossad whenever a covert operation was deemed too risky for the CIA. In 1964, Angleton directly contributed to the Israeli nuclear program, with the consent of President Johnson, whose grandmother was Jewish.

MAJOR JORDAN'S DIARY

At the outbreak of WWII, John J. McCloy was appointed assistant to the Secretary of War, Henry Stimson. From his Washington desk, McCloy played a crucial role in the conversion of the US economy from peacetime into high-gear wartime modus. He had his say in all major decisions taken in Washington at the time. And, of course, McCloy became involved in the Manhattan nuclear project. The plans to drop atomic bombs on two Japanese cities were hatched by Henry Stimson, John McCloy and their War Department staff.

The main subcontractor for the Manhattan project was the DuPont company, a client of McCloy. The essential DuPont company soon dominated the War Department. Some military insiders complained that DuPont *was* the War Department. The fact that Franklin D. Roosevelt junior had just married Ethel Dupont probably explained a lot. The connections between DuPont, McCloy and IG Farben were well documented.

When McCloy took up his job of High Commissioner in Germany in 1947, he installed his HQ in the beautiful IG Farben building in Frankfurt. Some of McCloy's Frankfurt staff had come under scrutiny from senator McCarthy for their pro-communist statements. McCloy used his position of power in Germany to influence the outcome of the Nuremberg trials. With his help, Nazi doctor Herta Oberheuser, who had conducted the most gruesome experiments on children, had come away unscathed. McCloy saved Fritz Thyssen, Friedrich Flick and even Klaus Barbie from the gallows. During the trial, very little transpired about the close wartime collaboration between DuPont and IG Farben, much to the relief of FDR and his daughter-in-law Ethel.

McCloy himself designated his successor for the position of High Commissioner in Germany: James Conant. The latter was one of the key figures of the Manhattan project. Both McCloy and Conant were great admirers of Robert Oppenheimer, the "great wizard" of the atoms and head of the secret nuclear project. Oppenheimer was known to have strong leftist sympathies. He had endorsed the Acheson-Lilienthal plan to share the non-military US nuclear technology with the rest of the world. At the time many still believed in the "Atoms for Peace" utopia.

In the meantime the Soviets had been working frantically on their nuclear bomb. To the astonishment of the Western world, the first RDS-1 nuclear device detonated in Kazakhstan on August 29, 1949, barely four years after the US had bombed Hiroshima.

Upon hearing the news of the Soviet nuclear bomb, Major George R. Jordan, a WWI hero of Eddie Rickenbacker's 147 Aero Squadron, contacted the FBI. He had witnessed first-hand the transfer of secret American nuclear technology and even plutonium to the USSR at the end of WWII. Jordan had been stationed at Newark airbase, New Jersey, where thousands of tons of military hardware were airlifted to Russia, via Great Lakes and Fairfax. These shipments included large quantities of cobalt, thorium and cadmium, all sanctioned by Harry Hopkins, FDR's personal assistant in the White House. They were part of the Lend-Lease deal with Stalin, who had been an ally of the West throughout WWII. Hopkins, who had started his professional career in 1912 in Christadora House in Lower East Manhattan, had succeeded in convincing FDR that Russia and China should be included in the US Lend-Lease program.

KATANGA BLESSINGS

One day before the nuclear attack on Hiroshima, General Leslie Groves placed a phone call to Belgium. The person he called was Edgar Sengier, one of the most powerful men in the Belgian Congo at the time. He was told by Groves to keep an ear to the radio for the upcoming news broadcasts. The next day, Groves uncorked a few bottles of champagne to celebrate the flawless operation of his nuclear darlings "Little Boy" and three days later, "Fat Man."

Sengier was the director of the Union Minière du Haut Katanga company, that was partly owned by Lazard Frères. Katanga was the mineral rich province of the Belgian colony in Africa. Under Sengier's direction the Union Minière company had grown to become the world's top producer of copper, zinc, tin, cobalt, radium and uranium. In secret deals, he had sold the entire uranium production to the US, thus making sure that the USSR could not lay hands on it. However, many years later it was uncovered that he had supplied uranium to Nazi Germany as well.

Sengier was invited to the White House. Groves introduced him to president Truman with the words "I want you to meet the man without whose assistance we could not have accomplished what we have done." From that moment, Belgium came under special scrutiny by US intelligence, fearing that a leftist Belgian government might renege on the exclusive Katanga uranium deal. In exchange, Belgium had its US-supervised Nuclear Research Center, founded in 1952, sponsored by the GE-Westinghouse cartel. Its security service was said to be a CIA antenna.

OIL, ARTILLERY AND DIAMONDS

In the 1970s and 80s, when it came to nuclear technology exchange, Israel and South Africa were on excellent terms. Both felt threatened by their neighbors. The Apartheid regime feared that continuous foreign encouragements could spark a black rebellion in the townships. Low-yield nuclear artillery promised to be best suited for containing a revolt. Both Pretoria and Tel Aviv showed great interest in Gerald Bull's extended range artillery that could fire conventional as well as nuclear charges with great precision. Bull's dreams of a supergun that could fire satellites into orbit ended when he was murdered in Brussels in March of 1990. As international pressure on the Apartheid regime mounted and the nation was struck with an arms and oil embargo, its Jewish friends did not stand by idly. Marc Rich, assisted by Bruce Rappaport, Ed Wilson and many others, turned out to be the key figure in illegally supplying South Africa with oil. Shabtai Kalmanovitch, Rich's agent in Africa, was instrumental in processing the illicit oil traffic through the West African nation of Sierra Leone. Kalmanovitch, member of the Mikhailov network, was given a hand in Sierra Leone by Brooklyn maffiya-boss Marat Balagula. The Red Maffiya literally took over the country and its exceptionally lucrative "blood diamonds" trade, undercutting the local Lebanese dominance.

THE SULEIMAN KILLING

The Sierra Leone connection left a trail all the way to Antwerp and to two Brabant Killings suspects: Robert Beijer and Dani Bouhouche. Both were ex-members of the Gendarmerie. Beijer had always insisted that he worked for the Russian GRU, which the police found hard to believe. Bouhouche was a weapons freak who loved practical shooting. He was always on the look-out for hard action. The B & B duo had been involved in the robbery of a shipment of diamonds in the Brussels National airport in October of 1982, which had left one security guard missing, presumed dead. His body was never found.

On Saturday September 2, 1989, B & B penetrated into the Antwerp apartment of Ali Suleiman Ahmad of the Lebanese Ahmad clan. They expected to find Suleiman alone at home. Officially, they were tasked to teach him a lesson for having failed to pay his dues. As it turned out, Suleiman had visitors. His son, his brother-in-law Ali Said, and his nephew were in the apartment when B & B busted in. The ensuing fight escalated into a fire-fight, leaving Suleiman dead and Ali Said badly injured. B & B escaped unscathed but were later arrested and convicted.

Asked about the motive of the raid, Beijer declared that he had acted on orders of the GRU to interrogate Suleiman on the whereabouts of an Israeli by the name of Mosseiev. It appeared that Beijer was well informed about the Blood Diamonds trade with Sierra Leone. Back in '89 this was still privileged information.

From his Lebanon residence, Suleiman's father informed the press that the Mossad was behind the murder simply because his son had been a competitor to the Israeli diamond traders in Africa. Said Ali Ahmad, who lost an eye in the Antwerp attack, had been involved in a failed coup in Sierra Leone in 1987. The Ahmad clan of Sierra Leone was linked to Amal and Nahib Berri in Lebanon. Until the start of the Momoh presidency in 1985, the diamond trade had been controlled by Lebanese businessmen. This had obviously put them in the line of fire of the Mossad, which was known to act in favor of the De Beers cartel. President Momoh, as we have seen, was coached by Kalmanovitch and Balagula. Under their control, loads of diamonds were shipped to Thailand where they were exchanged for heroin, that was sold on the European market with the help of the Genovese clan.

Mohamed Jamil, the former Lebanese "white" president of Sierra Leone had attempted to oust Momoh in the 1987 putsch that was thwarted by Kalmanovitch.

The Suleiman murder seemed to confirm Beijer's claim that he had been on the GRU payroll for some time. The Jewish Connection, the KGB-GRU complex and the Mossad overlapped to a great extent. If Beijer had indeed been a GRU agent, what did that say about the nature of the Brabant Killings and who commissioned them?

Martial Lekeu, an ex-gendarme just like B & B, had stated that, as a young man, he had been impressed by the Israeli forces' performance during the Six-Day War. He had volunteered to join the Israeli defense force, but he had been turned down. Whereupon an Israeli by the name of Uri had coached him to join the Gendarmerie, where he would be in a position to collect useful information. Lekeu's wife was Jewish. In one of his statements he explained that it was the Mossad who had derailed the planned 1980s coup in Belgium in which he was taking part. Apparently, a regime change was not in Israel's best interest at the time. Jean Gol, the Belgian minister of Justice in the 1980s, was of Jewish descent. He was no doubt an important actor in the 1980s dramas.

In 1983 Lekeu was starting to feel the heat. He wanted to get out of the country fast. Initially he had received permission to travel to Israel, via Paris. But his wife refused to spend the rest of her days in the Jewish state. Their destination of choice was America. To Lekeu's amazement it took quite a while to get the visas. The unexpected delay made him wonder about whose payroll he had really been on for the past decade. Justice minister Jean Gol must have known the answer, but he let it be known that sometimes the truth had to remain hidden in order to "prevent even greater calamities."

Baron Empain

CHAPTER 12

ENERGIYA CONFERENCE

THE ENERGIYA CONFERENCE

A 1993 study of the US Department of Energy showed that about 4000 criminal gangs controlled 40 percent of all private and 60 percent of public enterprises in Russia. One-out-of-two banks, hotels and restaurants was in criminal hands. When it came to securing the flow of oil and gas from the East to the West, negotiations with the leading figures of the Red Maffiya were inevitable. Leonid Minin, who has found his way into Belgian politics and diplomacy, was one of them.

In August of 1996 the Austrian embassy in Kiev telexed to Vienna that Minin, a prominent member of the Odessa maffiya was on the international "most wanted list." Minin financed and operated a small army of criminals, armed to the teeth. Belgian police suspected Minin, a known drug trafficker and oil smuggler, of being behind the attempt to assassinate Ukrainian President Pavlo Lasarenko. Lasarenko survived the attack. After his resignation in 1997, he emigrated to Geneva, where he soon landed behind bars for corruption.

The Belgian police were more than interested in what Minin had to say about the 1994 murder of businessman Vladimir Missiourin Kudelkina in Uccle, a suburb of Brussels. Missiourin himself was suspected of dozens of murders in Ukraine and Russia. He had been a business partner of Minin, who even lent him his Challenger-600 jet for a while. Then things had obviously turned sour between the two billionaires. Missiourin was shot dead with a Tokarev pistol outside his villa as he hurried to the Brussels airport to catch a flight to Caracas.

The murder investigation turned into a fiasco. How could a criminal like Missiourin have settled in Belgium without even being noticed? Maybe that had something to do with the fact that Missiourin was honorary consul of Costa Rica in Moscow. He must have had a little help from Don Felix. Minin was doing business on a global scale via some of the branches of the Griffon company, linked to baron Empain's Azur Trading Company ATCO. Baron Empain was one of the very few people ever to be photographed in the company of Don Felix. Waiving the evidence against Minin, Felix's friend Alfred Cahen had taken up his defense and shielded him from legal action.

One of Minin's lieutenants was Vadim Shpakovskyi, aka Shpakovski or Chpakovski, who had settled in a splendid villa near Vienna. His phone number turned up during a house search at the Mikhailov residence in Geneva. Chpakovski too was part of the Costa Rican diplomatic corps. He was the Tico consul-general in Geneva and later in Vienna. Johann Nitschinger, the former Tico consul in Vienna, remembered that Don Felix had always had excellent relations with Russia and that he had promised Chpakovski the Salzburg consulate. Some time later Costa Rican president Calderon had appointed Chpakovski to the office of consul of Tirol and Salzburg. When asked about his contacts with Don Felix, Chpakovski preferred to keep silent.

In a 1998 Austrian EDOK police report Don Felix was portrayed as a key figure of the drug trade, who had excellent contacts with Chpakovski, Ekhard Peters – "the most dangerous man in Germany" – and Mark Hibbs. The latter was a senior associate of the Carnegie Nuclear Policy Program in Berlin and Bonn and publisher of *Nucleonics Week* and *Nuclear Fuel*.

Although his attendance is well documented, Chpakovski refused to discuss the 1994 "Energiya Conference" that took place on November 23 in the Hilton hotel in Tel Aviv. Mikhailov, who was still a free man at the time, had checked in a day early. Don Felix too stayed at the Hilton at the time. One of the key participants was Joseph Kobzon, member of the Duma and personal friend of ex-president Boris Yeltsin. Gregori Lerner, a Russian emigrant who had settled in Israel under the Hebrew name of Zvi Ben-Ari, was there too. He was one of the richest men in Israel, owner of several banks and businesses in Moscow and Cyprus. He was a heavy sponsor of Likud, hoping that one day he would be part of the government. Instead he ended up in jail in 1998, on charges of murder and corruption.

Boris Birshtein, aka Bernstein, who had smuggled the money and the gold of the Russian Communist Party out of the country in the run-up to the Soviet collapse, was there too. Birshtein was known to be on excellent terms with Mikhailov. Another heavyweight checking in at the Hilton in November of 1994 was the Russian Viktorovitsh "Anton" Malewski, head of the Ismailovo gang, who had emigrated to Israel where he made a fortune trading diamonds and foodstuffs. In his home country Malewski was wanted for murder. He was spotted in the company of Mike Brandwain, an agent of Marat Balagula, who resided in Antwerp.

The real stars at the Hilton conference, however, were Grigori Loutchansky and Vadim Rabinovitch. The former was a close friend of Ukrainian President Leonid Kravchuk, of Kazach President Nursultan Nazarbaev and of Russian ex-Premier Viktor Chernomyrdin, of Gazprom notoriety. In 1991 he was a poor emigrant living off allowances in Düsseldorf, Germany. By 1993 Grigori "Lucky" Loutchansky was a billionaire, controlling dozens of companies. In 1995 he was a guest of the Clintons at the Hay Adams Hotel in Washington. Loutchansky was the founder of the Nordex company and a representative of the Itera group that got badly burnt in the shady Kazach deals with the Belgian Tractebel company. Media tycoon Rabinovitch, despite having spent several years behind bars, was a friend of the Clintons too. He had his picture taken with the presidential couple at a fundraising diner in the Miami Sheraton in 1995.

The Austrian police, investigating the consul Chpakovski case, picked up a trail leading to the Odessa Maffiya and to one of its capos, Nikolai Fomichev, who had made a fortune in the oil business. Fomichev was one of Minin's agents. He was said to be "armed and dangerous." Controlled by criminal gangs, Odessa was the main transshipping point for bootleg oil that was illegally sold to the West. In august of '98 Fomichev was spotted in the Penta hotel in Vienna where he was visited by two Ukrainians who arrived in Chpakovski's Land Rover. In December of 1997 Fomichev's lieutenant Igor M., residing in Antibes, was stopped in Ventimiglia by the Italian police for a routine check. In his brand new Ford Galaxy – a Christmas present from Fomichev – a list of phone numbers was found. One of which was that of Don Felix's villa Campanelle in Antibes.

PART III

Resurrection

"There is this very powerful club. High level industrialists and politicians are on its membership list. One could call it a sort of private intelligence service. A service at the very highest level, though. I am in charge of the operational section: intelligence collection. Cover-ups, counter-intelligence via the media, and operations. Anyone who disagrees is eliminated. We know a lot of things about the individuals at the top."

Hans Langemann, BND senior officer

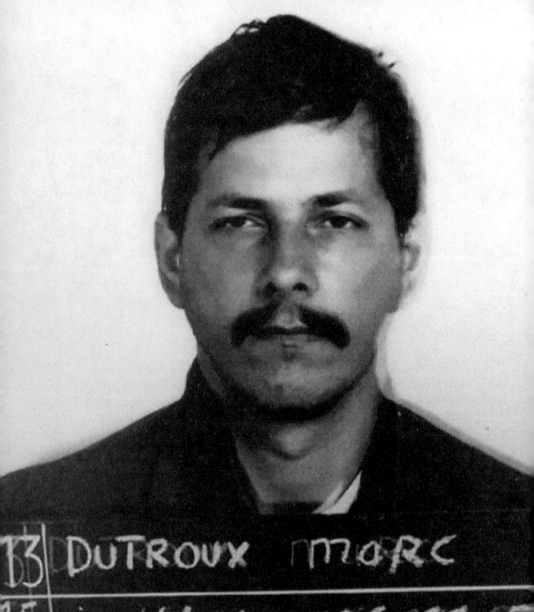

CHAPTER 13

ROYAL QUESTION

A ROYAL LEGACY

In February of 1979, Ulrich Lenzlinger was shot dead in his villa in Zürich. He was known as a rich, extravagant businessman who loved wildlife. He begged to be noticed. He had himself photographed while taking a stroll with his cheetah, in the company of his glamorous girlfriend. Lenzlinger had turned his villa into a fortress. The garden was like a private zoo. "When they kill me, one of these days, I'll have had a great life," he often joked.

In Zürich and beyond, Lenzlinger was reputed to be a chinchilla breeder and a pimp, who had his own brothel. Insiders described him as a ruthless criminal, who was doing business with East Germany: weapons, drugs and human trafficking. Lenzlinger was a known middleman for the ex-filtration of hundreds of disgruntled East Germans to the West. He was suspected of being an agent of the Stasi, who were "selling tickets" to the West to whoever could afford them. West German authorities too often sponsored this type of operation.

Lenzlinger had not limited his business to East German dissidents. On the side, he used his network to smuggle young women and even children, on his own account. They were lured to the West on the promise of freedom but were sold into prostitution and pedophilia networks instead. This line of business had made Lenzlinger a very wealthy man.

His death had some interesting aspects. Investigators uncovered a Belgian connection to the Lenzlinger murder. Lenzlinger had been in contact with Belgian Michel Nihoul, manipulator and extortionist, who was doing business with the notorious criminal and pedophile Marc Dutroux. Nihoul, a small-time drug dealer, was a regular visitor of sex parties in the Brussels area. He had many friends in high places. This had made him untouchable for a while. Nihoul and his concubine lawyer Annie Bouty were on record for assisting illegal immigrants, many of them out of Africa, who could afford the fees. When it came to visas, they could count on the kind assistance of ambassador Alfred Cahen, a close friend of Felix Przedborski's.

However, the clientèle of Nihoul and Bouty was not limited to Africans, they had business contacts in the former Eastern Bloc as well. This explains the contacts between Nihoul and Lenzlinger. Dutroux reportedly traveled to Eastern European countries on a regular bases, some say to pick up children. However, the international network aspect of the Dutroux scandal was suppressed by the police and the courts. Officially, Dutroux had acted alone. He was sentenced and jailed, but Nihoul's involvement was downplayed. Nihoul and Bouty were cleared of any involvement in the abduction and abuse of minors. The existence of a child abuse ring was out of the question.

This was 1996. Today, 20 years on, more and more evidence is surfacing in the USA, Belgium, Holland and the UK, pointing to the existence of a protected high-level pedophile ring. Child abuse seems to be the ultimate kick of the "Absolute Power" elites. Their impunity in the face of these unspeakable crimes confirms their superior, above-the-law status.

Child abuse also provides a powerful instrument for blackmail. Several witnesses had reported on the pedophile acts of Belgian politicians and magistrates, but these elements were suppressed in the investigation. José Happart, in his 1996 interview with Mister X, had expressed his dismay about the involvement of certain magistrates. They were almost certainly lured into compromising situations that were recorded on video so they could be manipulated. There are strong indications that this has been the case in the Brabant Killings investigations.

EVIL DOCUMENTS

The ex-wife of Belgian businessman E.B. had contacted the local police with the information that her ex-husband had confessed the Lenzlinger murder to her. According to E.B., the Swiss animal lover had blackmailed him and had threatened his family. To put an end to the blackmail, he had summarily executed Lenzlinger in his villa. Surprisingly, E.B. did not seem to worry about the consequences of his crime, nor, for that matter, of his confession. Rightly so. As it turned out, he was never bothered. The Lenzlinger murder remained one the most intriguing unsolved murders in Swiss criminal history.

E.B. too was portrayed by insiders as a ruthless brute, and, just like Lenzlinger, he was an animal lover who had made a fortune "somehow." He owned some rather exclusive real estate in the Belgian coastal resort of Knokke, in France and in the USA. After a few drinks he sometimes boasted about his immunity from prosecution. This fortunate state of affairs, he explained, was based on the "evil documents" he had in his possession.

These documents had been part of the legacy of a remarkable figure by the name of Willy Weemaes. Apparently he was another animal lover who had died without heirs. In accordance with his last will and testament, Weemaes' estate had ended up in the hands of E.B.'s well reputed Belgian animal rights protection group "V." As in many other cases, Weemaes' legacy benefited V's director, rather than the animals in his care. But who was this Weemaes figure anyway?

After the Nazi invasion of Belgium in 1940, Belgian king Leopold III, being himself of German descent, had officially been taken into custody by Hitler. The royal family had to spend some time in exile in the Hirschtein castle near Dresden. Young crown prince Baudouin would later admit that their stay in Hirschtein hadn't really been unpleasant at all. Under the false identity of "Count and Countess Gotenburg of Berlin," the royals were allowed to travel freely within the Third Reich. They loved their stays in Austria and even considered buying a castle there. But this was considered inappropriate, given the fact that Austria had been annexed by Hitler. Eventually they moved to neutral territory, to Switzerland, where they resided for the remainder of the war. Leopold III and his wife were allowed a single servant, attending to them and their children. This servant was Willy Weemaes.

Weemaes had been tasked by the king to take care of his personal archives, mostly confidential letters and documents, stored in 57 secured metal boxes. After Weemaes' death, these boxes ended up in the hands of E.B. Apparently, some of the documents proved to be more explosive than dynamite. With what he held, E.B. claimed, he could blackmail the entire Belgian upper class. If he published Leopold III's writings, the history of Belgium since 1935 would have to be rewritten.

Leopold III had been enthroned in 1934, after king Albert I died in a bizarre mountaineering accident near Marche-les-Dames, in the Belgian Ardennes. There had been speculations that Albert I, who was seeing his German mistress on many of his mountaineering trips, had been murdered. Indeed, Hitler may have preferred Leopold III over Albert I as king of the Belgians in view of the not so distant Blitzkrieg.

E. B. suggested that some of the archived royal letters to Chancellor Hitler had dealt with the future secession of Belgium, when under German rule. Allegedly, Leopold III had suggested to Hitler in a letter that "he could do with Wallonia – the Francophone part of Belgium – whatever he pleased," but that he, Leopold III, insisted on being appointed king of Flanders. E.B. revealed that the whole affair had been of the utmost importance to ex-SS leader Leon Degrelle, who resided in Spain. Incidentally, E.B.'s neighbor in Saint-Jeannet, in the south of France, was the ex-wife of Leon Degrelle, who stopped by regularly.

Degrelle's name popped up everywhere in the Brabant Killings and the Belgian Coup files. A private investigator who had attempted to uncover the link between E.B. and the main Brabant Killings suspects and their victims, had received death threats. He did discover however that E.B., to his surprise, had been in contact with the P2 Lodge and the French ultra-rightist group Le Cube, closely linked to the French Freemasonry. The key figure of Le Cube, as we have seen, was Jacques Médecin, the mayor of Nice aka "the godfather of the Rivièra." The town of Saint-Jeannet, where E.B. had his residence, is only a few miles away from Nice.

COLLABORATION-THE ROYAL QUESTION

Whoever ventures into the labyrinth of recent Belgian history will find the skeletons of war collaboration at every intersection. The vendetta between the "white" resistance fighters and the "black" collaborators, has been haunting Belgium ever since the end of WWII. Many "white" partisans were disgusted at the sight of documented collaborators, some of whom even had the guts to pose as resistance fighters, being left untouched and being pampered. Indeed, fascism hadn't died at all in 1945. Quite the contrary.

After the German invasion, Leopold III and the royal family were "taken in custody" by the Nazi's. In reality they were free to travel throughout the German Reich. On September 11, 1941, Leopold married his mistress Lilian van Rethy in total secrecy. Queen Astrid, princess of Sweden, Leopold's first wife, had been the darling of the Belgian people. Sadly, the revered queen and her unborn child had lost their lives in a terrible car accident in Switzerland, in 1935. A few years after the Queen's death, Leopold had fallen in love with Lilian, whom the Belgian people resented because of her lust for luxury and her blind ambition to become queen of Belgium. The chaos of war provided the smokescreen behind which the newly-wed royal couple could hide for a while.

However, when king Leopold returned to Belgium after the war, he had to face the wrath of his people. Many citizens questioned his marriage and his behavior in the face of the Nazi enemy. What had he been up to when he had traveled to Berchtesgaden to talk to Herr Hitler? Why had he not joined the government in London? The "Royal Question" caused great turmoil. It split the Belgian population in two vehemently opposing sides, for or against abdication. The majority vote decided against the king. His first-born son, crown prince Baudouin, was designated as his future successor.

In 1934, when Leopold III was crowned king of Belgium, parliamentary democracy was the subject of harsh criticism. Leopold resented the indecisive politicians and their endless talks. He too was attracted by the glamour of the most powerful men of his epoch: Mussolini, Hitler and Salazar. During the war, the Belgian government in exile had expressed its fears that the king might have made a deal with Berlin to grab power and establish a fascist regime.

This was not the first time rumors were flying about a coup in Belgium. In the late 1930s, there had already been a project to have SS officer Leon Degrelle take the position of prime minister in a government led by

Leopold III. This Belgian drive towards fascism mirrored the "Plan Bleu" and the Synarchist movement in France. Back in those days the Belgian ambassador in Berlin was Jacques Davignon, son of Foreign Affairs minister Julien Davignon, who had been a member of the Belgian delegation in Versailles, in 1919. Jacques was the father of the pipe-smoking Europeanist, CFR member and Opus Dei sympathizer Etienne Davignon.

Jacques Davignon had married the countess Jacqueline-Elisabeth de Liedekerke. Her family was related by marriage to the noble and very powerful d'Oultremont family, who were pulling some strings in the royal palace of Laeken. Prince Alexander, son of Leopold III and Lilian, was often seen in the company of Philibert de Liedekerke and his lovely bride Maria Teresa Cuevas, nicknamed "Kika."

The Liedekerke family were known to be more Catholic than the Pope. Kika was a member of Opus Dei and of the Nouvelle Europe Magazine (NEM) club. Count Philibert was co-president of the Mouvement d'Action pour l'Union Européenne (MAUE), which had strong ties with the Opus Dei power-brokers residing in Madrid. MAUE was headquartered in a Brussels house, address Belliard 39, owned by Baron Bonvoisin. MAUE was suspected of funneling Chilean money to Belgian ultra-rightist groups, but the Count was never bothered. He used to boast that "the Liedekerke dynasty was above the law."

In the 1970s and 80s, Philibert's friend Prince Alexander was often seen rubbing shoulders with Felix Przedborski. At the time, some even joked that Don Felix had hired a prince as his chauffeur. The pair were spotted visiting the Greenwood private club in Tervuren, where "Tuna" Israel used to hang out. Tuna was the mistress of Roger Boas, CEO of the Jewish controlled ASCO company that was involved in the Iran-Contra weapons deals. It's a small world.

NAZI HAVEN

The investigations into the Brabant Killings in the mid-1980s had unearthed yet another failed coup d'etat in Belgium in 1981. This time the projected putsch seemed to be linked with the ultra-right activists of the Westland New Post (WNP) and the Front de la Jeunesse (FJ), who in turn were somehow connected to the Brabant Killers. Actually the FJ movement was an early dissident spin-off of the pro-European NEM club.

Reading through the files, this author got the strong impression that these neo-Nazi groups were part of a bigger team that included Group G, Group M and even some members of State Security. The CIA, DEA and DIA were pulling some strings here too. Group G and M stood for the secret ultra-rightist clusters within the Gendarmerie and the Military. Had they been mobilized to prepare the coup? This modus operandi very much resembled that of the aborted P2 Borghese-coup in Italy in 1973. It was not unthinkable that the lower echelon of conspirators, having found out about their high-level protection, had gone rogue.

Through "Kika" Cuevas, the de Liedekerke dynasty had strong ties with Chile and its leader Pinochet. Chile had not only proved to be a safe haven for ex-Nazi's, it was also an anti-communist bulwark and the launching pad of the secret Operation Condor. Kika was an intimate friend of Pinochet's daughter. She often visited her in the Moneda palace. Next to Hitler, Pinochet was one of the main objects of blind adulation by the Belgian neo-Nazi and fascist milieus. When Paul Latinus, head of the WNP, was outed by the press as an informant of State Security, he fled to Chile in a hurry in 1980. He was welcomed there by relatives of Kika Cuevas, who at the time was working at the Chilean embassy in Brussels, where she headed the intelligence section. In other words, she was working for Pinochet's dreaded secret service DINA, a quasi-subsidiary of the CIA.

BURAFEX

When questioned Michel Libert, head of the FJ group, confessed that DINA was one of the important contacts of the Belgian ultra-right movement. (Appendix 15). Even more interesting was the fact that the WNP was being tasked by a secret agency that handed down the marching orders from the secret "principals" to the operators. This agency was code-named Burafex, for "Bureau des Affaires Extérieurs." It provided WNP with money, cars, weapons, and protection. Informants described Burafex as an "international criminal association of politicians and industrialists, not being leftists nor rightists, only in it for the money."

This statement is reminiscent of what the Insider Michel V had said about "all fish being of the same color," meaning that the bloody 1980s events had nothing to do with political ideologies of any color, but solely with money – and power. In a later statement on the Internet, Michel V, in his typical, sarcastic style, wrote:

"Gladio, Stay Behind … great story, isn't it? […] Great to see the reaction of the Belgian authorities when the Americans spit them in the face by refusing to deliver the names of the heads of the network! You can put that label on anything you want, the more so because each country of the new-born EU shelters parts of the network. It's almost as funny as the 'sniffer aircraft' story.

"Except when certain people, using the privileges, the contacts and the know-how that the network provides, exceeded certain limits just because the "straight, legit guys," promising total impunity, wanted it, and that this led to the killing of people who had nothing to do with it … including the killing of children, because they had enrolled psychopaths.

These were hired by guys who had some street credibility, who were attacking money vans, who supplied drugs, weapons, cars etc.… In essence the only trail you need to follow is tied to this: weapons, money and corruption! These elements are so ubiquitous, so blatantly present and so all-encompassing that they have become invisible. […]

"In 1980, Gorbachev, having been in the Central Committee for 10 years, was voted into the Politburo and this set the trend, namely…disarmament. At the time the deployment of ballistic missiles was a big topic. Imagine how many billions [of francs] were at stake and how many had already been spent. The process needed to be sped up in order to pocket some of it. On top of that the USA had announced that they would no longer be babysitting Western Europe at no cost. The US have better things to do, they need to protect their southern flank in Central-America. They demand something in return. What was offered to them in return were the arms deals. But in their haste, some have made mistakes, which the small fry has attempted to take advantage of. That was the true origin of when things went spinning out of control."

What Michel V is suggesting may at first sight seem outlandish, but he has a point. Where he mentions the "ballistic missiles," what he means is the nuclear "cruise missiles" that were projected to be deployed on the airbase of Florennes in the early 1980s. The project had met a lot of fierce, popular opposition. Unseen numbers of protesters, mostly linked to the socialist and green parties, had marched the streets of Brussels. This state of affairs must have infuriated some hardliners, who had been warning for years about the Soviet subversion via the ecological and leftist movements. As Michel V correctly points out, insiders must have sensed very early on that Mikhael Gorbachev's rise within the Polit Bureau – the highest Soviet instance – was a prelude to US-Soviet détente and mutual disarmament. In previous years Gorbachev had been traveling extensively throughout the West, where he had been labeled "a moderate."

Huge investments and speculation had taken place in anticipation of the actual US deployment, but to appease the popular resistance, the final "Go" for missile deployment as it had been agreed to in 1979 had been delayed by the government. What Michel V is suggesting is that, in the face of the weakening Cold War tensions, these investments were now thought to be in danger. That is why the cruise missile program needed to be implemented as soon as possible. As indeed it was.

In a surprise move in March of 1985, Foreign Affairs minister Leo Tindemans, bypassing the government, formally agreed to the missiles' deployment. Tindemans justified his bold decision by the rejection of his proposals by Soviet Foreign Minister Andrei Gromyko. By the time Prime Minister Wilfried Martens was informed of Tindemans' fiat, the first 17 of

48 cruise missiles were already airborne, on their way to Florennes. Someone had obviously been pulling some strings behind the curtain.

Interestingly enough, Michel V obviously links the cruise missile affair to the Brabant Killings. That is why his comments are worth exploring. There is reason to view this link as justified. In 1983, Jacques Fourez, a real estate agent, and his concubine, were executed by the Brabant Killers. It transpired that they had invested heavily in real estate in the Florennes area, anticipating a hefty benefit after the arrival of the US Detachment. The deal had been arranged through the office of a Brussels notary public by the name of Lefère. He was a personal assistant of the right-wing defense minister VDB. Incidentally, Fourez was also involved in the toxic and nuclear waste scandal around the Van De Voorde brothers and the Pakistani deal with the Belgian Nuclear Research Center.

Obviously Michel V was of the opinion that whoever was pushing the deployment of the cruise missiles was behind some of the Brabant Killers' attacks, that had taken place in two waves, with different actors in the second phase. These two waves, separated in time by over one year, were officially attributed to one and the same Brabant Killers gang after the discovery of a single batch of weapons that had obviously been used in both waves.

However, this "convenient" weapons find appeared to have been manipulated. Skeptical investigators concluded that the second wave perpetrators had been trying to piggyback on their less bloodthirsty predecessors, who had been guaranteed impunity. This impunity, according to Michel V, was promised by the "straight, legit guys" who had commissioned the black operations via the gang that "was attacking money vans." If by this he means the Haemers gang, then we need to take another look at Patrick Haemers' confession to his father that "they were paid for the attacks" on the Securitas money vans.

Too bad, the individuals he had named – top lawyers Vander Elst and Dumont; ministers Jean Gol, Willy De Clercq, André Cools – were all citizens above suspicion. They were never bothered.

Michel V continues:

> In fact, questions about the missile deployment to Florennes had already emerged around 1975. They became a real issue after the Caracas summit of 79 and the San José (Costa Rica) summit. In the wake of these summits, and given the huge amounts of money already spent, the deployment absolutely had to be expedited, even if it was all pointless. Funny, don't you think?

Here, Michel V is pointing out the change in US strategy, shifting its focus from Europe to Central and South America. This change coincided with the start of the Reagan presidency in 1980. Reagan had promised his Latin American friends, especially in Nicaragua, to crush the Soviet insurgency, even if that meant he had to bypass the US Congress that was no longer willing to finance the Contras. It was the start of the Contra affair that blended in with the Iran affair. According to Michel V, the US, leaving Europe to its own devices, had demanded something in return: weapons.

Belgium's notorious arms industry, in particular FN Herstal, centered near Liège, had a long tradition of arms deliveries to bellicose regimes. There was strong evidence that FN Herstal had been involved in the Iran-Contra arms shipments via Liège Airport since 1981. FN's Central American agent at the time was Juan "Tony" Mendez, who was murdered in January of 1986. His predecessor Ramon Davila, a known CIA agent, was involved in drug smuggling operations from Central America and in arms shipments to Beirut. Although many of the same actors were involved, the police and justice authorities for some reason obstinately refused to link the Mendez murder to the Brabant Killings.

As for the futility of the cruise missile deployment, Michel V was right. It was a political move rather than a military strategy, signaling that the US was no longer willing to use high-yield ICBMs to defend Europe. The tactical nuclear cruise missiles were – symbolically – taking the place of the ICBM shield. The targets they were aimed at were already "covered" multiple times by the NATO airforces' B61 and the Pershing missiles.

WNP was only one of many segments directed by Burafex. But who was pulling the strings within Burafex? Investigators came up with several names. One of which was that of the Countess de Liedekerke. Countess d'Oultremont was involved too. And Black Baron de Bonvoisin. The latter financed the pro-EU and Atlanticist NEM clubs. Head of the agency was said to be an unknown individual, code-name "Monsieur Guillaume." Allegedly only Latinus knew his identity, but he was suicided in 1984.

While in Chile, Latinus had been in contact with the local branch of the Rockefeller Foundation. The fact that his host family Liedekerke-Cuevas was in touch with the Rockefeller clan was no surprise. Kika and her husband Philibert were related by marriage to Etienne Davignon, a protégé of Kissinger and Rockefeller. Upon his return to Belgium, Latinus, obeying the instructions of "the Americans," had founded WNP, "in order to catch the KGB moles within the Belgian State Security apparatus." This suggested that State Security was behind the foundation of WNP. Initially Latinus had been convinced that his mate "the Duck" had joined WNP for that same reason. That turned out to be a big mistake.

Michel Libert, an insider of both FJ and WNP, had explained to the police that WNP was part of a "larger organization" whose structure was inspired by the Nazi model. This larger organization was compartmentalized and segmented on a need-to-know base. Within WNP, young new re-

135

cruits were indoctrinated with Nazi slogans, SS symbols and German mythology. Newcomers were submerged in heroic stories about the ancient Teutonic knighthood, the SS-Wewelsburg, the legend of Ygdrasil and pilgrimages to Bad Tölz, where the SS Junkerschule, the elite SS-school, had been erected in 1937.(Appendix 16).

In his statements, Libert explained that Burafex had been negotiating intensely with the Belgian management of Volkswagen and Mercedes. Apparently Volkswagen was interested in hiring WNP – in particular its SIPO section – for some unspecified job. SIPO stood for Sicherheits Polizei which in the Third Reich used to be the Gestapo unit that was responsible for political security in occupied countries. The original SIPO was engaged in counter-espionage and in the liquidation of local guerilla resistance.

Libert had been invited to a VW meeting by the Belgian ex-SS officer Karel De Lombaerde, "the ideologue," who had just joined the ranks of WNP in the early 1980s. The gathering had taken place in the VW offices in the Rue du Mail in Brussels. There, Libert had been introduced to a rotund German ex-SS officer, whose name he had forgotten.

Among the guests, Libert had recognized Charles Verpoorten, son of the late Belgian Nazi Albert Verpoorten, who had died fighting the Russians on the Eastern Front. Charles, a protégé of De Lombaerde, was the director of the press agency, Way Press, that had excellent contacts in the US, in particular with CNN. Libert learned that many ex-SS officers and collaborators were employed in the VW staff in Belgium and that they were "still active."

GLADIO

Karel De Lombaerde was born in 1909 on the island of Java. At age ten he had been enlisted in the Belgian military. By 1934 he had been promoted to the rank of lieutenant in the Belgian army. In 1940 he was arrested by the Germans and deported to Lückenwalde. After his release in 1941, he joined the Waffen SS. Promoted Major of the Luftwaffe, he was dispatched to the Eastern Front. In 1945 he was sentenced to life imprisonment for having collaborated with the enemy. However, he was released from jail as early as 1951. He joined the ranks of the Eastern Front Nazi-veterans, where he met Charles Verpoorten. He also kept in touch with ex-SS-officer Verbelen, who had been sentenced to death, but who had fled to Austria, where he was recruited by the CIA.

In the mid-1970s De Lombaerde's protégé Charles Verpoorten had his name added to the members lists of the Catholic Ordre du Rouvre and the Cercle des Nations.

In other words, Verpoorten had strayed into an orbit around Unilever millionaire Richard Van Wijck. The Ordre du Rouvre was founded by Van Wijck, while still a student, in 1960.

At the time his anti-abortion initiatives had been supported by the Catholic University of Louvain. His Ordre du Rouvre, aiming at safeguarding Western Catholic values in Europe and in Latin America, soon openly engaged in anti-communism. Rouvre entered into an alliance with the violent Militia of Jesus Christ (MJC). One of its members was jailed for a double murder. MJC openly advocated the installation of a "strong regime" in Belgium.

Belgian State Security had never intervened to stop the rise of WNP at any time. Which was odd, given the fact that State Security claimed to have infiltrated WNP. The agent who had allegedly spied on the WNP from within was CS, nicknamed "the Duck." This all proved to be a lie when it was revealed that the Duck and Latinus had been friends for a long time. Latinus had known all along that his friend CS was working for State Security. In fact, Latinus himself was recruited by the same agency. Interestingly enough, the head of State Security from 1977 to 1990 was Albert Raes, who at the same time commanded the section STC-MOB of the military intelligence service SGR/SDRA. STC-MOB was the top military staff section that "supervised" the Belgian branch of the NATO-Gladio network.

Gladio was suspected of being involved in the Brabant Killings. Raes and the military top brass never bothered to conceal their contempt for the democratic institutions of the country. When appearing before the Parliamentary Commission, they were signaling that Gladio was a top secret "patriotic" military operation that politicians had no "need to know" of. Even behind closed doors they refused to name the members of the Stay-Behind network to the Commission. Curiously, none of them were ever officially reprimanded for this.

It was much more probable that the Duck was the liaison agent between WNP and the head of State Security. Officially, the Duck had no mandate for his membership of WNP. He reported directly and unofficially to Albert Raes, but not in writing. This type of modus operandi could hardly be called "standard operating procedure" and soon speculation arose about WNP being a "dirty tricks department" created by Albert Raes. If so, what could have been its goal?

Was it "the destabilization of the country and the elimination of witnesses in pseudo hold-ups"? Witnesses to what? If the execution of banker Leon Finné by the Brabant Killers was any indication, the background for the attacks could have been the failed coup. When Latinus found out that he and his WNP were being used, he probably threatened to spill the beans. Shortly before his death, he scheduled a meeting, not with State Security or the Gendarmerie, but with a Brussels police officer. At the time, federal police and Gendarmerie were still two separate, completely different and above all competing law enforcement structures.

Otto Skorzeny and Adolph Hitler

Otto Skorzeny and Léon Degrelle

CHAPTER 14

NAZI UNDERGROUND

THE PALADINS

The Nazi-fascist character of the "organization" described by Libert made one wonder whether it had been an affiliate of the underground Nazi-continuum. After all, the Portuguese section of Skorzeny's Paladin cluster, Aginter Press, was demonstrably involved in the NATO-Gladio operation. Everything was connected. The CIA, NATO and Gladio, to a great extent, were Nazi products. If Aginter Press was a Paladin subsidiary, then WNP could have been its Belgian equivalent. WNP was preceded by the PIO, the Public Information Office, that organized public conferences about the Soviet threat. Its name sounded harmless enough but in reality, the PIO was a façade for the ultra-rightist protégés of VDB, including high-ranking military, who were gearing up for action.

Also, let's not forget that Skorzeny had been strongly advocating the return of his close friend Leon Degrelle to Belgium. Belgian judge Schlicker had stated before the Belgian Parliamentary Commission that he had found out in 1986 that WNP had indeed been part of a much larger, important organization, but he failed to name it.

Latinus talked a lot about his contacts with "the Americans," probably the DIA. The affiliation of WNP with the Nazi underground was in no way contradictory to its allegiance to the American intelligence services. They were all connected. Remember the words of ATLAS Report key witness Michel V: *"there is this structure that is well organized, well equipped and well trained. Its existence is justified by the paramount interests of the nation states. For a number of reasons, this structure is accountable to no-one. This structure had its origins in history and it is so well established that nobody really directs it any longer, while nobody knows all its intricacies any more. The more so because anyone in the know keeps silent or lies about it."*

BORMANN

In the immediate post-war years, Martin Bormann had become a mythical figure. He had been Hitler's private secretary and director of the NSDAP party headquarters. Although he was pronounced dead, he was said to have flown to Argentina on orders of Hitler, whose testament he was carrying on him. Allegedly, Bormann was tasked with the clandestine organization of an economic underground Third Reich. The concept was less absurd than it may sound. The German bankers and industrialists had realized that the war was lost long before the allied landing in Normandy.

In 1944 a meeting of German top industrialists and top military had taken place in Hotel Maison Rouge in occupied Strassbourg, France. The object of the meeting was the immediate implementation of a "Plan B," that had been hatched out in anticipation of the worst-case scenario. The plan entailed political, economic and para-military aspects.

During the war, German U-boats had already shipped tons of gold, diamonds, cash and documents, mostly German industrial patents, to Argentina.

Whether Bormann was really alive or dead was only of symbolic significance, but a 1947 CIA document, only recently released under the FOIA, made reference to "agent BC364" who reported that Bormann lived in Argentina and that Leon Degrelle resided in Spanish Morocco. The report also warned that the "organization" had built a research lab for bacteriological warfare. (Appendix 17). The fascism-friendly atmosphere in Europe and North and South America after the war greatly alleviated the task of the Bormann network, as witnessed by the great German "economic miracle" of the 1960s and the unchecked expansion of giant chemical and pharmaceutical companies whose origins can be traced back to IG Farben.

One of the most successful German agents was Klaus Barbie, "the butcher of Lyons," who had been instrumental in the expansion of the Colombian drug trade and the rise of the Medellin cocaine cartel. Barbie, aka Altman, was a key figure of Operation Condor, the tracking and killing of Latin American "leftists" and dissidents on a global scale. At some point, the Colombian drug traffickers had joined forces with the Jewish-Italian mob of Lower East Manhattan, who had switched from bootleg whiskey to cocaine.

The collaboration of Nazis and Jews may seem surprising, but it was not. Documents released in 2016 showed that Skorzeny in person had been contracted by the Mossad for the killing of a German scientist by the name of Heinz Krug in 1962. Krug was working on a rocket program on behalf of the Egyptian government, which was viewed by Tel Aviv as a serious threat. According to the *Haaretz* newspaper, Mossad agents Isser Harel and Yitzhak Shamir played an important role. After the more recent German Dolphin U-boat revelations, it has also become clear that Germany and Israel had been working together on a nuclear program since 1949.

THE SWEDISH COUNT

A police informant who had been part of the Burafex security team, insisted that a figure by the name of Carl Magnus Torsten Armfelt had been a key figure of the organization. Armfelt was portrayed as a Finnish-Swedish-American Count who was linked to the WACL, the CIA and the Sveaborg network, the Scandinavian equivalent of Gladio. In Holland, Armfelt collaborated with Interdoc, an anti-Marxist "information office" of the Aginter Press-type. He had been an adviser to Chiang-Kai-Shek and knew CIA boss William Colby personally. One of his contacts was Oliver North. For a while the Swedish Count had set up headquarters in an antiques shop in Knokke, Belgium. The informant suggested that it was Armfelt who had co-founded WNP and the Communist Combatant Cells (CCC) in order to destabilize the country "in times of emergency." He added that it was Armfelt who had financed Latinus' trip to Chile.

In the mid-1970s, Armfelt, in association with Saudi agent Al Ajjaz, had been involved in shipments of weapons and military technology to Lebanon, Israel, Libya, Iraq and even to the ETA, the IRA and the PLO. This type of clientèle suggested that Armfelt may have been in contact with the Genoud network. Genoud was Hitler's Swiss banker. Together with Hjalmar Schacht, he had continued to finance the Muslim Brotherhood in Egypt after the war. At the same time Skorzeny had been busy organizing the Egyptian armed forces and the intelligence services.

The influence of the underground Nazi team Genoud-Skorzeny-Schacht on the history of North Africa and the Middle East cannot be overestimated. Genoud's anti-British alliances with Nazi-Arabs and with the Muslim Brotherhood would ultimately result in the Israel-Palestine conflict and the founding of the PFLP, the PLO, Hamas, and Al Qaeda. Genoud's Al Taqwa bank had financed the terror operations of Carlos "the Jackal." It was Genoud who first made use of Muslim extremism to further the Western political, military and economic agenda.

Hitler himself had always spoken of Islam with great admiration. He often referred to the high level of sophistication of the Muslim culture, that had found its expression in the southern part of Spain. As far as religion was concerned, Hitler preferred to take a neutral stance. He respected the religious fervor of Leon Degrelle, who had posted several Catholic chaplains among his troops fighting on the Russian East Front. Degrelle too had expressed his admiration for the Muslim Nazi divisions who he had seen marching into combat against the Russians in temperatures of minus 42°C. Degrelle would stay in contact with the Genoud network, Amin von Leers, Ahmed Huber and ex-general Otto Remer, until the 1960s. Von Leers had converted to Islam. He was an intimate friend of the Great Mufti, Hitler's Muslim ally. Being an adviser of President Gamal Nasser, Von Leers resided in Cairo until his death in 1965.

PRELUDE TO A COUP

At the start of the 1980s, Armfelt had contracted WNP for a coup d'état against Desi Bouterse in Surinam. A Dutch informant explained that he had personally been in the thick of things from the Dutch end. Around the time the coup was to take place, US troops invaded the Island of Grenada. There was definitely something going on in that region. The informant had briefed the Belgian justice authorities about this because one of the hired mercenaries heading "the liquidation team" was Bouhouche, a prime Brabant Killings suspect. However, the Belgians did not act on the information. The Surinam operation was eventually canceled, after Bouterse had sniffed out the conspiracy.

According to the informant, Saudi agent Al Ajjaz was financing the operation.

Was Ajjaz acting on the orders of Bush, the Safari Club and the parallel CIA that was financed by Saudi Arabia? It certainly looked like it.

Armfelt had made it quite clear that the Surinam coup was but a prelude to the planned coup in Belgium. The gold stolen at Brussels National Airport in late 1982 was probably to be used to finance the putsch. Bouhouche had been involved in that robbery, which left one security guard dead. His accomplice, Belgian-American pilot Francis Buslik, a CIA agent, was sentenced to death in Belgium but escaped to the USA. He changed his name to Somerville and was never bothered.

In December of 1985, Armfelt, who was said to be pulling the strings of Burafex, suddenly left Belgium for Canada. The Brabant Killers had struck for the very last time on Friday November 9, 1985, killing eight people. Belgian prime minister Martens first heard about the bloody attack on the news while driving to the coast, where he had hoped to pass a quiet week end. In his memoirs, Martens wrote:

> All of a sudden the urgency of the situation occurred to me as I was reading through the press reports. The consequences of the terror attack were horrible. The Belgian people was in shock. Even more so because the CCC had staged four bomb attacks in that same week and two people had been killed in a brutal attack on an armoured money van.[…] Something had to be done quickly. This form of criminality in our country could no longer be tolerated. We were confronted with a national emergency.

If destabilization of the nation was the aim of the attacks, the operation could be qualified as successful by the end of 1985. The prime minister clearly qualified the killings as "terror attacks" that had pushed the country to the brink of martial law.

Armfelt was never questioned. His story, if genuine, provided yet more evidence of the connections between the Brabant Killings and the CIA-Gladio operation.

CHAPTER 15

"GEOZENTRALE"

COREA

On December 21, 1988, a bomb explosion ripped apart the fuselage of a Boeing 747 in flight over Scotland. Wreckage and bodies rained down on the sleepy village of Lockerbie. Two-hundred-and-seventy people died. The investigators soon pointed their finger at the Libyan head of state Gadhafi. In 1986, President Reagan had ordered the US Air Force to bomb the Libyan capital Tripoli. One of Gadhafi's daughters was killed in the attack. The press bull-horned that Lockerbie was Gadhafi's revenge. However, Ex-DEA agent Lester Coleman told a different story.

Before starting on its transatlantic flight, the 747 had made a stop at Frankfurt, where the bomb had been placed aboard the aircraft, probably in an unchecked diplomatic suitcase. The CIA agents who died in the crash had been on their way to Washington to blow the whistle on the illegal drug trafficking by CIA and DEA agents from Beirut. The *Observer* reported that a secret, autonomous CIA unit by the name of COREA had made a deal with Syrian arms dealer Monzer Al Khassar, who was given carte blanche for the import of heroin into the US. In turn, Al Khassar was to mediate the release of Western hostages in Beirut. In Frankfurt, someone had swapped one of Khassar's drug cases. This is how the bomb case passed security unchecked. Lester Coleman confirmed the role of the COREA agents in the plot. The German BKA had noticed the Frankfurt swap on CCTV and had reported it to the CIA. The reply from Langley was "Let it go!"

Who or what in hell was COREA? An "autonomous" CIA unit? Could there be any such thing as a CIA branch that acts on its own? According to DEA officials COREA had never existed. In the meantime, the investigation had revealed that the bomb could be traced back to the Abu Nidal terrorist group.

DVD

Fast forward to the year 2006, when Christopher Adward Harle Story published his book *The New Underworld Order*. Story was a British Russia expert and intelligence specialist who had been an adviser to the Thatcher government. He was the author of *The Perestroika Deception* and publisher of the reputed *International Currency Review* magazine, in which he had extensively reported on Leo Wanta and his Ruble-transactions.

According to Story COREA was a section of the secret Nazi-underground, which he labeled the Abwehrcontinuum, or Deutsche Verteidigungsdienst (DVD). After the war, the DVD had remained operational in Germany, under the supervision of Nazi generals Gehlen and Canaris. In fact, the DVD was the intelligence service of the underground Bormann network to which Skorzeny's Paladins belonged. It's HQ was established in Dachau, near München. The Nazi underground had established its outposts in Italy, Switzerland, Egypt, Portugal, North America and even in the Eastern Bloc countries.

Story further reported that the DVD had been activated in 1944 by the German "Geozentrale," the German global underground headquarters in Madrid. Various branches of the DVD were known under the names Die Spinne, Edelweiss, Konsul, Sechsgestirn, Scharnhorst, Leibwache, Lustige Brüder and Odessa. The latter was the code-name for the organization of the Nazi Elite Guard.

Story had taken this and other information from the work of T.H. Tetens, a Jewish German journalist and author who was born in Germany in 1899 and who emigrated to the United States after the Nazis had seized power in Germany in 1932. Tetens was the author of *Germany Plots with the Kremlin* and *The New Germany and the Old Nazi's*, in which he details how "Hitler's own had managed to return to power in almost all walks of German life ... including the foreign office, justice, the police." This postwar Nazi revival was confirmed by German journalist Jurgen Roth, in his 2016 book *Der Tiefe Staat*, or "Deep State." On May 29, 1951, *New York Times* correspondent C. L. Sulzberger reported the existence of a group that had revived the Fascist International in various countries "from Malmo to Tangier, and from Rome to Buenos Aires."

In his first book of 1953, Tetens explained how the German Geozentrale in Madrid was used as an instrument of foreign policy by Chancellor Adenauer. Furthermore, Tetens aimed to "show how the Nazi masterminds, long before the German collapse, had established a well-financed headquarter in Madrid and how another group of German diplomats went underground after the collapse and continued to operate a skeleton foreign office in Stuttgart, effectively camouflaged under the phony name of Evangelic Relief Organization. This Ribbentrop outfit was later taken over by Dr. Adenauer as his new Foreign Office."

And Tetens continues:

> In this way the Germans transferred thousands of experts, technicians, military instructors, political planners and propagandists

to Spain and Latin America. Long before the war ended, a sort of geo-political general staff had been organized in Spain which operated on a world-wide scale from its center in Madrid. The German planners in their lush offices in Madrid, Barcelona and Seville are not burdened with administrative routine work as are their counterparts in Washington, Paris and London. They enjoy a luxurious life and they devote their entire time and talent to one task only: to resurrect a powerful German Reich. The German Geo-political Center in Madrid and the other German planning agencies are well-camouflaged as commercial enterprises or as German relief organizations.

GEOZENTRALE MADRID

The Madrid HQ regularly circulated letters and magazines like "Christ und Welt" and "Der Weg" to its various branches worldwide. According to Tetens, Adenauer had used these channels to discretely pass his insights and orders to the German underground community. In his books Tetens warned the Americans that Germany, in reality, was more interested in an alliance with the East than with the West. But first, Tetens pointed out, Germany would play the game and take the American money for its reconstruction before turning to the Kremlin. To illustrate the aim of the underground Reich, Story in his book quoted one of the famous Madrid Circular Letters, issued by the Geozentrale:

> We must never let ourselves become befogged by Washington's stupid and meaningless slogans about the so-called "Struggle of Democracy versus Communism." The so-called American democracy does not deserve the sacrifice of the bones of even a single German soldier. In the age of regimented and militarized economy [sic], the US babbling about democracy and so-called "free enterprise" is such nonsense that we do not need to squander a single moment in refuting this American propaganda swindle.[...] What Germany needs in the future is not democracy but a system of statecraft similar to that of the Soviet dictatorship which would enable the political and military elite in Germany to organize the industrial capacity of Europe and the military qualities of the German people for the revival of the German race and the re-establishment of Europe as the power center in the world.

The German post-war plans were also laid out by Curt Reiss in his book *The Nazis Go Underground*. General Franco, who had been brought to power with Nazi help, had welcomed the Geozentrale in Madrid. In his book, Reiss refers to the Tetens' text where it says:

> According to the Madrid Circular Letter, referred to above, the German planners have never ceased their political warfare against

the Allies. They admit that they had "blueprinted the bold plan and created a flexible and smoothly working organization," in order to safeguard Germany from defeat and to bring Allied post-war planning to naught. They boast that they were able to create total confusion in Washington, and that they saved German heavy industry from destruction: "By no means did the political and military leadership of the Third Reich skid into the catastrophe in an irrational manner as so many blockheads and ignoramuses often tell us. The various phases and consequences of the so-called 'collapse' ... were thoroughly studied and planned by the most capable experts ... Nothing occurred by chance; everything was carefully planned. The result of this planning was that, already a few months after Potsdam, the coalition of the victors went on the rocks...'"

The Madrid Circular Letter goes on to set forth the course to be pursued by Germany.

In view of the present political situation ... the policy of orientation towards the West has lost all meaning or sense.... We must not forget that Germany has always considered orientation towards the West as a policy of expedience, or one to be pursued only under pressure of circumstances. Such was the case in Napoleon's time, after 1918, and also after 1945. All of our great national leaders have constantly counseled the long-range policy of close cooperation with the East...

Fear of this dynamic drove the U.S. to accede to all of Germany's demands for renewed power. "Anti-Communism Uber Alles!"

DOROTHY SAYS

Frontrunning the Tetens and Reiss books by many years, journalist Dorothy Thompson published an astonishing article in the the *New York Herald Tribune* of May 31, 1940, in which she analyses Germany's plans for world dominance by a centralized European economic union. While working in Munich, Thompson had met and interviewed Adolf Hitler for the first time in 1931. She had described him as "the very prototype of the little man." She was the first journalist to be kicked out of Germany by the Nazi regime. She was featured on the cover of *Time* magazine naming her the second most popular and influential woman in the country behind Eleanor Roosevelt. She radically changed her pro-Zionism views after a trip to Palestine in 1945, concluding that Zionism was a recipe for perpetual war. As a consequence, she was accused of anti-Semitism.

Thompson, drawing on the plans of pan-German theoretician Friedrich List, as realized by the European Monetary Union, wrote:

The Germans have a clear plan of what they intend to do in case of victory. I believe that I know the essential details of that plan. I have heard it from a sufficient number of important Germans to credit its authenticity. Germany's plan is to make a customs union of Europe, with complete financial and economic control centered in Berlin. This will create at once the largest free trade area and the largest planned economy in the world. In Western Europe alone there will be an economic unity of 400 million persons...To these will be added the resources of the British, French, Dutch and Belgian empires. These will be pooled in the name of Europa Germanica. [...] The Germans count upon political power following economic power, and not vice versa. Territorial changes do not concern them, because there will be no "France" or "England," except as language groups. Little immediate concern is felt regarding political organizations. No nation will have the control of its own financial or economic system or of its customs. The Nazification of all countries will be accomplished by economic pressure. In all countries, contacts have been established long ago with sympathetic businessmen and industrialists. As far as the United States is concerned, the planners of the World Germanica laugh off the idea of any armed invasion. They say that it will be completely unnecessary to take military action against the United States to force it to play ball with this system. Here, as in every other country, they have established relations with numerous industries and commercial organizations, to whom they will offer advantages in co-operation with Germany.

US MARSHAL
TAMPA FLORIDA

Carlos Lehder

2 5 87

CHAPTER 16

YELLOW FRUIT, WHITE POWDER

EL PUMA

Story had noticed that Kintex, the Bulgarian state company, had continued its "business as usual" even after the collapse of communism. The cleansing of the KGB had caused many agents to join either the DVD or the Red Maffiya, which was now closely collaborating with ex-Eastern Bloc political heavyweights. The ancient Kintex drug trail from Afghanistan to Beirut had left it's marks in Belgium too. In the 1970s quite a few people had been involved in it, including the Belgian police's narcotics section, dubbed the "François Network." For the most part, these drug-runners were protected by the DEA and the CIA.

According to Story, the DVD was part of the CIA structure. After all, the Agency had been built by Nazi General Gehlen. In other words, the CIA was the US branch of German intelligence. The illicit drug trades financed part of its operations, which therefor required no funding nor the green light, for that matter, from the Congress. The CIA, in other words, had spun out of control. This global drug network had been constructed on the foundations of the early Jewish-Italian drug trails from Latin America and the Golden Triangle. The names of Meyer Lansky, Robert Vesco, Klaus Barbie, Auguste Ricord, Bronfman, Pasqua, Vesco and Przedborski spring to mind.

In Belgium in the 1970s, the drugs-for-arms trades had taken truly industrial proportions. Truckloads of firearms and grenades, many stolen from Army depots, were shipped to Lebanon via Antwerp. The ministry of justice and the Gendarmerie were well aware of the operations, which were sanctioned by the CIA. The Gendarmerie even escorted the convoys to a particular quay of the Antwerp port on more than one occasion.

Many of the Beirut deals originated in the Brussels bar El Puma, situated near the Grand Place. The bar was a meeting place for Latin American expatriates. The place was run by Carlos Davila, a Peruvian ex-military who had been the representative in Latin America of Belgian arms producer FN Herstal. He had been fired because of his close links with the CIA. In reality, Davila was deeply involved in the protected arms and drug trades with Beirut. Interestingly, Davila's successor at FN Herstal, Juan "Tony" Mendez, was shot dead in his car in January of 1986. The murder was never officially linked to the Brabant Killings although some of the same main suspects were cited in both cases. Bouhouche, for one, was a close friend of Mendez. Both of them were arms freaks and collectors. The Mendez murder was never resolved. Incidentally, Bouhouche and his buddy Beijer, while still serving in the Gendarmerie in the 1970s, had been involved in the El Puma investigation. Martial Lekeu too had been one of the El Puma investigators. All three later became main suspects in the Brabant Killings case.

Around the corner from El Puma was the Latino club El Machado, owned by Roberto Marin, the Costa Rican cultural attaché to Belgium. Marin had married a wealthy daughter of the owner of the Mayfair Hotel on the Avenue Marie-Louise in Brussels. She was on excellent terms with the Belgian-Jewish justice minister Jean Gol.

Felix Przedborski, being a Tico diplomat himself, was well introduced in those circles. He was a friend of Tico diplomat Miguel Bourla, who had written a few books on the subject of the cultural exchange between France and Latin America. Bourla was cited in police report PV18367/2001 as being involved, together with Don Felix, in the drugs traffic between Vietnam and the US. Both of Bourla's sons-in-law, Zev Klausner and Charles Bercovitch, were of Jewish descent.

Legal council to the Costa Rican embassy was Michel Vander Elst, a notorious ultra-rightist and "friend of VDB," whose name popped up regularly in the Brabant Killings files. Vander Elst was suspected of being in contact with Costa Rican CIA station chief Joe Fernandez, who was involved in the Yellow Fruit and Iran-Contra operations, including the Santa Elena "tourist project" mentioned in the ATLAS Report. The exact role of Vander Elst, who obviously was one of the few "accredited counselors" of the Absolute Power cartel, remained veiled in secrecy. According to an American source he had stated in 1993 *that the Costa Rica operations were now completed and that his group would now proceed to rearm Iraq."* Which was quite a remarkable statement from the mouth of a lawyer. According to suicided gang leader Patrick Haemers, Vander Elst had been one of the sponsors behind his gang's bloody hold-ups.

HERR LEHDER

Drugbaron Carlos Lehder was introduced to Fidel Castro by Robert Vesco. Carlos was the son of the German immigrant Wilhelm Lehder, who had married a Colombian. Lehder senior was selected, recruited and trained by the CIA on the basis of his German origins. Awaiting his CIA mission overseas, Lehder senior settled in Michigan where he made a living as a car salesman and small-time drug dealer.

In Colombia, Carlos had followed in his father's footsteps. But he had visions of greatness. He started using the Norman Cay airstrip to fly drugs into the US on account of the CIA, or, according to Story, of the DVD. Lehder's business was thriving. In no time he had put into operation a small fleet of light aircraft and helicopters. In Colombia he was suspected of being involved in a series of attacks against policemen and magistrates, but he was not bothered.

Carlos could soon call himself rich and powerful. He became arrogant. He seemed to have forgotten who he was working for. Carlos was becoming a risk. In 1988 he was arrested. Whereupon Carlos spilled the beans on the Panamanian leader Manuel Noriega, a CIA-Mossad puppet controlled by Mike Harari. As a consequence Washington and Langley now turned their backs on Noriega.

Mike Harari was the key figure and liaison officer for the Israeli side of the Iran-Contra trafficking in Latin America, that made use of the existing Jewish-Italian network. Story connected the Lehder-Noriega episode to Operation Watchtower, as reported on by Desirée Carone. Her father, Colonel Albert Carone, was deeply involved in the operation. He had been working with and for the CIA and the Italian mafia at the same time.

By 1996, Carlos Lehder was a free man again. According to Story he was escorted to Germany, where he lived happily ever after, having been allowed to keep the proceeds of his drug business. Talking about a happy ending! While Carlos was in shackles, his wife Coral Talavera Baca had managed the family fortune well. Coral invested the money wisely. She landed a job at AIG, the world's biggest insurance company, directed by Maurice "Hank" Greenberg, a Goldman Sachs confidant. AIG, according to Story, was a giant drug-money laundering machine, that also involved ADFA, the Arkansas Development and Finance Authority.

GO2

In England, Story wrote, the DVD had set up shop within the intelligence service MI6, General Operations section 2, called GO2. MI6 was accused by Story of acting on behalf of the French-German alliance that was lobbying to drag the UK into the EU and keep it there. GO2 was supposedly coordinating the "war against drugs." In reality it was facilitating the drugs contraband to the British Isles. The profits of which were funneled to the Conservatives and to Labor. This financial support guaranteed the temporary survival of both rapidly shrinking pro-EU parties. Among the British people there was a strong anti-EU sentiment, as it was feared, and rightly so, that the UK would lose its sovereignty under EU-rule. The binding of the UK within the EU structure, according to Story, was part of the long-term German strategy.

Conservative figureheads Edward Heath and Geoffrey Rippon, who in 1972 had signed the UK's accession to the EU, had acted on the orders of the DVD, against the will of the people. Heath had already been a laureate of the German Karlspreis in 1963. Hitler's adviser and EU architect Walter Hallstein had been awarded the Karlspreis two years prior. Geoffrey Rippon was appointed president of the European Documentation and Information Center CEDI in 1979. CEDI was the catholic pro-EU think-tank centered on Otto von Hapsburg and Generalissimo Franco.

According to Wikipedia: "The Karlspreis is one of the most prestigious European prizes. It has been awarded annually since 1950 by the German city of Aachen 'for distinguished service on behalf of European unification.' It commemorates Charlemagne, ruler of the Frankish Empire and founder of what became the Holy Roman Empire, who resided and is buried at Aachen."

In 2015, in the wake of the Jimmy Savile child-abuse scandal, ex-prime minister Ted Heath, aka "Mister Eddy," was accused of pedophilia by one of his early 1970s victims. Child abuse evidence has proved to be a powerful instrument for political blackmail on more than one occasion. Tim Fortescue worked as a whip in Edward Heath's government between 1970 and 1973. Here is what he said In a 1995 BBC documentary about what party whips would do for MPs in trouble:

> For anyone with any sense, who was in trouble, would come to the whips and tell them the truth, and say now, I'm in a jam, can you help? It might be debt, it might be … a scandal involving small boys, or any kind of scandal in which, erm er, a member seemed likely to be mixed up in, they'd come and ask if we could help and if we could, we did. And we would do everything we can because we would store up brownie points… and if I mean, that sounds a pretty, pretty nasty reason, but it's one of the reasons because if we could get a chap out of trouble then, he will do as we ask forever more.

CHAPTER 17

HEARTLAND

SCHNEZ

The existence of the German partisan group Schnez Truppe, an early version of Gladio, was revealed in May of 2014. Albert Schnez was a colonel in Hitler's army who had remained in service after the war. Under defense ministers Strauss, Schmidt and Brandt the Nazi colonel was promoted to general and even to "Heeresinspecteur," the highest rank within the German army. The Schnez Truppe had been in permanent contact with the Skorzeny headquarters. Schnez' underground army was not the only stay-behind militia in postwar Germany. It co-existed with the "Brüderschaft," the Brotherhood of Nazi officers, and the "Technische Dienst." They too must have been in contact with the Paladins and the Madrid Geozentrale.

Also part of the larger Bormann network was the revived Ribbentrop diplomatic network that was coordinating its actions with the Nazi headquarters in Madrid and Buenos Aires. It was looking at forging alliances with Russia, thus working towards the German dream of "Osterweiterung" or "expansion to the East" into what Mackinder had called the Heartland.

One of the early editions of *Der Weg* magazine, explained that the Yankees were obviously prepared to spend huge amounts of money to keep Germany from going East. This confidential information had been forthcoming from the office of the US High Commissioner, John J. McCloy. According to *Der Weg*, this was the best possible scenario for Germany to regain her sovereignty in all aspects of defense and rearmament. "That would put Germany in a better position to negotiate with Russia."

Der Weg continued ...".we must insist that Germany will not lead the defense of Europe as long as we are being treated as a defeated nation. The Americans have forfeited peace, the Cold War and their future, but they haven't realized that yet. Economical problems will topple the USA sooner or later. This sort of catastrophe can be accelerated by manipulations and synthetic crises, which are common practice in the international power struggle. It is not unthinkable that a weakened America will one day request assistance from a reborn Germany. This expectation promises great prospects for our future position of power when the new world order will be established."

NAUMANN

Roscoe Hillenkotter, the first CIA director, was a product of Navy intelligence. Between 1933 and 1941 he served in the office of the US military attaché in France. He witnessed first-hand the manipulations of the Synarchists and their Cagoule in the run-up to WWII. During the war, his office was acting as a liaison between the US and the fascist Vichy government. With double-agent Allen Dulles heading the CIA – that had been organized by general Gehlen – and given the fact that thousands of Nazi's were recruited by the US services, one could not dismiss Christopher Story's allegation that the CIA was but a DVD subsidiary.

As early as the 1950s, the CIA was involved in illegal operations, drug running, arms deals, political murders and coups d'etat. More often than not, the US Congress was not aware of the CIA's dirty business. Over time the Nazi influence inside the Agency had somewhat waned, but it still very much looked as if there was a "CIA within the CIA." President Kennedy pledged to break up the CIA in a thousand pieces. He sacked Allen Dulles, but didn't live to keep his promise. After the shocking revelations about the CIA's dirty tricks, its MkUltra mind-control program and its biological weapons projects, the agency's wings were finally clipped in the mid-1970s.

And then, in 1976, along came George Bush, who launched the Enterprise and the Safari Club as CIA surrogates. According to Story, George Bush succeeded general Canaris as head of the DVD, after Canaris – again, according to Story – had died in 1975. This appointment of George Bush Sr may seem odd, but wasn't. Prescott Bush, in association with Harriman, had been in cahoots with the Thyssen dynasty, who co-financed Hitler. The confiscation of the Bush-Harriman Union Banking Corporation and the reasons behind it are well documented. In the post-war years Prescott had been the US Senate's liaison with Allen Dulles' CIA, that had just been organized by Nazi general Gehlen.

George Bush Sr was parachuted into the CIA in 1976, seemingly "out of the blue." What Story is suggesting is that it may have been his Nazi ties that had Bush appointed head of the Agency. His arrival at the CIA coincided with the founding of the secret Enterprise and the Safari Club. Bush's secret pact with the Saudis to help finance covert operations closed the loop with the Nazi Arab League tied to the Genoud network.

Skorzeny's mission was not only about para-military training, sabotage schools and terror operations. He was one of the key figures of the "centers for industrial coordination," linked to the Bormann network. Among the industrial giants belonging to the network were obviously the IG Farben spin-offs but also Mercedes and Volkswagen. There was one visible element that linked the network to Skorzeny's project "Stille Hilfe" ("Silent Help"): the Naumann Circle.

Doctor Werner Naumann was a war hero who had been promoted to the rank of general before he had reached the age of thirty. He had been in battle on the Eastern Front. He had been wounded several times and faced death on more than one occasion. He was Joseph Goebbels' personal assistant. After Goebbels' suicide he had even taken over his job for a while.

Naumann's name was cited in the 1956 CIA memorandum titled "The Fascist International." "Item 108 – Skorzeny" explains that Naumann was in contact with Skorzeny and Schacht. (Appendix 18). Right after the war, Naumann had attempted to found a Nazi party in Germany. His associates succeeded in infiltrating the governing liberal FDP party, a coalition partner of Adenauer's CDU. Naumann's influence within the FDP was growing rapidly. So much so that the British intelligence service had to step in to end Dr. Naumann's political ambitions in 1953.

Outsiders viewed Naumann as a quiet businessman who managed a Dusseldorf company by the name of H.S. Lucht. This import-export company was headed by Lea Lucht, the daughter of a Belgian general. She was the widow of Herbert Lucht, a war hero and one of Goebbels' aides. Lea Lucht was a truly remarkable lady who had close ties with Leon Degrelle. Some even speculated that it was Degrelle who directed the Lucht company. Ernst Achenbach, legal advisor of the company, had been Otto Abetz' political adviser during the war. Abetz had been the German wartime ambassador to Vichy. The British searched Naumann's house and offices and found documents proving the links between the Nazi refugees in Argentina and fascist figureheads in Belgium, England and France. The British also came up with evidence that the H.S. Lucht branch in Madrid was being run by Otto Skorzeny.

Naumann's attempt to revive the Nazi party so soon after the war had not gone unnoticed. In the US, the Society for the Prevention of WWIII in a pamphlet expressed its doubts about the de-nazification of Germany. The Society also warned about pro-Nazi manipulations by the Dulles brothers, their Sullivan & Cromwell law firm, and the J. Henry Schröder Banking Corporation in New York. Sullivan & Cromwell was legal counsel to Rockefeller while the Schröder Bank had financed Himmler's SS. The Society went so far as to subpoena Allen Dulles. He had been the director of Schröder Bank New York up until 1944. His brother John Foster had traveled to Europe on many occasions in the 1930s. He had been the driving force behind the ascension of two cartels: the Belgian Solvay cluster and International Nickel of Canada, both connected to IG Farben.

The Naumann papers had the British government worried. Foreign Affairs minister Herbert Morrison admitted that the Nazi movement had been on the rise since 1952, not only in Germany but in Argentina, Brazil, the Middle East, the Far East and in Indochina too. Fritz Klein, for instance, who had worked for Hjalmar Schacht's Octogon Trust in Liechtenstein, had been dispatched to Shanghai in the late 1940s to assist Chiang Kai Shek. The British reported that the Naumann clique was collaborating with Vincenz Muller, the "brain behind the East German police," and with two Russian generals named Bulganin and Kuvalov. Churchill himself expressed his fear that the Nazi underground, financed by the industry barons of the Ruhr, could topple the Adenauer government. As a result of pressure from the American side, the arrested Naumann group members were soon released.

What was most astonishing was the extent of Naumann's influence in the Middle East. In 1953 it was reported that Doctor Gustav Scheel of the Naumann Circle was a close associate of the Grand Mufti of Jerusalem. Any German company wishing to do business in North Africa or the Middle East had to talk to Naumann, Scheel, Skorzeny or the Mufti. Scheel was especially close to Mossadeq, head of state of Iran, whose plans he supported to nationalize the oil industry. In Egypt, Naumann and Skorzeny had ignited the pro-Nasser revolution.

FAT ALEX

What was particularly intriguing was the Nazi Underground activity behind the Iron Curtain. With the consent of Moscow, Skorzeny had set up a special unit in Leipzig with the aim of recruiting military technicians for service in Egypt. Apparently the Skorzeny network did not perceive the Iron Curtain as an obstacle to its operations. The old German stay-behind structure from WWII, that had been activated behind the Eastern Front, could obviously still be relied on. The idea of the Eastern Expansion of the Reich was still very much alive. For the Bormann strategists the reunification of East and West Germany was only a matter of time.

The Nazi brotherhood had infiltrated the Stasi and the KGB as well. Just like their American counterparts, both agencies had recruited many Nazi experts. This explained the unusual West German business deals with Imes, a Stasi company headed by "Fat Alex" Golodkowski. Fat Alex was a high ranking Stasi officer who had been tasked by President Erich Honecker with collecting "strong" foreign currency, particularly dollar and deutschmark.

And so Golodkowski had engaged in the sale of anything he could lay his hands on, from AK47s to gold, artwork, antiques, cars, drugs...He was also involved in the business of selling "visas" to freedom-loving East German citizens for their flight to the West. Fat Alex was a regular guest of Franz Josef Strauss, the ultra-rightist Lion of Bavaria, who arranged a huge loan for Honecker.

After the collapse of the Berlin Wall, Golodkowski was allowed to settle down in southern Germany without ever being bothered. The loan could be seen as an early down-payment for the re-unification of Germany and its expansion to the East, in accordance with the pre-war "Lebensraum" concept of Karl Haushofer, one of Hitler's early mentors. Haushofer had visited Hitler in his Landsberg prison cell in the 1920s. The future Führer had been impressed by his visionary exposé. The new danger, Haushofer insisted, would not emanate from Russia, but from the USA.

THIRD WORLD

While Skorzeny, Schacht and Gehlen were rearming Egypt, the Nazi Geozentrale developed the concept of using the Third World as an instrument of power that could strategically be placed in between the East and West. In association with Werner Von Hentig, Genoud, Skorzeny and Schacht, its staff worked feverishly to establish reliable points of contact in Saudi Arabia, China, Indonesia and Ghana. The 1955 Conference of Bandung had greatly accelerated the process of emancipation of Third World countries. It was the prelude to a series of African colonies demanding their independence.

In that same year 1955, Werner-Otto von Hentig, Bonn's ambassador to Indonesia, became King Saud's principal adviser while Egypt, with the help of Skorzeny and the Genoud-sponsored Muslim Brotherhood, was making plans to get rid of the British rule.

One of the Waffen SS officers who sympathized with the Genoud branch of the Nazi underground was Jean-Robert Debbaudt, a Belgian collaborator and close friend of Leon Degrelle. Debbaudt's name was listed in a 1956 secret CIA document titled "The Fascist International," that also mentioned Skorzeny and Degrelle, among many others.

This document alone proves that the Nazi Underground did indeed exist and that the CIA was well aware of its existence. (Appendix 18)

Debbaudt was also cited in a 1970 CIA telex about the "Blue Division" preparing the return to Belgium of the Rexist leader. This brings us back to the subject of the planned Belgian putsch in the 1970s and 80s. Burafex, the international criminal organization that allegedly issued the WNP marching orders, had come under scrutiny of the Brabant Killings investigations team. Judge Willy Acke, one of the magistrates in charge of the Brabant Killings case, who committed suicide in 1994 at the age of 39, made an intriguing note about the German federal police BKA in reference to Burafex. In this context, BKA could only stand for BundesKriminalAmt. (Appendix 19). Judge Acke made these notes on May 11, 1989, while being briefed by investigators AM and LM about their contact with Michel Libert, former head of the FJ, who was deeply involved in WNP. Oddly, the notes seem to suggest that the BKA could somehow have been involved in the tasking by Burafex of WNP and the Brabant Killers.

The middle of the text reads:

> [Libert] hands us a picture he received from an unknown person in the GB [shopping center] of Kraainem in 1986, before arrest; it shows a person carrying a riot gun; allegedly the killer of Aalst [Brabant Killers' most deadly attack of November 9, 1985]; =in the context of marching orders for Burafex via BKA.

CHAPTER 18

BONESMENS' PLEDGE

THE GERMAN DISEASE

In 1998, Kay Griggs, wife of Special Forces Marine colonel George Griggs, was interviewed by Eric Hufschmid. The eight hour interview was videotaped and posted on YouTube later. Kay had volunteered to speak out about the criminal operations and weird practices her husband had been involved in. As a practicing Christian, she thought the public should know what was going on in the Special Operations (SO) milieu, so it could be stopped. She had gotten in trouble after making pictures at a SO party that had degenerated into total sexual debauchery. Her husband had tried to take her camera away from her. He beat her, but she fought back, had the pictures developed and sent them to the Base Commander. That's when she had "fallen out of grace" with the SO community.

In her exposé Kay connects the dots between the Jewish-Italian mob, Zionism, Nazism, NATO and terrorism. In her interview she often refers to homosexual practices, pedophilia, Skull & Bones, Yale, mind control, mercenaries and random killings. She also refers to the German Nazi backgrounds of the "SO cult" and its rituals.

On the subject of her husband's background, Kay said:

> … And so. But he was a little boy when he was… it's mind control. Mk Ultra somebody said. They had a group of men, psychiatrist in New Jersey. I don't know where this place was but they would go and… even his roommates in Princeton told me about it. George never in, intentionally, he never introduced me to any of his friends so I had to cold call all these people. I got their names, addresses, telephone numbers, I called all his roommates at the Hun School at Princeton. They tell me things about George and, you know, holding hands with, you know, with Caddock and other people about being a cheerleader and going off and so forth…
>
> And that's what George would tell me, it was like, killing is just like, you know it's nothing, there's no emotion involved, you just get rid of some body and he said he was an existentialist and that these murders were necessary and, you know it was very matter of fact, and I would sort of go, "Uh-hum, yeah" and we'd be eating dinner and I was trying to get him to be, to know Christ, you know, sort of understand a little bit about my, my background and Ameri-

ca's background but he, his group are, they are not Christians."

They're what he calls existentialist. And they study German Clausewitz [Carl Philipp Gottfried von Clausewitz], Nietzsche [Friedrich Nietzsche], Sartre [Jean-Paul Charles Aymard Sartre], Camus [Albert Camus], er, Montesquieu [Charles-Louis de Secondat, Baron de La Brède et de Montesquieu] and his thesis at Princeton, which is a written for him by a very good friend of his named Todave, who is a French count, and his thesis was on this.

This is what Kay had to say about the SO agents and links with the mob:

> I'm talking about the Brooklyn/New Jersey mob. My husband, Al Gray, Sheehan, they're all… Brooklyn, Cap Weinberger [Caspar W. "Cap" Weinberger], Heinz Kissinger. There's the Boston mob which were shipping weapons back and forth to Northern Ireland. And I don't want to get too deeply involved in that but it goes… Israel, some of the Zionists who came over from Germany, according to my husband, were… see he works with those people. They do a lot of money laundering in the banks, cash transactions for the drugs that they're bringing over, through Latin America, that the southern Mafia, the Dixie Mafia, which is now my husband's involved with in Miami. The military are all involved at once they retire. They, you know, they go into this drug and the secondary weapon sales. And, before I forget, I want to find the name of this Russian who worked with Al Gray, who was my husband's boss, and [looking through her notes] trying to see where I wrote it. I may have to look and find that another…

When referring to her husband's diary, which she is holding in her hands, Kay explains that George was working with Robert McFarlane. This is interesting because this puts George Griggs in the Enterprise milieu, headed by George Bush Sr, in the Beirut years, when tons of weapons were illegally shipped from Antwerp to Beirut. These weapons were paid for with drugs, corrupting the Belgian police force and the magistrates. According to Kay, general Haig was in the same tightly knit club called "the Brotherhood," which reminds us of the post-war German Brüderschaft. George Griggs, Kay explains, was of German descent. He and all the others were above the law. They could kill a person without blinking and walk away scot-free.

> And it's in his handwriting. The Beirut diary tells how the intelligence community the Army and Marine Corps assassins, snipers are, how they operate in the city during a crisis. My husband was the liaison between the White House and president Gemayel. So

he, my husband is a friend of spoke of Scowcroft [Lieutenant General Brent Scowcroft], McFarlane [Colonel Robert C. McFarlane], Ledeen [Michael Ledeen] all of these men are personal friends of George's. Colby [William Colby], I spoke with personally on the phone. Two weeks later was murdered. He went to Princeton, my husband knew him, he knew my husband. He told me, Colby told me that...

EH: This is General Colby?

KG: No, this is William Colby who was head of the CIA.

KG: Of course. And the head, Krulak, who is the commodore of the Marine Corps, his father, Victor Krulak, worked with this Russian/Czechoslovakian double agent who was, worked with Al Gray, who is enlisted at that time, rose right up to the top because they were involved with [Buchann?] and this whole crowd that was trying to pick fights. And they were not, they were Army and Navy together. Joint. And George kept saying, George calls them "the members of the firm." He calls them "the members of the firm" I've heard the Brotherhood. They're very close. It's a small group and it's very hierarchical. I had Caspar Weinberger's bodyguard "farm" me when I was at Sarah McClendon's.

EH: Alexander Haig, he rose from nothing to top dog just overnight that's 'cause he's in the club.

KG: Oh, of course. He's in the club. Now how he's in the club, you see...

EH: Now all these guys...

KG: Henry Kissinger, Heinz Kissinger... Oh, I have a story, this...

EH: Oh, we all suspect Henry's a queer but...

KG: Oh, well I have first, I have a first-hand story from Bob who was a bear in Cambodia with Heinz.

EH: Okay... you call him Heinz.

KG: [nodding] Henry."

Alexander Haig and Heinz "Henry" Kissinger both served in US intelligence in Germany at the end of WWII. Kissinger became the protégé of the mysterious German character Fritz Kraemer. Kay refers to the Brotherhood "initiation rituals," reminiscent of the Yale University Skull & Bones rites, as being "a German thing." George Bush Sr, who had taken over the command of the DVD according to Christopher Story, had been a member of the select Skull & Bones society.

In a coffin and it's even now coming in to the military totally. The Chiefs do that, they put them in the coffin, they do the bowling ball trick...

161

EH: Okay, you're going to have to explain this. What happens when you get the coffin, why do you get in a coffin?

KG: Oh. They get… When you get your eagles [points to shoulders], that's a German thing, you know. It's what the German high did and most of them had the boyfriends and stuff. The Krupps and all that. It is a German thing that they say goes back to Greece and it's all the male Marine looking men that they do it with, you see.

EH: Uh-huh.

KG: So, now the Chiefs have to do that. What they do is, they get… George said it's like a zoo. They get everybody really drunk and they sometimes call it "Dining in" or "Shellback" is another time is another time that they do it. Not everybody does it but the ones who do it, if they're young, they, they get right to the top. It's a…

EH: Okay, well what actually do they do? They've got a coffin they get in…

KG: Anal sex. Oh, oh that. They do, they put them in the coffin and they do things."

Indeed, "the Eagle," the US military symbol for the rank of full colonel, is a German thing. The Nazi spread-winged "Adler" was visible on all Nazi-standards. When referring to homosexuality, Kay uses the term "German disease."

Yeah, the German disease is what the pink triangle boys were. Colonel Rob Ray [Colonel Charles Rob Ray] writes about this. He's a Marine Colonel who's a Christian who's writing about the 'Cherry Marines' a homosexuality in the group sex orgies and so forth, which brought down the German government because Naples, which is where all of the Navy is doing their playing. I mean today, in Naples, these orgies are going on it was where Krupp, the weapons manufacturer, used to take the German High Command and they would go into, on the allied Capri into the Blue Grotto and they would have big orchestras and they bring in a little boys, little Italian boys, who would be raped. They'd give them trinkets and, of course, the mother's gradually found out and just like me it was one thing when there was just one of me, now there are a lot more of us wives who were talking and telling truth. And it took those Italian, those Italian women went to newspapers in Italy; they wouldn't listen. But when they went to the wives of these guys, in Germany, it brought it all out. It brought the German government down because they were duplicitous in it, you know. But what they were doing was pedophilia; they were raping bringing in little boys. They involve the catholic priests, you

know, who were bringing it all, anyways. So, but what happened
was this whole group came over to the United States and they…
it's a, it's an old culture. But it is the reason there are a lot of things
going on with children these days.

As for the connections with the old Jewish Lower East gang and
NATO, Kay continues:

And, of course, drug money to pay for the weapons, which are
brand new weapons. This, the Bosnia… bizarre this is the reason we
had the war in Bosnia. The war in Bosnia is simply a stage to train
assassins, to be a market for brand new weapons, to be a market
place so the drug money can be used and the Army runs the whole
show. It's, it's totally run by the army. The CIA is a bogus thing,
you know, it's, it's training in doctoring command. It's NATO. It's
SHAPE -Supreme Headquarters Allied Powers Europe – Started
by Eisenhower [President Dwight David "Ike" Eisenhower]. It's a
totally independent corporation. Its main function is to sell weapons and laundered money.

EH: You're talking about the CIA?

KG: No, [I'm] talking about SHAPE.

KG: It's all being done by Army people who are, now joint,
'cause word joint comes from the group that brought over
a lot… and a lot of good people came over but they came out
over illegally from, to kind of escape Nazi Germany and stuff, I
don't know that much about it, but I do know that the funding
organization, one of the funding organizations was out of New
York and it was called 'The Joint.' And Meyer Lansky [Meyer
Suchowljansky]… see, our mob, the organized crime, the Jewish Kabalalist group, who don't believe in god really, well they
do, they look at god as a kabalalic like kind of thing, the opposite
of good is bad and they had to get rid of all that, all the good
people and kill them and then, you know, I mean they really do
this. They're killing people, who are good, on purpose and they
get brownie points with their little cult. But this funding group
in New York they would pay for passports, which were illegal,
in fact Grandfather was involved with that, that's how I know so
much about it because my Grandfather was told to keep silent
and not to tell anybody but of course he told my Grandmother
and my Grandmother told me and I've told my children. Everybody knows that they brought in, probably, more than two hun-
dred thousand Nazi soldiers and SS [Schutzstaffel – Protection
Squadron] and, you know, wacko scientists and psychologists
and, and all of the, most of them had the German disease. You
know, because it was their culture.

In a separate interview Kay Griggs answered the question "Who are these people?

> In general, they are first generation German sons, mostly who run things in the military through tight friendships made in Europe and at war colleges. Psyops is a controlling group and Paul Wolfowitz is a major player, as are the many Zionists on this side of the Atlantic.

Back to Belgium , the Brabant Killings, the projected coup, and the WNP. If it was true that Latinus was in contact with "the Americans," who he thought were the DIA, and he was an admirer of general Haig, then he and his WNP may have been working with and for "the Brotherhood," aka "the Joint," via the mysterious Burafex agency. Kay Griggs' following words can be read as a description of the Brabant Killings, all you would need to do is to replace "Stuttgart (airport)" by "Chièvres (airport)."

> The taxpayers are paying young men, who are not citizens of the United States, to kill innocent people, women and children. They get on a flight from Norfolk and Oceania, they fly to Stuttgart, and I was told this, this is what they do. Then they go by a special heli-copter to countries like Turkey, like part of Iraq, to Algeria, to parts of Africa and they do wet ops, you know, murder five, ten, twenty people and then they blame it on the Arabs or they blame it on somebody else but it's actually NATO rogue assassins. Because they are men from Australia, South Africa, Britain, that I've been able to determine, and a lot of these other little countries that are sort of wanting to get into NATO ...

PART IV

Trumped

Roy Cohn and Donald Trump

CHAPTER 19

THE ROAD TO THE WHITE HOUSE

"We now live in a nation where
doctors destroy health,
lawyers destroy justice,
universities destroy knowledge,
governments destroy freedom,
the press destroys information,
religion destroys morals,
and our banks destroy the economy."

Chris Hedges.

In previous chapters we have studied the emergence of power centers around the Russian-Jewish Maffiya and the Nazi undergroud. At first sight these appear to be two totally separated and even opposing forces. Really, they are not. The case in point to demonstrate their overlap is the ascent to the presidency of the USA of Donald Trump. The forces behind Trump can be traced back to the Nazi ideology, the Red Maffiya and even to the Vatican.

Before we elaborate on this, it is necessary to revisit the role of the Vatican, and more specifically that of the Sovereign Military Order of Malta (SMOM) aka the Knights of Malta, in global politics. The SMOM can be considered to be the 'armed forces' of the Vatican that once saved Catholicism and Western civilisation from the invading Muslim 'barbarians'. The Knights are operating next to and on order of the religious, political and financial sections inside the Holy See. The Order of Malta is directly linked to the Christian Crusaders and their Hospital Knights who set out to liberate the Holy Land one thousand years ago.

After WWII the new global threat as perceived by the Vatican was Communism, for different reasons. One reason was that Communism, on paper, was an atheïst and anti-religious ideology. A second reason was that Communism was a Jewish enterprise and Judaïsm had clearly set out to destroy Christianity. This Jewish-Marxist alliance was seen as a serious threat, but over time this alliance had also teamed up with Freemasonry and Protestantism. Judaïsm, Protestantism, Marxism, Freemasonry, for differing reasons, all shared a common goal: the abolition of Christianity.

In the early 1950s the Vatican decided to take action, tasking the SMOM with setting up a full-blown campaign against Communism.

US Senator Joseph McCarthy, who was looking for an issue that would inspire his re-election campaign, was found to be willing to 'hammer the commies' who had infiltrated many US institutions. It should be remembered that Uncle Sam and Uncle Joe (Stalin) had been wartime allies against Germany for four years. This state of affairs had put the commies in a privileged position in the USA.

Before long senator McCarthy was accused of working together with the Nazi underground. This accusation was in part based on the involvement of Roy Cohn in McCarthy's legal staff. Legal counsel Cohn was said to be a Jewish Nazi – member of the 'Kosher Nostra' – who was a top figure of the Meyer Lansky crime ring. Roy Cohn was a very close friend of Lewis Rosenstiel, who was in turn a friend of Sam Bronfman. Lansky and his lieutenant Robert Vesco were later involved in the Latin American cocaine trafficking operations via Costa Rica, where Felix Przedborski joined in. Cohn's law partner Tom Bolan was a Knight of the SMOM.

Indirectly, the accusation that McCarthy and Cohn were working with the Nazi's was justified, as Roy Cohn worked with Frank Wisner's secret Office for Policy Coordination that would later be absorbed by the CIA. 'Whiz' Wisner was at the basis of Operation Paperclip that recruited thousands of ex-Nazi's. Next to Wisner the OPC was directed by Allen Dulles, James J. Angleton and Carmel Offie. Dulles was known to have interests in the United Fruit Company that was behind the Guatemalan coup in 1954 and involved in the Latin American cocaine trafficking on behalf of the Jewish-Italian mob. The 'dirty tricks' OPC, in its covert war against Communism, had made a pact with the Nazi underground. Francis Parker Yockey, a prominent American Nazi kingpin, called this Nazi secret organisation the SD (Sicherheidsdienst) or The Order. The Order was linked to the Skorzeny's underground Nazi headquarters in Madrid and Buenos Aires.

In an article dated March 31st, 1954, the *Chronicle Telegram* of Ohio, reporting on the Naumann Cercle, wrote:

> Naumann used a Dusseldorf export-import firm, the H. S. Lucht Company, as a front for a world wide political network which kept in touch with Nazi exiles in Spain and Argentina, as well as pro Nazis in other countries. For example, Col. Otto Skorzeny, the rescuer of Mussolini, and Dr. Hjalmar Schacht, Hitler's former financial wizard, are connected with the company in Spain [where Skorzeny ran an underground mercenary group called Paladin, in Madrid]...
> Two members of the Nazi-Communist underground in Spain also took in Senator McCarthy's two junior G-men. Roy Cohn and David Schine, during their comic-opera, spy-hunting junket throughout Europe last year."

This is the Naumann Cercle that had planned, as seen in a previous chapter, to infiltrate and take over the German governing FDP party in order to turn it into a post-war crypto-NSDAP. Werner Naumann, as mentioned earlier, was in touch with the Belgian ex-SS general Léon Degrelle, who was said to secretly run the Lucht company as part of the Nazi underground economic empire. Lea Lucht, daughter of Belgian general Dievoet, had been a member of Goebbels' Nazi propaganda staff in Paris.

Another interesting aspect of the Roy Cohn character was his affiliation with Robert Gray, the most powerful lobbyist and PR man in Washington, head of 'The Powerhouse' Hill & Knowlton. Gray was gay and involved in pedophile sex blackmail operations. He was said to conclude most of his deals not in his office but next to his swimming pool, where young flesh was always available. Gray was a Special Forces veteran who had seen hard action in Asia. He knew what financed the anti-Communist army of Chiang Kai Shek.

Interestingly, his name was mentioned in the Belgian Brabant Killers files. In late 1982 he had negotiated with weapons expert Daniel Dekaise about the purchase of a batch of silenced Ingram machine guns. Shortly thereafter Dekaise's shop was raided by armed men who stole Dekaise's prototype. A policeman was killed during the attack.

Gray knew his way around in anti-Communist circles, he was a friend of John Singlaub, who headed the World Anti-Communist League (WACL). Like Ed Wilson and his mate Frank Terpil, Gray was an expert in sexual blackmail, often involving minors of both sexes. The first president of the George Town Club, where Ed Wilson's sexual blackmail operations were reportedly run, was Robert K. Gray. Ed Wilson had learned the tricks of the trade in the 1950s from Roy Cohn who was then taking part in McCarthy's witchhunt. It is important to remember that Ed Wilson later teamed up with Baruch 'Bruce' Rappaport in the maritime logistics operations in support of the Iran-Contra operations. Rappaport had close ties with Edmond Safra. Rappaport was the mastermind behind the Bank of New York, the favourite bank of the Brighton Beach Red Maffiya headed by Balagula, who had ties to the Belgian M & S International company and to the Comuele debacle.

Citing the former head of the vice squad for one of America's biggest cities,

> Cohn's job was to run the little boys. Say you had an admiral, a general, a congressman, who did not want to go along with the program. Cohn's job was to set them up, then they would go along. Cohn told me that himself.

Cohn's sexual blackmail operation was linked to the cult involved in the Son of Sam killings. This cult was the Process Church of the Final

Judgement. According to David Berkowitz, one of the participants, the Process provided children for sex at parties held by wealthy people. Berkowitz stated that one of these parties was held at Cohn's house in Connecticut where he first met Roy Cohn.

One of Cohn's close friends was Catholic Cardinal Francis Spellman, better known in the gay milieu as 'Franny', who seemed to like Broadway chorus boys. Spellman was described as one of the most sexually voracious homosexuals in the history of the American Church. Still, the mainstream press kept silent for fear of revenge from the Vatican. His Eminence Cardinal Spellman was a Knight and "Grand Protector" of the Order of Malta. He had assisted Pope Pius XII in setting up the ratlines that helped Nazi war criminals escape justice. At this point it is interesting to note that Nazi general Gehlen, and the Dulles brothers too were Knights of Malta, as were the three Bushes, Bill Casey, and William Colby.

In later years, Donald Trump called on Roy Cohn for his legal defense in a case involving charges of racism on the part of Trump. Cohn and Trump would remain allies and friends. As columnist Ian Greenhalgh commented:

> Trump is 100% a creature of the mob, he was created by mob kingpin Roy Cohn, everyone he has been in business with was mobbed up. We are talking of course, not of the Italian-American Mafia, but of the real mob, the true organised crime syndicate in the US, the largely Jewish network once run by Meyer Lansky and Roy Cohn with close ties to the Jewish mobs in Russia and Israel. Sheldon Adelson, the Koch Brothers, the Bronfmans, they too are all a part of this network. [...] This is what some call the Rothschild Khazarian Mafia. Trump is their creation, their candidate, their Golem to terrorise the goyim with.

In his own memoirs Trump described how he got into the casino and gambling business in 1987, when he purchased the majority of the voting stock in the Resorts International concern. Resorts International had known historical ties to the Jewish-Italian Mafia network of Meyer Lansky. Its origins were to be found in the Mary Carter Paint Company that proved to be a CIA-funded instrument in the anti-Castro operations of the early 1960s. Incidently, Roy Cohn was a member of the board of Permindex where he rubbed shoulders with Clay Shaw, another Knight of the SMOM. Permindex was suspected of being deeply involved in the Kennedy assassination.

One of the principal investors in the Resorts venture was Meyer Lansky, 'chairman of the board'. Lansky had ties with both the CIA and Mossad. Other Resorts investors were David Rockefeller and Tibor Rosenbaum of the infamous Investors Overseas Services that was funded by

Edmond Rothschild. After the death of James Crosby, head of Resorts International, rising real estate star Trump made his move.

By 1990, Trump was virtually bankrupt. According to Ian Greenhalgh that was when he was chosen to be instrumental in the skinning of the Russian Bear. Christopher Steele's dossier revealed that Trump had started working with the Russian Alfa Bank, owned by Russian-Israëli oligarchs. This bank was used as a conduit for the laundering of billions of stolen Russian money. This brings us back full circle to the Red Maffiya in Belgium and their sanctuary in the South of France, on the Riviera coast.

A key link in the Alfa Bank chain was Felix Sater, one of Trump's advisers. Felix Sater was an immigrant who landed behind bars for having stabbed a man in the face with a broken glass. He had emigrated to Brighton Beach from the Soviet Union when he was eight years old. Sater was also involved in a securities fraud by the White Rock and State Street brokerages. Their illigal activities involved four different Italian mafia crime families: the Bonnano family; the Colombo family; the Gambino family; and the Genovese family.

Felix Sater, like his father Mikhail, had become a federal informant. When Sater junior's past became known, Trump denied even knowing the man with whom he had earlier set up several SoHo New York hotel deals. Sater, on behalf of Trump, was party to a round of pseudo-diplomacy in an attempt to topple Ukraine's president Poroshenko and put an end to the war with Russia. Felix's father Mikhail, aka Michael Sheferofsky, was indicted in 2000 on two counts for extorting restaurants, stores, and a medical clinic in the Russian enclave of Brighton Beach. In separate court documents, Sater was named as an accomplice of Semion Mogilevitch, one of Russia's most notorious mobsters who, up until 2015, was on the FBI's Most Wanted List. Note that this was the same Mogilevitch that obtained a European visa with the help of the Belgian ambassador in Paris, Alfred Cahen. Mogilevitch was implicated in a massive money laundering scheme that saw more than $7 billion laundered through the Bank of New York. By 2011 it had become clear that Moscow would not move against Mogilevitch, who would face no charges at all, given his importance to the Russian government. This Mogilevitch connection brings us close to the Mikhailov network with which Felix Przedborski was collaborating.

Edmund Safra, whose name was mentioned in the ATLAS Report, was clearly part of this machination. Safra's Republic National Bank was implicated in the Red Maffiya money laundering scandal via the Bank of New York. Safra had been working with Rappaport, Wilson, the Gokal brothers, and Marc Rich. Soon after that scandal broke in 1999, Safra was murdered in his Monaco apartment.

Abbas Gokal and Rappaport had introduced Mikhail Fridman to the Bank of New York. Fridman was head of the Alfa Bank that entered into business with Donald Trump. Safra and Fridman were believed to have co-orchestrated Vladimir Putin's rise to power in 1999. Dave Emory, who has been tracking the underground Nazi continuum for over 35 years, on the subject of the Alfa conglomerate commented:

> It appears to be Underground Reich, all the way, with evidentiary tributaries running in the direction of: the Iran-Contra scandal; the Iraqgate scandal; the oil-for-food scam vis a vis Iraq; malfeasanace by a coterie of GOP bigwigs including Dick Cheney and others close to George W. Bush, and Haley Barbour; money-laundering by powerful international drug syndicates; Chechen warlords and drug-trafficking syndicates; the Royal family of Liechtenstein; the Bank al-Taqwa (which helped finance al-Qaeda); the Marc Rich operations; Eastern European and Russian associates of Wolfgang Bohringer, one of Mohamed Atta's close associates in South Florida; and the Carl Duisberg Fellowship, which brought Mohamed Atta to Germany from Egypt and may have helped him into the U.S.

Trump's fascination with fascism – or a peculiar variant thereof – was inspired by the rethoric of his adviser Steve Bannon, actually acting as the assistant to the President and White House chief strategist. Speaking of Bannon, former Ohio Governor Ted Strickland said that he is *"a dangerous person driven by an authoritarian ideology who, I fear, has more influence than anyone in the administration. This is a mean, vicious, intolerant group. I've never seen anything like this in my political life."*

This authoritarian ideology appears to be at least in part inspired by the little known writings of Julius Evola. After his appointment to the White House, Bannon spelled out his world views. The message he conveyed apparently corresponded with what he had put forward earlier in his 2014 speech where he talked about his admiration for the Italian fascist theoretician Julius Evola. He also pointed out that Vladimir Putin too was basing his 'Eurasianistic' and Traditionalist, nationalist views on Evola's insights. The fact alone that Bannon referenced the little known, tabooed Italian Nazi-thinker astonished his audiences. The Eurasia theme refers to old Mackinder's Heartland doctrine that was later revived by US presidential adviser Z. Brzezinski.

EVOLA

Julius Evola had been cited by insiders and experts as having decisively influenced Freemasonry as well as Nazi-fascism. These may at first sight appear to be incompatible, but are not. Nazi and fascist occultism overlaps to some extent with that of Freemasonry.

Today, Evola seems to be rising in popularity in several parts of the world, including Russia, where he is being reflected in the views of Alexander Dugin, who, according to Bannon, is Putin's most influential thinker, sometimes called "Putin's Rasputin." It would seem that Donald Trump and Vladimir Putin have found some common ground in this Evolian Traditionalism.

But who was Julius Evola?

Baron Giulio Cesare Andrea Evola was born in Rome in 1898. He was a philosopher, a Dadaist painter, a poet and an esotericist, who promoted Guénon's 'Traditionalism' or the return to the basic, natural, pagan, pre-Christian spiritual undercurrent of humanity that modern Western man had lost sight of. Changing the system, Evola argued, was not a question of words but of "blowing everything up." Evola's ideal order was violent and based on "hierarchy, caste, monarchy, race, myth, religion and ritual." Evola expressed his radical views in several books, one of which was titled *Rivolto Contro il Mondo Moderno* (*Revolt Against the Modern World*).

Evola's writings on racial theory had impressed Mussolini, who supported the launch of Evola's *Blood and Spirit* journal. In 1942 Evola traveled to Germany where he gathered support from the main Nazi race theorists. Even after the war Evola's views remained in high esteem by the neo-fascist community in Italy, in spite of the fact that Evola himself had rejected Italian fascism for being too passive. Evola had come to prefer Nazism and its anti-Semitism instead.

Evola had been fascinated by knightly orders as expressions of the warrior caste of the aristocracy. The formal structures of the SS, he hoped, would give birth to a new Ordenstaat, a State ruled by an Order. He saw great advantages in the transnational nature of the medieval orders of chivalry. The Knights Templar and the Knights of Saint John of Jerusalem, were pan-European, organized in national sections presided over by a Grand Master. Such a knightly new Order, Evola argued, would be required after the collapse of fascism.

In his 2013 article "Freemasonry, Traditionalism and the Neo-Caliphate," David Livingstone, who saw Julius Evola as the main source of inspiration for the underground fascist Gladio networks, bluntly wrote

> After World War II, the pretext of a Cold War with the Soviet Union was used by the US to carry out covert action in all countries of the world. CIA chief Allen Dulles devised a plan whereby on the explicit request of the Pentagon, secret armies of fascist terrorists, including many former leading Nazis, were set up across Western Europe with the coordination of NATO, known "Stay Behind" units. The most infamous "stay-behind" unit was Operation Gladio of Italy, which was responsible for the Strategy of Tension, which carried out false-flag terror operations to discredit the popular communist party, culminating in the assassination of Aldo Moro by the Red Brigades and the Bologna train station massacre of 1980."

According to author and researcher Kevin Coogan, who investigated the American top fascist Francis Yockey in great detail, Julius Evola, an admirer of Yockey, had become involved in the Nazi underground SD network, dubbed The Order.

In his excellent 1999 book *Dreamer of the Day*, Coogan explains:

> Evola's SD work at the end of the war is shrouded in mystery. Historian Richard Drake says that while he was in Vienna, 'Evola performed vital liaisons for the SS as Nazi Germany sought to recruit a European army for the defense of the Continent against the Soviet Union and the United States.' According to his own account, Evola spent his time living incognito while doing 'intellectual' research. But what kind of research? [...] While Evola was in Vienna, the SD supplied him with a series of arcane texts plundered from private libraries and rare book collections. The SD bureau that provided him with these documents was Amt VII, an obscure branch that served as an RSHA research library. With this precious archive, Evola closely studied Masonic rituals and translated certain "esoteric texts" for a book called *Histoire Secrète des Sociétés Secrètes*.[...]
>
> But why would the SD actively involve itself in Evola's arcane research at a time when hundreds of thousands of Russian soldiers were sweeping into the Reich? And why would Evola choose to live in Vienna under a false name and devote his time to such a strange project? Could the answer to this question be found in the cryptic reference to Evola's 'efforts to establish a secret international order' in the 1938 SS report?
>
> I believe that Evola's Vienna project was intimately linked to the development of what I will call "the Order," a new kind of Knights Templar designed to successfully function sub-rosa. Well before the end of World War II, the intelligence and financial networks of the Third Reich were hard at work preparing underground networks to survive the coming Allied occupation. Escape lines to South America and the Middle East were organized. Bank accounts were created in Switzerland and other neutral nations to finance the underground with plunder the Nazis had looted from occupied Europe. But how was this secret empire to be managed, except by a virtually invisible "government in exile"?

Coogan adds that his interpretation was speculative but that Evola's unique talents were exactly what the SD required:

> With his extensive knowledge of matters esoteric and occult; his fascination with secret societies and knightly Orders; his Waffen SS transnationalism; his ties to some of the highest figures in fascism, Nazism, and movements like the Iron guard; and his loyal

service to the SD, Baron Evola was a perfect candidate to help the-orize a new underground Order. As the SD's equivalent of Albert Pike, the former Confederate Army general who designed the ritu-als for the Scottish Rite Masons in the late 1800's, Evola's task was to help create the inner organizational and ritual structure for the Grand Masters of a secret Shamballah whose financial nerve center was carefully hidden away in Swiss bank accounts."

What was significant in Coogan's exposé were two aspects.

The first being the Masonic character of Evola's work.

The second being that The Order appeared to have overlapped, and also worked with, elements of the East Bloc, including former Soviet and East German national security officials. The organization also maintained contacts with "anti-imperialist," Third World liberation movements, in-cluding the Muslim Brotherhood in Egypt and the Middle East. This confirms that that The Order was part of the Nazi underground, dubbed Deutsche Verteidigungs Dienst or DVD by Michael Shrimpton. The Nazi continuum acted worldwide and used both sides of the Iron Curtain to its advantage. Skorzeny's Paladins worked with the CIA and Wisner's OPC as well as with the East German Stasi. The alleged East-West schism obvious-ly did not affect its operations. In fact Evola and Yockey were against any occupation of Europe, be it by gum chewing American capitalists or Rus-sian Bolshewiks. Of the two, America seemed to pose the biggest threat.

This rejection of both the USA and the USSR incited the followers of Yockey and Evola to seek influence in Cuba, North Africa and the Mid-dle East, where Skorzeny, Schacht and Naumann – in cooperation with François Genoud – had made significant progress. Genoud in turn re-mained in permanent contact with Léon Degrelle in Spain.

In Belgium, after the war, this 'third way' fascist faction found its personification in the 'obscure fascist thinker' Jean-François Thiriart, who continued Yockey's efforts to incorporate Russia into a geopolitical axis with European fascism. In the 1960s Thiriart supported de Gaulle's anti-American policy and sympythized with Che Guevarra, Fidel Cas-tro and Juan Peron, who at the time lived in exile in Spain. Like Yockey, Thiriart saw Europe not as a Greater Reich but as a proud Imperium in its own right, free of American and Russian domination. Thiriart established a 'new fascist' network in Algeria, Libya, and China. In 1992 Thiriart was invited to Moscow for talks with the high-level officials.

GLADIO REVISITED

On the subject of Evola being at the roots of the 'stay behind' concept that had given birth to Gladio, David Livingstone wrote:

The Turkish Gladio, known as Counter-Guerrilla, have exerted great influence over the country's Cold War history, and were responsible for numerous unsolved acts of violence. Counter-Guerrilla were responsible for the development of the Ergenekon, the name given to an alleged clandestine, Kemalist ultra-nationalist organization in Turkey, with ties to members of the country's military and security forces. Ergenekon is a name deriving from a supposed Turkish legend describing it as a mythical place located in Eurasia, in the inaccessible valleys of the Altai Mountains, serving as a model for the synarchist idea of the mythical underground realm of Agartha. The Ergenekon connection to Agartha is related to the Pan-Turkism movement, which the US sought to exploit after World War II in their continuing fight against communism. [...] US support of Pan-Turkism in bolstering Turkey's role in NATO came in the person of a right-wing extremist named Colonel Alparsan Turks, who during World War II had been the contact person of the Nazis in Turkey. After the war, Turks made contacts with the CIA in 1948 and set up a secret anti-Communist stay-behind army in Turkey, eventually renamed the Special Forces Command, which operated Counter-Guerrilla. To staff the Counter-Guerrilla, Turks had recruited heavily among the Grey Wolves, a right-wing terrorist group which he also ran. The Grey Wolves derived their name and flag from the mythological legend of the grey wolves that led the Turk peoples out of Asia to their homeland in Anatolia. The Grey Wolves' dream is to create the "Turan," the "Great Turkish Empire," to include all Turkic peoples of the Central Asian countries of the former Soviet Union, as well as the Caucasus and the Uighurs' homeland of East Turkestan in the Xinjiang, China.

According to investigative reporter Lucy Komisar, the 1981 attempt on John Paul II's life by Grey Wolves member Mehmet Ali Agca may have been related to Gladio.

Livingstone wrote:

> Alexander Dugin is the suspected leader of Ergenekon. But Dugin is not a Turk. He is a Russian, and the most popular ideologist of Russian expansionism, nationalism, and fascism. Dugin likes to see himself as the inheritor of the "ancient Eurasian order," elements of which were already present in the Sicherheitsdienst (SD), the secret service of the SS. Like Zbigniew Brzezinski, Dugin is also a follower of Sir Halford Mackinder, seeing Central Asia as a key aspect of geopolitics, but taking the reverse view, where he sees Russia as needing to create a Eurasian block to impede American imperialism.... Dugin's call for an alliance with Islam is reflected in his associate Gaydar Jamal, a Muscovite of Azerbaijani origin, who exemplified the relationship between (Evolian) Traditionalism and Islamic extremism.

This "Agartha" that Livingstone was talking about was a legendary underground city linked to the Shambhala myth that had been popularized by Madame Blavatsky, who described the city as the ancient home of the Aryan race. Blavatsky was inspired by a novel by Bulwer-Lytton, titled *Vril: The Power of the Coming Race.* According to the myth, both Agartha and Shambhala were situated in Central Asia.

John Loftus discovered that Hitler had mandated Husseini al Banna to found the Muslim Brotherhood, that was later supported by Nazi banker François Genoud. The Brotherhood was to serve as an intelligence collecting unit for Germany in the Middle East. No surprise here, Livingstone posits, as Hitler's Nazi party was the result of a fusion of Aleister Crowley's Ordo Templi Orientis and the German Thulé Society, that derived its racial Aryan superiority theory from the writings of Blavatsky and Bulwer-Lytton.

This meeting of Evolian Traditionalism and radical Islam was also personified by Claudio Mutti, born in Parma, Italy, in 1946, whose works have been promoted by Dugin. Mutti showed a great interest in all matters esoteric, symbolistic and religious. He studied Nietzsche and Evola and converted to Islam. In 1976, having joined Italy's ultra-right movement, he translated and re-published the Protocols of the Elders of Sion, inserting Evola's views on the 'Jewish question'. Mutti was a friend of Belgian ex-Green Beret Luc Jouret, the founder of the notorious Solar Temple mass suicide cult with links to Gladio. In 1980 Mutti was arrested and indicted for having participated in the Bologna bomb attack of that same year. He was later acquitted and took interest in the history of the Rumanian fascist 'Iron Guard'. Evola himself, having been disappointed by Nazism, which he found 'overly lame', had turned his back on this kind of fascism and had turned to the SS and the Iron Guard specifically, which he deemed fit to act as the uncompromising, ruthless knightly orders he was dreaming of.

March 22. 2016 Brussels Airport explosions

CHAPTER 20

THE ROAD TO THE ELYSÉE

At the end of the previous century, globalization may have looked like a new phenomenon to many, but it wasn't. Around 1900, industrial and financial power was already concentrated in a few cartels that were acting on a truly global scale, from Shanghai to Buenos Aires. The industrial revolution had seen the rapid growth of the coal and steel industries, which produced the rail tracks, locomotives and the luxury ocean cruisers that made fortunes for their owners.

Lenin in his 1916 book *Imperialism, the Highest Stage of Capitalism* had correctly predicted the rise of the financial industry on the back of the heavy industries. Lenin's reasoning was simple and accurate: the banks determined who was getting credit and who wasn't. They had the power to throttle unwanted competition and support the companies whose stock they were holding. Consequently, over time, they had gradually maneuvered themselves into a leading position at the helm of the global economy. Money can be moved around the world much faster than blast furnaces or assembly lines.

By the end of the 20th century, the financial industry had definitely become the dominant force of global economic activity. To make a fortune, you no longer needed to start up a production plant. You simply speculated your way to riches.

When examining the French political system, Lenin borrowed the words of Lysis from the 1908 book *Against the Financial Oligarchy*: "The French Republic is a financial monarchy. It is the complete and utter dominance of the financial oligarchy that controls the press and the government."

By 2007, 100 years after the financial crash that precipitated the installation of the Federal Reserve in 1913, things had only gotten worse. Much worse. After the collapse of communism in 1991, any form of opposition to the rogue capitalism that Lenin had predicted, has been swept away. The post-war take-over by the new "Atlantic ruling class," thriving on dollar hegemony, has proved to be a complete success. The financial industry not only trumps productive industry but clearly also dominates world politics. Political regimes have become mere instruments of the global banking cartel. Wherever governments fail to hand over the riches of their nations, politicians are being replaced by technocrats. "Non-political governance" is becoming the new buzzword. Technocrats are taking over from the elected to "straighten out" things in favor of the banks, while the press and the media are seeing to it that the masses remain largely uninformed and constantly entertained.

President de Gaulle proved to have been right as well. Indeed, he was the last great statesman of Europe. After him the French Republic declined rapidly. His successor Pompidou was a Rothschild pawn, who tried hard to undo the "damage" done to the progression of the Atlantic project in France. Europeanist Giscard d'Estaing was a product of the de Wendel dynasty and Opus Dei. Mitterrand was a faux-socialist who by the end of his life had come to the conclusion that France was at war with the voracious American imperialists who wanted everything for themselves. In this respect he seemed to agree with de Gaulle. Yet, he had supported the Atlantic cartel by turning his socialist party against the communists, who had animated the Resistance during the war. By the time Mitterrand wrote his memoirs, the great nation of France had lost all of its luster, as de Gaulle had predicted. After the loss of its colonies in the 1960s, France had gone from the leading nation of the early "Europe of Six" to a minor regional entity being directed by unelected EU technocrats under German tutelage. As a consequence the prestige of the presidency had taken a steep dive as well, reaching all-time lows with the lackluster 2012 election of François Hollande, a spineless and powerless socialist.

His predecessor Sarkozy had been an ambitious opportunist, a product of the CIA, the Canadian Desmarais dynasty, and the Corsican mob's Charles Pasqua. Pasqua was linked to both the Bronfman-Lansky and the Guerini clans, exponents of the Jewish and the Italian mob respectively.

In late 2015, ex-president Sarkozy came under investigation for his alleged involvement in the smuggle of 1500 pounds of cocaine out of the Dominican Republic. The drugs were hidden on board a French private jet in 2013. The Dassault Falcon 50 jet had been regularly used by Sarkozy. The pilots were arrested and sequestered, but they escaped on board a speedboat that had been sent to pick them up in Santo Domingo. A trail of paperwork connected Narco-Sarko and his associates to the aircraft. Sarkozy lashed out at French authorities for having put him under investigation, tracking the GPS locations of his cell phone. It was all business as usual. Sarkozy, although innocent until proven guilty, seemed to have followed in the footsteps of his mentor Pasqua and the Bronfmans. Despite his clash with French justice, Sarkozy plans on running for president again in 2017. As we all know, a decent election campaign requires lots of money.

By 2015 Russian godfather Patokh Chodiev had acquired Belgian nationality. Chodiev wasn't just a Belgian citizen, he was the second richest man of the country, next to Albert Frère of the GBL Group. To accommodate the billionaire, the Belgian legislature had hurriedly pushed through a new law that kept him out of jail. It turned out that it was Sarkozy who had pressured the Belgians into voting the law into existence, securing a French-Kazakh helicopter deal in the process. Obviously "Sarko" had learned all the tricks of the trade from his Corsican mentor Charles Pasqua. Sarkozy, of Hungarian descent, even considered changing his name to Sarkozi, which would definitely have given a Corsican ring to it.

Charles Pasqua had been close to the French Connection, the Guérini clan, and the Corsican thugs Léandri and Peretti. Léandri was the French "ambassador" of Lucky Luciano and the Genovese clan, who were collaborating with the CIA. Pasqua's friend and business partner Jean Venturi had been exposed as a Mafioso by *Time* magazine in Canada. The Guérini's, having been recruited by Dubinsky and Irving Brown, had been instrumental in the breaking-up of the Marseilles harbor strike of 1947. Léandri had exactly the right underworld contacts to select a team of tough guys for President de Gaulle's Praetorian guard, called SAC, that had been set up by Pasqua and Peretti. The latter was running the day-to-day operations of the SAC.

Peretti's secretary was Christine de Ganay, who would later become Sarkozy's stepmother. After her divorce from Pal Sarkozy, she married Frank Wisner Jr in 1977. Wisner was the son of the legendary boss of the early CIA dirty tricks department.

In 1982, Sarkozy married one of Peretti's nieces. Pasqua was his best man at the wedding. In the early 1990s Pasqua, honorary officer of the Mossad, could be found in the Elysée, where he acted as Foreign Affairs minister. His protégé Sarkozy was managing the budget of the République. In the meantime the SAC had allegedly evolved into the Elysée's underground intelligence service that was being financed with drug money.

Around the turn of the century plans were drawn by the Wisner-Desmarais milieu to bring Sarkozy to power.

Léandri hadn't done too bad either. As the war came to an end, he had gone "in business," after having been cleared of collaboration charges with the help of his American friends. Very soon he was negotiating on behalf of big companies like ELF, Thomson, Alstom and CGE. Léandri became a socialite figure, driving around in a chauffeured Bentley. In the early 1990s CGE, the second largest company in the world next to General Electric, was in the cross-hairs of French justice on charges of corruption of civil servants. The French press now dubbed the company "Corruption Générale des Elus," which translates as "General Corruption of the Elected."

LIQUORMAN DIVERSIFIES

In October of 2003 the *New York Times* headlined "G.E. Finishes Vivendi Deal, Expanding Its Media Assets":

> General Electric, owner of television's most profitable network, NBC, completed its agreement yesterday to acquire the entertainment assets of Vivendi Universal in a deal that executives said would create a new entertainment conglomerate better able to compete with media giants like Viacom, Time Warner, the Walt Disney Company and the News Corporation. The new entity, to be called NBC Universal, will be 80 percent owned by G.E., with Vivendi retaining the rest. […] Clearing the way for its hand off of control of NBC Universal, General Electric Co. this week spent $3.8 billion to buy out the remaining interest of its French partner, Vivendi.

Vivendi was the new name for the old CGE, that had gone on a wild acquisition spree, expanding into waste-management, media and entertainment. The project was carried out under the direction of "business guru" J-M Messier, who nearly ruined the company in the process. To cover the huge debt created by the take-overs, Vivendi was forced to sell-off some of its assets. Enter General Electric and … the Bronfmans.

> The board of the French media and utilities giant met in Paris to weigh bids from two final suitors for its U.S. entertainment businesses. One was General Electric Co.'s NBC; the other a group led by investor Edgar J. Bronfman Jr.

In January of 2011, the *Guardian* wrote:

> The Warner Music Group chairman, Edgar Bronfman Jr., was convicted today of insider trading and fined €5m (£4.2m) over his conduct as vice-chairman of French company Vivendi nearly a decade ago. Jean-Marie Messier, the former Vivendi chief executive, was convicted on charges of misleading investors by the same Paris court.
>
> Bronfman Jr, who was vice-chairman of Vivendi until 2003, received a 15-month suspended sentence and a €5m fine. Messier, the former high-flying chief executive who from the mid-1990s to 2002 built Vivendi from a French water utility company into a global media giant, received a three-year suspended sentence and a €150,000 fine.

It was as just business as usual, but on a much bigger scale now.

FAILED STATE

The French Sarkozy-Eurocopter affair spilled over into Belgium. It became obvious that several politicians were involved in the pampering of Patokh Chodiev and the "Kazakh Trio." Serge Kubla, mayor of Waterloo, where Chodiev resided, even ended up behind bars for a while. Armand De Decker, a lawyer by trade, who had lobbied to push the "Chodiev law" through Parliament, came under fire as well. He had a long history of strong ultra-rightist sympathies and an outspoken aversion to communism. He had received quite a handsome amount of money for his intervention, which he claimed was nothing more than his fee. It was the umpteenth case of corruption in Belgium that was going to end up unsolved on the scrapyard of history.

The synthetic nation of Belgium had demonstrably been a cesspool of corruption and perversion since the "Golden Years" of the 1960s. There had been the aggressive real estate sharks who forever changed the Brussels skyline with their illicit concrete-and-steel high-rises. There had been the suspicious fire in the Innovation shopping mall, killing 350 people; the Lockheed bribery scandal; the scandals surrounding Defense minister Paul VDB, drug trafficking and fiscal fraud; the deadly stampede in the Heyzel football stadium; the artillery shells procurement scandal; the Agusta bribery scandal; the Mirage jet electronic self-defense system scandal; on and on…culminating in the Brabant Killings, the "war of the Police Forces," the murder of Andre Cools, the Dutroux affair and finally the terror attacks of March 22, 2016.

Belgium, the international press concluded, was a "failed state," a basket case. Yet, this country is like paradise for the thousands of expats, lobbyists, NATO bigshots, EU-technocrats and criminals that have swarmed to Brussels. They enjoy life in a grand style: excellent restaurants, lots of culture and history, Paris and Rome are only a few hours away. For the average citizen though, life is not so easy. Each and every one of them has been meticulously registered and spied upon for many years. Contrary to the tax exempt NATO and EU gangs, they are slaves to one of the harshest taxation systems in the world, from which there is no escape. After the Kredietbank Luxembourg fraud, Swiss-Leaks and LuxLeaks, the Panama Papers made the gap between the Belgian haves and the have-nots abundantly clear yet again.

NAZI OFFSHORE

Incidentally, Jurgen Mossack, one of the directors of the Panamanian Mossack-Fonseca (MF) cabinet that leaked the off-shore companies data, was born in Fürth, Bavaria, on 20 March 1948. His father, Erhard Mossack, was a Rottenführer in the Waffen-SS during the war. He offered to spy for the Americans after the war. The Mossack family moved to Panama in 1961, from where Erhard Mossack was collecting intelligence on Communist activity in Cuba. In 2016, Germany's Federal Intelligence

Service BND would not release documents relating to Erhard Mossack due to "security risks." Jurgen's brother Peter is honorary consul of Panama in Germany. The MF cabinet has been an "integral part of the underground economy" for over 40 years now. It was in the 1970s that Panama decided to become a fiscal haven for the rich. The cabinet had really taken off under Manuel Noriega, who was very close to MF. As law professor Miguel Bernal explained, in Panama "there is complete convergence of interests between the political power and the big companies." Some call that fascism.

While trying to downplay the fall-out of the Panama leak, the actual Belgium rightist government, clearly the weakest ever, raises taxes yet again and considers abolishing the 38-hour work-week. At the same time the finance minister refuses to collect 700 million Euros in back-taxes from various multinational companies, while Defense mulls the acquisition of 5 billion worth of F-35 jet fighters to replace the F-16s. Utter madness!

The 3/22 terror attacks at Brussels airport, barely twenty years after the Dutroux scandal, exposed Belgium yet again as a failure of titanic proportions. Decades of corruption and incompetence have taken their toll. The Belgian populace, internally fractured and accustomed to the political profiteering, shows no sign of revolt.

CHAPTER 21

THE MUSLIM CONNECTION

The Belgian capital has a long tradition of Islamist extremism. Some blamed the late King Baudouin for having invited Wahhabism into Belgium as a gesture of gratitude following the Saudi charitable donations to the victims of the 1967 fire of the Innovation shopping center.

By the 1990s, the city had become a safe haven, hiding place and transit zone for members of the terrorist GIA Armed Islamic Group. GIA, via Farid Melouk, was linked to the Paris subway attacks in the mid-1990s. Melouk and his GIA accomplices were jailed after a fire-fight in Brussels in March of 1998. One of the people arrested in the wake of the incident was Essousi Laaroussi, who was complicit in the Maâche-gang attacks on armoured money vans. Maâche was financing Muslim terror cells.

Those who knew him described Hassan Maâche as an elegant, charming and witty individual. Hassan Maâche, aged 48 when he was arrested in 2014, had spent half of his life in prison. He and his accomplice Abderrahim Bekhti had been involved in armed hold-ups since the early 1980s. The latter's brother, Abdelatif Bekhti, convicted for terrorism, was doing 30 years in a Moroccan cell in the company of professional killer Khader Balirj, better known as Belliraj, a Belgian national of Moroccan descent. Belliraj had been an informant of Belgian state security for years until it was exposed that he had killed 6 people. It was hard to believe that state security had not been aware of Belliraj's violent criminal past. Surprisingly, after his extradition to Morocco, Belliraj confessed. It became apparent that he had managed to infiltrate the Abu Nidal terror group, probably on order of the Mossad. Allegedly the Belgian authorities had paid "protection money" to Abu Nidal in order to keep Belgium off its terror target list.

A few weeks before 9/11 Belliraj had had a meeting in Kabul with Al Zawahiri, the second in command of Al Qaeda. This again raises the question of how much the Western intelligence services knew about the planned attacks of September 2001.

THE HAEMERS CONNECTION

Laaroussi had been working at the Bird's Nest Tavern in a Brussels suburb, owned by Denise Tyack, the widow of gang leader Patrick Haemers, who was found suicided in his Belgian cell in 1993. This was no coincidence. Apparently the Haemers network had been used by the Maâche gang for the transfer of stolen money in the 1990s.

The Haemers gang gained notoriety in the 1980s on account of their brutal attacks on vans transporting cash and valuables and especially their kidnapping of ex-minister Paul VDB in 1989. At some point Haemers was even suspected of being the leader of the Brabant Killers, at least on some occasions. Everything seemed to be connected somehow. The VDB kidnapping for ransom had seemed odd to many insiders, suspecting VDB of having staged the event.

A huge ransom was handed to Haemers in Geneva, Switzerland, by VDB's friend Jean Nathan, who reportedly had received the money from Israel, "for services rendered." These "services" may have had something to do with the mysterious account 1114 at the Banque d'Investissements Prives, the Caisse Privee subsidiary in Geneva. Asked about the money in the account, VDB answered that he was only a proxy and not the owner of the account, adding that he could not discuss the matter any further lest he trigger a "diplomatic incident." The only person who knew who was behind 1114, VDB said, was Jean Nathan, a Yom Kippur veteran.

Patrick Haemers told his father that he and his gang had been paid for the attacks on the armoured vans. According to Haemers, attacks were commissioned by top lawyers Vander Elst and Dumont, linked to the rightist VDB milieu; and ministers Jean Gol, Willy De Clercq and André Cools. According to the ATLAS Report, liberal minister Willy De Clercq had been eating out of the hand of Felix Przedborski. Haemers' statement was never taken seriously.

If Haemers' statement was anywhere near the truth, the attacks must have been an inside job. The security company that operated the vans was Securitas, later renamed G4Securitas or G4S. Interestingly enough, G4S would later be put in charge of the security of the NATO HQ compound in Brussels. There is no doubt that G4S was and is a parallel "private" intelligence agency, just like its American counterparts Wackenhut and Kroll.

The Belgian branch of Securitas had been founded in 1962 by … André Moyen, aka Captain Freddy, a wartime partisan who hated communism. In the run-up to WWII he had been employed in the infamous "Second Bureau," the intelligence section of the Defense ministry. After the war he had been instrumental in setting up the Belgian section of Gladio, and, of course, he had been behind the killing of communist leader Julien Lahaut in 1950. Moyen had been an advisor to the Kuomintang forces in China. He must have known some of the infamous China Cowboys like Jack Singlaub and Ted Shackley. Here too everything seemed to be connected.

If the hold-ups by the Haemers gang had been commissioned then what was the money intended for? Was it for the funding of ultra-right wing operations in Belgium, including a coup?

A more than interesting connection of the Haemers gang had been the mysterious Italian Elio Ciolini, aka Colonel Baccioni. He was first introduced in the Brussels right-wing political circles by Robert Wellens, whose correspondence with ex-SS officer Leon Degrelle was discovered during a house search. Ciolini had infiltrated the Haemers gang in1984. He was labeled a terrorist by the Italian authorities for his involvement in the 1980 Bologna bomb attack. (Appendix 20).

Ciolini was an agent of the CIA and probably of the Mossad. He had a half-sister named Marina Fabienne Cohen, who lived in Moron, a suburb of Buenos Aires, Argentina. Ciolini was a close friend of Stefano Delle Chiaie, the terrorist connected to the P2 Lodge. Another friend of Ciolini's was Volcker Flick, of the German Flick dynasty who had co-founded and financed the NSDAP. Was Ciolini on the payroll of George Bush's parallel Saudi-sponsored CIA, that was acting in concert with the Safari Club?

Ciolini had joined the Latin American Nazi "Special Commando" team headed by Klaus Barbie, SS-colonel Schwend and Joachim Fiebelkorn that had been advising the regimes of El Salvador and Honduras. In 1980, this Nazi clique was instrumental in the Bolivian cocaine coup. That same year Fiebelkorn had been dispatched to Italy for the Bologna attack.

Ciolini was obviously operating at the intersection of the Skorzeny network, the CIA, the P2 Lodge, Gladio, and possibly some Arab terror groups. The latter could well have been part of the Genoud-Schacht Arab League network, the Islamic branch of the Nazi underground. A 1978 telex linked Ciolini to Salah El-Chouk, aka Lorenz, who had attempted to recruit him, probably to carry out terror attacks in Israel.(Appendix 21).

In Belgium, Ciolini, using the alias Roland Baccioni, had co-founded a private investigations service called SIS, Special Intervention Service. SIS badge number 0018860 shows the picture and a fingerprint of "lieutenant-colonel Baccioni," born 18 August 1946. Which is Ciolini's real date of birth. (Appendix 22).

In an e-mail to an anonymous investigator, dated October 14, 2013, Ciolini's female companion codename "Vérité" ("Truth") wrote (Translated from French):

> Yes! Global government does exist and it is functioning. I would like to discuss these matters with you, but in writing it's too complicated. [...] As you know public opinion and journalism only create smokescreens. These people know it and they use it to hide from sight so they can continue to fool us. But he [Ciolini] and me have a powerful weapon: irrefutable proof of who is who, and who are the real crooks on the political and justice level. And so we will leverage this information [to get Ciolini out of jail]. We are fed up with these benumbed people believing whatever nonsense

they are being told. The truth is completely different. There is only one true world government. We shouldn't discuss this on a public forum because that would be too dangerous for me. Just one other thing: Elio is like a caring brother to me, he is not the person they would have us believe he is.

Somehow the surfacing of Ciolini in the Haemers gang was odd. Was he to assist in the preparation of a Bolivian-style coup in Belgium? Or was he the liaison officer for the Maâche-gang's Islamist terrorist connection? If the latter was the case, was Elio Ciolini somehow connected to Saudi secret agent Al Ajjaz – married into the Krupp dynasty – and his boss, Prince Turki? If so, Ciolini's operations in Belgium could have been linked to the Genoud-originated Islamic terror groups that produced Al Qaeda, which in turn evolved into ISIS. Which brings us back full circle to the 3/22 Brussels terror attacks and, of course, to the 9/11 attacks, in which the Saudis were deeply involved.

In the early postwar years Genoud had supported the "Ikhwan," better known as the Muslim Brotherhood (MB). After it was ousted from Egypt, the MB had settled in Saudi Arabia, where it formed an alliance with the Wahhabi movement. Many of the fanatic Muslim Brothers were recruited into the mercenary army of Osama bin Laden to fight the Russians in Afghanistan in the early 1980s. The Ikhwan was founded in 1928. Their leader was Al-Husseini, the Grand Mufti of Jerusalem, who, in an anti-British move, offered his support to the Nazi's. Hitler turned the Ikhwan into his Muslim SA division in the Arab region. The Mufti was put in charge of his own Muslim Nazi death squad in the Balkans, that decimated the Serbian population.

In the early post-war years, the US government, fearing the communist influence in the colonies that were moving towards independence, resolved to fight Soviet power in the Third World. The French debacle in Dien Ben Phu in 1954 had seen the USA scramble to fill the vacuum. In the Middle East, US oil corporations were taking over the role of the former colonial powers. Soon, the US was labeled the "new colonizer." Plans had already been made by the Truman administration back in 1953 to use Islamic fanaticism as a weapon in Third World countries. Truman's Psychological Strategy Board had warned that Islam was not a "natural barrier to communism." Some work needed to be done here.

The CIA had learned of the work of Turkic studies expert Gerhard Von Mende, who in the Nazi era had pioneered the use of Muslim extremism against the Soviets and who was running a similar intelligence office in West Germany. Not only the US but West German authorities as well started to cooperate with Von Mende's Muslim agency. Theodor Oberländer, head of the German refugee ministry, saw great opportunities in the use of muslim extremism for the re-unification of Germany and for the re-annexation of former German territories. Oberländer was the farthest right member of the FRG government. He had participated in Hitler's 1923 Beer Hall putsch in Munich. He had led one of the first Wehrmacht units made up of disgruntled Soviet emigrants. Oberländer would later become a member of the Anti-Bolshevik Bloc of Nations and of the WACL. In 1956 he sent a memo to Von Mende. It was the start of their anti-Soviet offensive that put some of the Muslim Brothers to work as propaganda broadcasters at Radio Free Europe and Radio Liberty.

The Muslim effort was rewarded with the construction of a mosque in Munich. After the death of Von Mende and the collapse of the Berlin Wall, the Muslim cells were of no further use. With Von Mende dead, German authorities lost control over the Muslim Frankenstein they had created. Left to their own devices, the Muslim Brothers started to turn the Munich mosque into a bulwark from which they would direct their conquest of the West.

Dave Emory, who has been tracking the Nazi Underground for over 30 years, has been reporting about his well-documented findings on a weekly basis. On 26 March 2016 he published his analysis of the Brussels 3/22 attacks under the heading "Brussels 'Blowback'" Background: The Belgian Muslim Brotherhood (The Killer B's)."

In his article Emory links the Brussels Islamic extremists involved in the attacks to the Muslim Brotherhood.

> The Syrian bloodbath stems from the use of the Syrian Muslim Brotherhood and al-Qaeda-Linked combatants backed by Turkey, Saudi Arabia and Qatar by elements of the CIA to remove the Assad regime in Syria. ISIS is a direct outgrowth of the so-called Arab Spring and the Syrian covert ops. An examination of the Muslim Brotherhood in Belgium highlights the profound presence of that organization there, its infiltration of government and civil society and links between its leadership and the milieu of the Bank al-Taqwa and Youssef Nada. Al-Taqwa cements the Nazi/Islamist relationship that is at the heart of the power group we have analyzed.

The bank Al Taqwa, it should be noted, was founded by François Genoud. What Emory is saying is that the recent ISIS terror attacks can be traced back to the Nazi origins of the Muslim Brotherhood.

Emory, citing from the Global Muslim Brotherhood Watch website, more specifically from an article by Steve Merley, titled "The Muslim Brotherhood in Belgium," dated December 4, 2008, writes:

> A 2002 report by the Intelligence Committee of the Belgian Parliament explained how the Brotherhood operates in Belgium:

The State Security Service has been following the activities of the International Muslim Brotherhood in Belgium since 1982. The International Muslim Brotherhood has had a clandestine structure for nearly 20 years. The identity of the members is secret; they operate in the greatest discretion. They seek to spread their ideology within the Islamic community of Belgium and they aim in particular at the young people of the second and third generation of immigrants. In Belgium as in other European countries, they try to take control of the religious, social, and sports associations and establish themselves as privileged interlocutors of the national authorities in order to manage Islamic affairs. The Muslim Brotherhood assumes that the national authorities will be pressed more and more to select Muslim leaders for such management and, in this context, they try to insert within the representative bodies, individuals influenced by their ideology. [...] A January 2007 article posted on the Internet describes a Bassem Hatahet as a member of the FIOE [a Brotherhood affiliate in Belgium]. He is 43-years old and was born in Damascus, Syria, where he likely still has relatives. Various sources list a residential address for Mr. Hatahet in northwest central Brussels. Security sources in Belgium describe Mr. Hatahet as the most important Muslim Brotherhood figure in Belgium, and a Bassem Hatahet was listed in a 1999 phonebook belonging to Youssef Nada, a self-described leader of the Muslim Brotherhood who was designated by the U.S. in 2002 as a terrorism financier.

The importance of Hatahet was confirmed by the Belgian magazine *Le Vif/l'Express* in its April 25, 2008, edition:

"Brussels resident Bassem Hatahet, 43 years old , is the son of a big shot of the Syrian branch of the Muslim Brotherhood, whose attempt at a coup d'etat was embedded in blood, in Hama, in 1982. After his arrival in Belgium, via Germany, he started studying dentistry in 1985. He is behind the origin of a series of associations, dedicated to the collection of funds (for example Foundation Al Aqsa), and many mosques, like Khalil (last in the hands of the Moroccan Brothers Justice and Development Party), in Molenbeek, or Assahaba, in Verviers. Presenting the profile of financier he is active today in the European headquarters of the Brotherhood (Federation of Islamic Organizations in Europe), located in Brussels. However, he never succeeded in obtaining Belgian citizenship."

The *New York Times*, in its March 26, 2016 edition, wrote:

Acting with uncharacteristic – and still unexplained – swiftness, Belgian security forces sealed off the area around the apartment in Schaerbeek within 90 minutes of the airport attack. The authorities attributed their speedy reaction to a tip-off from the taxi driver.

NYT's skepticism was justified, there was something definitely fishy about the whole affair. Salah Abdesalam, the most wanted terrorist after the Paris attacks, had quietly retreated in his apartment in Molenbeek. He was seen walking the streets without being bothered, his neighbors reported. It very much looked like Abdesalam was a police informant. He should have died in the Paris suicide attacks, but he "had changed his mind in order to save lives." When the SWAT team finally raided his apartment, Abdesalam was dressed in white, wearing a white cap, signaling "don't kill the guy in white." After he was arrested, Belgian police obviously failed to extract from him the information that could have prevented the Brussels attacks. Either he did not know about the planned attacks or the police failed to act on his information. Yet, 90 minutes after the Brussels Airport bombing, the Belgian police were able to pinpoint the Schaerbeek apartment?

The *New York Times*, criticizing the "dysfunctioning of the Belgian state," continues:

> How was it possible, members of Parliament asked, that two of the suicide bombers in the Brussels attacks, Ibrahim el-Bakraoui and his younger brother Khalid, both residents on Max Roos Street since the beginning of the year, had managed to go undetected for so long? And all this despite a record of violent crime in Belgium and, in the case of the older brother, a clear warning from Turkey in June that he was on his way back to Europe after being arrested as a suspected terrorist while on his way to Syria? And was it really true, the lawmakers demanded, that the authorities had received a precise tip in December about the possible whereabouts of Salah Abdesalam, the only known survivor among the terrorists responsible for the Paris attacks, who was finally captured in Brussels on March 18? He was found at the address cited in the December tip-off, which had not been acted on because it had not been passed up the police chain of command.

It would seem that early warnings of the attacks had been thrown to the wind by Belgian authorities. Much as had been the case on 9/11.

9/11

The early hours of 11 September 2001 were bright and sunny, as forecast. Anyone involved in air operations knows that the weather is the main factor in making the "go/no-go" decision. The same goes for location movie shooting. By the time the second airplane hit the WTC tower, dozens of camera's were pointed at the towers. The images they recorded, repeated on millions of screens over and over again, had a vague familiarity to them. The 9/11 pictures, masterpieces of Hollywood propaganda, stunning and hypnotising, were like a mix of cheap Godzilla movie scenes and a TV ad. Being constantly bombarded with these terrible visual imprints, the public at large, as expected, soon acknowledged two basic facts. First, that this was an act of war against America. Second, that Muslim extremists did it. The American "Hawks" finally had their new Pearl Harbor. The Evil Empire of the Soviets that had collapsed 10 years earlier had been substituted with the Devil himself, Osama bin Laden.

This was extremely good news for Israel, as president Netanyahu himself would later acknowledge. On the day of the attacks, five "dancing Israeli's" were arrested while filming the burning towers. In their home country they were hailed as real heroes. Larry Silverstein, the owner of the WTC towers, made a fortune on 9/11. On "Ground Zero" – an expression normally used in military jargon for the exact geographical location of a nuclear explosion – a new tower would arise. The creation of architect Daniel Libeskind. Although very few Jewish people perished in the attacks –"miraculously," as some suggested – the new building could be understood as yet another Holocaust monument on US soil, dedicated to the victory of money over truth. As the new tower slowly but surely rose into the New York skyline, gambling billionaire Sheldon Adelson was buying his way into US Congress, that now, like Napoleon two centuries ago, crawls at the feet of the moneymen.

With the WTC rubble still smoldering in the background, President Bush junior explained to the world that the attacks should be understood as "acts of war" against the United States. The wording was carefully chosen, as it implied that Article 5 of the Washington Treaty was now in force. This meant that all NATO allies were now at war with the new Islamic "terrorist enemy." NATO, having remained idle for 10 years for lack of enemies, not only sprang back into action, but also shed its old, defensive skin. The Alliance had just been promoted, without any political debate, to "global enforcer" of the Pax Americana. This uncontested state of affairs made the acquiescing European nations accomplices of the planned American criminal wars in the Middle East. As usual, the press and the media supported and reinforced the new post-9/11 paradigm. Samuel Huntington's 1996 book *Clash of Civilizations,* an instant bestseller after 9/11, was frequently quoted to convince the public of the fact that the Muslim culture was the new enemy of the West, as it had been for centuries since the time of the first Crusades around 1100 A.D. Now, we are told, Western values are at stake again.

François Genoud, who financed the Muslim Brotherhood and later Hamas, had strong ties to the Geneva law firm Magnin, Dunand & Co. Baudouin Dunand was a good friend and advisor of the Nazi banker. Incidentally, Dunand was co-director of the Saudi Investment Company (SICO), in which the bin Laden family had a big stake. SICO had several "undisclosed" accounts at the Clearstream clearinghouse in Luxembourg. This type of account allowed giant illegal financial transactions to be effected by means of invisible compensatory barter within the clearinghouse. These transactions would leave no traces in the normal banking system. Ernest Backes, ex-Clearstream director, who exposed the fraudulent system in his 2001 book *Révélation$*, stated that "he wouldn't be surprised if the 9/11 trails would lead directly to the Swiss bank accounts operated by Genoud." If true, this would mean that there was a German Connection to the 9/11 terror attacks.

And indeed there was. In the run-up to the September attacks, some of the 9/11 hijackers had demonstrably been operating out of Hamburg. And there was the strange story of the prescient buying of airline "put options" ahead of the attacks, involving Deutsche Bank Alex Brown.

In fact Alex Brown, a subsidiary of Deutsche Bank, where many of the alleged 9/11 hijackers handled their banking transactions, had acquired massive put option positions on United Airlines Cy through the Chicago Board Option Exchange ahead of September 11. On September 12, the chairman of the board of Deutsche Bank Alex Brown, Mayo A. Shattuck III, suddenly and quietly renounced his post.

Financial journalist and ex-Wall Street trader Max Keiser commented:

> There are many aspects concerning these option purchases that have not been disclosed yet. I also worked at Alex Brown & Sons (ABS). Deutsche Bank bought Alex Brown & Sons in 1999. When the attacks occurred, ABS was owned by Deutsche Bank. An important person at ABS was Buzzy Krongard. I have met him several times at the offices in Baltimore. Krongard had transferred to become executive director at the CIA. The option purchases, in which ABS was involved, occurred in the offices of ABS in Baltimore. The noise which occurred between Baltimore, New York City and Langley was interesting, as you can imagine, to say the least.

HARD ROAD

As to the EU, Trilateralist Richard Gardner in a 1974 article in the CFR's *Foreign Affairs* magazine, wrote:

> In short, the "house of world order" will have to be built from the bottom up rather than from the top down. It will look like a great "booming, buzzing confusion" … but an end run around national sovereignty, eroding it piece by piece, will accomplish much more than the old-fashioned frontal assault.

Gardner's words remind us of a statement made by Martial Lekeu, thought to be a key figure in the Belgian coup project of the early 1980s.

Lekeu once said that "a slow motion coup was underway." It was slowly but surely progressing, he said, and in the end it would prove to have been more effective than a tank brigade in the streets of Brussels. If by this "stealthy coup" he meant the construction of the EU, which has indeed proved to be an insidious, undemocratic and slow process, bypassing the "No"-vote of the European people with a series of sneaky "faits accomplis," then this tells us something about those who are behind it. Namely the modern-day globalist Synarchists and their Cagoule, serving the Atlantic dollar hegemony.

In 2011, two Belgian names appeared on the Trilateral Commission member list. One is that of Luc Coene, director of the National Bank, the other is that of Thomas Leysen, the son of André Leysen, a former SS collaborator. Citing Andrew Marshall from his January 14, 2015 article "Global Power Project: Bilderberg Group and the Central Bankers" on the Occupy.com website:

> Luc Coene, the governor of the central bank of Belgium and a member of the governing council of the ECB since 2011, attended Bilderberg meetings in 2009 and 2011. In a May 2012 interview with the *Financial Times*, Coene explained that in the European Union, "We have lived beyond our means for the past ten years and now there needs to be a correction somewhere," noting that the main crisis was "a crisis of confidence," with the issues being about fiscal policy, growth prospects, [and] the soundness of banking systems.

The job of central banks and monetary policy, Coene stressed, was to "provide breathing space to implement all these things." In an October 2012 panel debate on the Eurozone Coene stated: "To think that austerity could be avoided is naïve." In June of 2014, Coene stressed the need for Belgium to impose further austerity measures and structural reforms on its population, stating that "we absolutely must carry on with structural reforms." This, he added, is not the central bank's job, it is the government's job, and if this isn't done financial markets might push Belgium into a crisis.

In essence, this banker is telling the government what to do. The "soundness of the banking system" must be guaranteed by the political authorities. This very much sounds like the Banque de France talking to Napoleon, back in 1805. If they refuse, they will be punished by "the markets."

What markets? The free market mechanism is dead. Even the basic Libor yardstick interest rate is being manipulated. In real life the ECB and the FED impose the interest rate upon the markets. The ECB is buying the treasury bonds being floated by the European states, thus bypassing the markets. Where does the ECB get the money, you might ask ? Well, it just opens the spigot of the FED credit pipeline, et voilà! This is how interests rates have been kept much too low for much too long, ignoring the creeping inflation. Yet, Coene insists on austerity. If banks are "too big to fail" then, one could argue, surely a whole nation state couldn't ever fail either!

But that is not how central bankers see it. It's the old story repeating itself: in a crisis, in order to save the profit margins of the corporations – and consequently the dividends they pay – you just crush wages, abolish workers' rights, prohibit strikes. And above all ... you, gentlemen of the governments, must save the banks.

The ECB's monetary moves mirror those of the Rothschilds financing the young Belgian government back in the 1840s. The Belgians, dubbed "stupid donkeys" by Rothschild for buying into his scheme, had realized early on that their deal with the Jewish money masters would result in a snowballing composite interest debacle. When the government decided to go it alone and float the Belgian treasury bonds directly on the market, the Rothschilds refused to buy any of them. This signaled to the markets that Rothschild obviously had his doubts about the credit worthiness of the Belgian nation. As a consequence, other institutional investors shied away from the bonds and the operation failed, driving the Belgian donkeys back into the arms of the Rothschilds, where they have remained since.

And so Coene would have us believe that it's all about credit worthiness. What makes a nation credit worthy? The ability of its government to extort yet more taxes from its population to ensure the pay-back of interests to the banks. In Coene's sophisticated banker speak this is translated into "a correction of fiscal policy." In this current year 2016, the Belgian debt-to-GDP ratio still stands at 100 percent, among the highest in Europe. Due to this, objectively speaking, Belgium did not qualify to enter the Euro zone in 2002. The need to reschedule and service this debt keeps the Belgians hooked on the banking cartel's line forever.

The other name on the 2011 Trilateral list was that of Thomas Leysen. His father André had joined the Hitlerjugend during the war. His uncle Siegfried "Fritz" was an SS officer. Leysen's successful post-war career was typical of many collaborators. The Belgian industrialists, who had tasted the benefits of the German centrally guided economy with its fixed prices and guaranteed profit margins, were not intent on returning to a system of pure competition.

Leysen, who hated the workers' unions, had married Elisabeth Gertrude Ahlers on 23 August of 1953. She was the daughter of German shipping agent Herwig Ahlers, who resided in Antwerp. During the war Ahlers had been appointed "Deutscher Verwalter" or "German Administrator" of all Belgian shipping companies. In the early 1950s the Ahlers group employed over 1000 workers.

Leysen used his father-in-law's company as a launchpad for his business career. In 1970, the Ahlers company was integrated in Leysen's IBEL holding. In 1976 the Ahlers fortune helped Leysen acquire the VUM publishing company. In the so-called "silver putsch" of 1979, Leysen, squeezed by the skyrocketing price of silver caused by the Hunt brothers, sold the Agfa-Gevaert photo company to the salivating Bayer corporation. Agfa-Gevaert, it should be noted, was part of the Almany holding that was deeply involved in the financial shenanigans of the Vatican.

Leysen was one of the captains of industry who joined the European Round Table, where he rubbed shoulders with Etienne Davignon. Leysen demonstrated his contempt for workers' rights by sacking 3,000 employees at the Agfa Munich plant. Soon he was filling seats on many company boards, one of which was that of GBL, the holding of Frère and Desmarais. He ended his career as the top dog of the association of Belgian employers. Other collaborators like Vlerick, Collin, Bekaert, Lannoo and Santens enjoyed similar successes in the decades following the German "demise" in 1945.

WAYNE MADSEN REPORT

This book started with a reference to Wayne Madsen's 2011 comments on the ATLAS police report, that this author had e-mailed to him. In closing I would like to thank Wayne for his support. Wayne's contribution in exposing the Nebula came in the form of his Special Report of October 2015, that reads as follows:

> October 22-26, 2015 – Special Report. A little-known Israeli-Zionist power syndicate exposed publication date: Oct 22, 2015
> Belgian author Walter Baeyens has published an exposé of a little-known Europe-based Israeli-Zionist power syndicate titled "The elites of power. The power of the elites." The book is a follow-on to a Belgian police investigation into the business dealings of a gang of wealthy Jewish business tycoons who have engaged in deep state operations in a number of countries. The Belgian police report, called the ATLAS report, was detailed in a September 2, 2011 report by WMR.
> The ATLAS report dealt with the assassination of former Belgian Deputy Prime Minister and Belgian Socialist Party leader Andre Cools in a gangland-style murder in 1991. Our 2011 report stated: "Before Cools' murder, Belgium had been wracked by Italian Gladio-style "strategy of tension" (or, as in Turkey today, Ergenekon) right-wing terrorist attacks, including death squad hits and bombings, which were initially blamed by authorities on leftist guerrilla groups such as the Communist Combatant Cells. Cools' hometown of Liege was the center of the nexus of organized crime syndicates and the right-wing Gladio cells. However, it was not the

revelation that Cools and other top Belgian politicians were in-volved in Belgium's right-wing 'deep state' that brought down their house of cards but the infamous Agusta helicopter scandal."

Our report continued: "Agusta, the Italian helicopter manufac-turer and a licensee of Bell helicopters of the United States, bribed Socialist Party leaders, including Cools and then-NATO Secretary General Willy Claes, a friend of Cools, to cement a Belgian Army contract for 42 helicopters, which would replace the Army's aging French Alouette helicopters. Cools was to have received $10 mil-lion in bribes but the cash he received turned out to be counterfeit. Cools, in retaliation, threatened to tell all he knew about the Agusta deal and much more. It was Cools' threat to go public that earned him two bullets while he was sitting in his car next to his girlfriend. One bullet struck Cools in the head, the other to his chest. His girl-friend was also hit but she survived. What Cools threatened to ex-pose was an intricate network of terrorists, nuclear smugglers, drug dealers, diamond and gold smugglers, and weapons merchants who were ultimately tied to Mossad and a shadowy network of in-fluential European Jewish Zionists, a network known as 'Nebula.' The details on Nebula are contained in the ATLAS report.

The ATLAS report identified one of the key Nebula leaders as the "éminence grise" of Nebula, the "de facto director of most of the big multinational companies whose structures are being used to launder large amounts of capital. This person is: PRZEDBOR-SKI, Felix, born 12 December 1930. Przedborksi, a Polish Jew, is a dual national of Belgium and Costa Rica who maintains residences in Brussels; Antibes, France; San Jose, Costa Rica; Miami; and Tel Aviv.

The Belgian police identified Przedborski as a kingpin in nucle-ar material, diamond, and heroin smuggling. Linked to a number of noted Israeli smugglers, including one-time Manuel Noriega friend Mike Harari, and Bill and Hillary Clinton pal, the late Marc Rich, "Don Felix," as he is known, apparently does not like any me-dia attention, even at the age of 85. WMR has learned that Don Felix sued the late Belgian investigative journalist Walter De Bock and his Costa Rican colleague for libel. However, the threat did not deter journalists from delving into Przedborski's murky business dealings over several decades. For example, German author Juer-gen Roth published a book under the title "Die graue Eminenz" ("The grey Eminence"), in which Don Felix is the main character. However, Przedborski used his influence to have the book recalled with only a few copies remaining in circulation.

Belgian author Baeyens has resurrected the investigation of Przedborski in his new book, which relies, to a significant extent, on the personal archives of Walter De Bock, which are now stored at the Catholic University of Louvain in Belgium. Przedborski has led a charmed existence in Costa Rica and, although he has been involved in nuclear smuggling, was appointed Costa Rica's ambassador to the International Atomic Energy Agency (IAEA) in Vienna.

A 2001 Belgian police (PV 13867), unearthed in the course of Baeyens' research, documents Przedborski's links to the late international fugitive and Central Intelligence Agency – and Richard Nixon-linked Robert Vesco. Vesco was also a lieutenant of Jewish mafiosi boss Meyer Lansky. Vesco was involved in an early 1970s grand swindle targeting Investors Overseas Services, Ltd., a firm managed by jailed financier Bernard Cornfeld and linked to Prince Bernhard of the Netherlands, a founder of the Bilderberg Group. Vesco attempted to buy the island of Barbuda from Antigua and establish an independent state. A fugitive from justice in the United States, Vesco reportedly died in Cuba in 2007, although some doubt that he is actually dead.

"Smoking gun" Belgian police report linking Costa Rican Jewish syndicate chief Don Felix to Robert Vesco and Marc Rich.

The police report, which is in French, links Przedborski to Alfred Cahen and his son, Max-Olivier Cahen. Alfred was a former Belgian ambassador to Zaire, now Democratic Republic of Congo, and a NATO official. The Cahen connection clearly involved the smuggling of "blood diamonds" from the killing fields of Congo/Zaire. In 1997 Max-Olivier came under investigation by the FBI for trying to sell classified intelligence documents from the defense Intelligence Agency and Drug Enforcement Administration to the daughter of Zaire's dictator Mobutu Sese Seko. The FBI probe centered on President Clinton's former National Security Council adviser on Africa, Shawn McCormick, who was also a close friend of Max-Olivier. Max-Olivier appeared to throw his friend McCormick under the bus when he revealed that he a had a copy of a $10,000 check made out in 1995 by the lobbying firm of Barron-Birrell Inc. to McCormick while he worked at the National Security Council. The payment was allegedly made on behalf of the former president of the Republic of Congo (Brazzaville) Pascal Lissouba. The "pay to play" operations in the Clinton White House closely match those involving the Clinton Foundation, the lobbying group Teneo, and Hillary Clinton's tenure as Secretary of State.

Also named in the Belgian police report are American Levant Industrie; a Liechtenstein-based company Anstalt Tradin and Serdan, owned by Przedborski; Global Bank, partly owned by Przedborski; Kuhne & Nagel, a transport company also partly owned by Przedborski that was involved in the Iran-contra affair; former Lufthansa CEO Herbert Culmann; and Marc Rich.

Culmann was involved with Przedborski and SABENA Belgian Airlines to sell tens of thousands of cheaply-made linen travel bags to Lufthansa and SABENA at overly-inflated prices. After defrauding Belgian tax authorities in the 1980s, Przedborski fled to Israel, the preferred refuge for Jewish gangsters and criminals worldwide. Przedborski eventually paid a $3 million fine to the Belgian government.

Przedborski also allegedly was involved in trafficking nuclear material to the Pakistani nuclear scientist A Q Khan. This smuggling reportedly involved the Belgian nuclear center SCK Mol and the German enterprise, TransNuklear.

The Przedborski syndicate in Costa Rica is similar to the Rosenthal criminal family in Honduras. Headed by former Honduran Vice President Jaime Rosenthal, who is of Romanian Jewish extraction, the syndicate owns Banco Continental, part of Grupo Continental. On October 7, 2015, Rosenthal was named by the U.S. government as a "specially designated narcotics trafficker." As it is normal with the Zionist-founded and -controlled Wikipedia, Rosenthal's close connections to wider Jewish global gangsterism is not to be found in his Wikipedia entry.

Rosenthal, who once met President Ronald Reagan in the White House, owns over 20 businesses in Honduras, including cattle ranches and alligator farms. Rosenthal's Inversiones Continental controls banking and financial services companies, as well as real estate, media, agriculture, and construction interests in Honduras as well as three off-shore firms in the British Virgin Islands. On October 7, 2015, Rosenthal's nephew, former Honduran Investments Minister Yankel Rosenthal, was arrested, along with his lawyer, at Miami International Airport and charged with providing "money laundering and other services that support the international narcotics trafficking activities of multiple Central American drug traffickers and their criminal organizations." His uncle Jaime and cousin Yani were similarly charged although Jaime remains in Honduras.

As with the Rosenthals, who used Honduran government and diplomatic offices to further their criminal operations, Przedborski relied on the help of Costa Rican officials, including the former Costa Rican ambassador to Belgium and Austria. Przedborski's international facilitators also include a number of influential Russian-Ukrainian Jewish mafiosi, referred to by Roth as the "Odessa Mafia," many of whom live in Israel but travel abroad freely. These include Mikhail Chernoy, an Israeli industrialist born in Uzbekistan; Ukrainian-Jewish mobster Semyon Mogilevitch, arrested in Moscow in 2008 for tax evasion; Anatoly Katric, a Ukrainian-born Israeli Jew and front man for Mogilevitch; Sergei Mikhailov, the head of the Solntsevskaya Brotherhood, the most dangerous Russian mafia syndicate and linked to Mogilevitch; Vadim Rabinovich, head of the All-Ukrainian Jewish Congress and 2014 Ukrainian presidential candidate who attended a fund raising dinner for Bill Clinton in 1995 at the Sheraton in Bal Harbor, Florida, where Przedborski also maintains a residence; and Lithuanian Jewish double agent for the KGB and Mossad, Shabtai Kalmanovich, who was, interestingly, a former honorary consul for Costa Rica in St. Petersburg, Russia.

Kalmanovich was assassinated in 2009 in Moscow by a passing vehicle that hit him 10 times with gunfire. Mossad is suspected of carrying out the hit that Moscow police termed "very professional."

The renewed focus on the Odessa or Russian-Ukrainian-Israeli Mafia may spell trouble for the Hillary Clinton presidential campaign. Many of the key members of the syndicate, including Marc Rich, Grigori Loutchansky, and Vadym Rabinovich, were donors to Bill Clinton's political coffers. Part of the current congressional investigation of Hillary Clinton's activities at the State Department involve her shake down of foreign political and business leaders for donations to her and her husband's Clinton Foundation. And none of these leads have anything to do with Benghazi.

EPILOGUE

Felix Przedborski passed away in Monaco on 9 March 2016 at the age of 86. His remains were cremated in the strictest discretion, the *Nice Matin* newspaper reported.

He survived "the Insider" Michel V, who died in an accident in 2014, by two years. Michel V's last Facebook Timeline entry was dated 1 March 2014.

Business is now being taken care of by Felix's son and successor Daniel, heir to an immense fortune that has its origins in Don Felix's hazy past. From this hazy past the Przedborski's, like the Bronfmans before them, have emerged victorious, respectable and very wealthy. In these days of unbridled egocentric materialism, power and money have become the only means and measure of all things. How they were acquired does not matter. In this Age of Fake, real history has become a thing of the past.

In November of 2015, 30 years after the last attack of the Brabant Killers, the Belgian government has voted a law to push back the legal time limit date to the year 2025.

Some critics say this will allow the political class to hide the truth behind the "secrecy of the official investigation" for another decade.

Angelo Codevilla in his book *The Ruling Class* phrased it this way: "Consensus among the right people is the only standard of truth. Facts and logic matter only insofar as proper authority acknowledges them."

"LIKE"

Today, the brave new world of Facebook allows us a brief look into the private world of the Przedborskis. Felix's descendants do not seem to share his urge for privacy. They do not know any better than that they were born into the upper class. As such they think of themselves as being above the law. They are the people whose consensus now decides on what the truth is. They just go on living their privileged little lives of luxury. The crimes of their fathers are of no concern to them.

From the looks of it, the Przedborski's are doing very well, thank you. Anyone peeking into the "Friends" list of lawyer Daniel Przedborski today will recognize the familiar names that have colored Felix's life. Krygier, Salik, Goldschmid, Goldman, Kriwin, Borenstein, Perlmutter, Libeskind. From the diplomatic circles: Calderon, Esquivel, Ortiz. The Geneva

Connection: Neyroud, Dwek, de Picciotto, Zwirn, Pinto. The business connection: Dassault, D'Ursel. The Iran-Contra affair: Rappaport. The Roman catholic old money connection: De Grunne, De Bassompierre, De Kerchove. From the ATLAS Report: Empain, Afschrift, Le Hodey, Linker.

Unexpectedly, some other well-known names pop up. Harari, for one, the former top Mossad agent. And Luc Hennart, the Belgian judge who mishandled the Brabant Killings case.

Respectable citizens each and every one.

BIBLIOGRAPHY

Honey, Martha, *Hostile Acts. US Policy in Costa Rica in the 1980s*, University Press of Florida, Gainesville, FLA, 1994.

Friedman, Robert, *Red Maffiya. How the Russian Mob has invaded America*, Little, Brown and Cy, Boston, 2000.

Henderson, Dean, *Big Oil and their Bankers in the Persian Gulf*, Bridger House Publishing, Carson, City, NV, 2010.

Mullins, Eustace, *A Study of the Federal Reserve and its Secrets*, Wilder Publications, Blacksburg, VA, 2010.

Leese, Arnold, *Gentile Folly: the Rothschilds – uitgave door de auteur*, White House, Pewley Hill, Guilford, 1940.

Corti, Egon Caesar Count, *The Reign of the House of Rothschild*, Cosmopolitan Book Corporation, New York, 1928.

Ferguson, Niall, *The House of Rothschild. The World's Banker. 1849-1999*, Viking Penguin Group, New York, 1999.

Ferguson, Niall, *The House of Rothschild. Money 's Prophets 1798-1848, 1849-1999*, Viking-Penguin Group,New York, 1998.

Morton, Frederic, *The Rothschilds. A Family Portrait*, Atheneum, Curtis Publishing Co, NY,1962.

Spingola, Deanna, *The Ruling Elite. The Zionist Seizure of World Power*, Trafford Publishing, Bloomington, IN, 2012.

Knuth, E. C., *The Empire of The City*, The Book Tree, San Diego, CA, (1944), 2006.

Guenther, Leonhard, *A German Ace tells Why. From Kaiserdom to Hitlerism*, Sci-Art Publishers, Cambridge, MA, 1942.

Lazare, Bernard, *Antisemitism. Its History and Causes*, (1894), Cosimo NY, 2005.

Stolfi, R.H.S., *Hitler. Beyond Evil and Tyranny*, Prometheus Books NY, 2011.

Griffin, G. Edward, *The Creature From Jekyll Island*, American Media, Westlake CA, 1994.

Duke, David, *The Secret Behind Communism*, Free Speech Press, Mandeville LA, 2013.

Mercier, Vincent, *Prins Diamant*, Van Halewyck, Leuven Belgium, 2013.

Evans, M. Stanton, *Blacklisted by History. The Untold Story of Senator Joe McCarthy*, Three Rivers Press NY, 2007.

Gordon, Sarah, *Hitler, Germans and the Jewish Question*, Princeton University Press, 1984.

Zinsser, Hans, *Rats, Lice and History*, (1935), Read Books, 2008.

Allen, Gary, *None Dare Call It Conspiracy*, Concord Press, Rossmoor CA, 1972.

Christianson, Scott, *The Last Gasp. Rise and Fall of the American Gas Chamber*, University of California Press, 2010.

John J. McCloy Papers 1897-1989, Five College Archives-Amherst College Archives.

Bower, Tom, *Blind Eye to Murder*, Granada Publishing Ltd, London-1981-1983.

Lacroix-Riz, Annie, *Le Choix de la Défaite*, Armand Collin, Paris, 2012.

Roth, Jürgen, *Die Gangster aus dem Osten*, Europa Verlag, Hamburg, 2003.

West, Diana, *American Betrayal*, St. Martin's Press, NY, 2013.

Gillingham, John, *Belgian Business in the Nazi New Order*, John Dhondt Stichting, Gent, 1977.

Naylor, R.T., *Hot Money and the Politics of Debt*, Unwin Hyman Ltd, London, 1987.

Booker, Chris/North Richard, *The Great Deception. Secret History of the EU*, Continuum, London, 2003.

Bülow, Andreas von, *Im Namen des Staates*, Piper Verlag, München, 1998.

Herman, Edward/Brodhead, Frank, *The Rise and Fall of the Bulgarian Connection*, Sheridan Square Publications NY, 1986.

Lernoux, Penny, *In Banks We Trust*, Anchor Press / Doubleday NY, 1984.

Wisnewski, Gerhard, *Verschlussache Terror*, Knaur München, 2007.

Roth, Jürgen, *Die Graue Eminenz*, Hofman & Campe, Hamburg, 1999.

Havaux, Pierre/Marlet, Pierre, *Sur la Piste du Crocodile*, La Longue Vue Bxl, 1994.

Teacher, David, *Rogue Agents. The Cercle Pinay Complex 1951-1991*, download http://www.cryptome.org/2012/01/cercle-pinay-6i.pdf, 1993 revised 2008.

Centre de Recherche et d'Information Socio-Politiques, *Structures Economiques de la Belgique- Morphologie des Groupes Financiers*, CRISP, Bruxelles, 1966.

Executive Intelligence Review, *The case against Kissinger for the murder of Aldo Moro*, Volume 9, Number 36, September 21, 1982.

Executive Intelligence Report, "George Bush and the 12333 Serial Murder Ring,"Oct. 1996.

Ehrenfeld Rachel, *Evil Money*, HarperCollins NY, 1992.

Bichler, Shimshon & Nitzan, Jonathan, *New Economy or Transnational Ownership? The Global Political Economy of Israel*, CCGES conference, York University, Toronto, 2002.

Ryssen, Hervé, *La Mafia Juive*, Editions Baskerville, Levallois France, 2008.

Brenner, Lenni, *51 documents. Zionist collaboration with the Nazis*, Barricade Books, Fort Lee NJ, 2002

Pietrusza, David, *Rothstein: The Life, Times, and Murder of the Criminal Genius*, Basic Books NY, 2011.

RAGGRUPPAMENTO OPERATIVO SPECIALE CARABINIERI "Procedimento penale contro Rognoni Giancarlo ed altri. Annotazione sulle attività di guerra psicologica e non ortodossa, (psychological and low density warfare) compiute in Italia tra il 1969 e il 1974 attraverso l'" "AGINTER PRESSE"- Rome, 23 juli 1996.

Gijsels, Hugo, *De VlaamSSche Kronijken. De Zwarte Jaren van André Leysen*, EPO/Halt, Berchem, 1987.

Gijsels, Hugo & Willems, Jan, "HALT aan Verrechtsing en Racisme," *Halt Magazine* jaargang 4, nr. 2.

Schrijvers, Klaartje, *l'Europe sera de droite ou ne sera pas! Netwerking van de neo-aristocratische elite in de korte XXe eeuw*, Proefschrift 2007-2008, Universiteit Gent.

Poppe, Guy, *De Moord op Rwagasore*, EPO, Berchem, 2011.

Van Esbroeck, Leopold, *De Opdrachtgevers. Popolino over de Bende van Nijvel*, Van Halewyck, Leuven, 1999.

Trepp, Gian, *Swiss Connection*, Unionsverlag, Zürich, 1996.

Verduyn, Ludwig, *De Discrete Charme van een Luxemburgs Bankier*, Van Halewyck, Leuven 1997.

Van Bosbeke, André, *Opus Dei in België*, EPO, 1985

Bruck, Connie, *The Predators' Ball. The inside Story of Drexel Burnham*, Penguin Books NY, 1989.

De Jonghe & Van Brussel-, *Les Années de Plomb. Contacts d'information*, politierapport, 1989-2009.

Watson, Sabrina Roxanne, *Public Person Libel Standards in the British Commonwealth Carribean versus the United States*, Doctorthesis filosofie, University of Florida, 2006.

Cohen, Bernard L., *The Myth of Plutonium Toxicity*, University of Pittsburgh, Physics Dept., 3 januari 1989.

Douglass, Joseph D Jr, PhD., *Red Cocaine*, Edward Harle Limited NY, 1990, 1999.

Sejna, Jan, *We Will Bury You*, Sidgwick & Jackson, London, England, 1982.

De Bock, Walter, *De Mooiste Jaren van een Generatie. De Nieuwe Orde in België, voor, tijdens en na WOII*, EPO Berchem, 1982.

Raes, François, *Rijkswachter als Don Quichot*, EPO Berchem, 1983.

Starr-Miller, Edith, *Occult Theocrasy*, private edition, 1933.

Lee, Martin, *The Beast Reawakens*, Routledge, Taylor & Francis Group NY, 2000.

Higham, Charles, *Trading with the Enemy. An Exposé of the Nazi-American Money Plot 1933-1945*, Dell Books NY, 1983.

Tetens, T.H., *Germany plots with the Kremlin*, Henry Schuman, NY, 1953.

Gijsels, Hugo, *Netwerk Gladio*, Kritak, Leuven 1991.

Nefors, Patrick, *Industriële Collaboratie in België*, Van Halewyck, Leuven, 2000

Wood, Patrick, *Technocracy Rising. Trojan Horse of Global Transformation*, Coherent Publishing, Meza AZ, 2014.

Damseaux, Gérald, *Les Années Noires Vous Intéressent?*, Société des Ecrivains, Paris 2014.

Van Der Pijl, Kees, *The Making of an Atalantic Ruling Class*, Verso, NY, 2012.

Roth, Jürgen, *Der Tiefe Staat*, Wilhelm Heyne Verlag, München-2016.

Chaussy, Ulrich, *Oktoberfest. Das Attentat*, Ch. Links Verlag, Berlin, 1985.

Baeyens, Walter, *De Elite van de Macht. De Macht van de Elite*, Van Halewyck, Leuven, 2015.

Webster, Nesta H, *World Revolution. The Plot against Civilization*, Small, Maynard and Cy, Boston, 1921.

Faligot & Kauffer, *Le Croissant et la Croix Gammée'*, Albin Michel, Paris, 1990.

Livernette, Johan, *La Franc-Maçonnerie, 300 Ans d'Imposture'*, Editions Saint-Rémi, Cadillac, 2017.

Laïbi, Salim, *La Faillite du Monde Moderne*, Editions Fiat Lux, Marseille, 2013.

Story, Christopher, *The New Underground Order*, Edward Harle Ltd, London, 2002.

Reed, Douglas, *The Controversy of Zion*, Omnia Veritas, 1978.

Reisman, Judith, *Kinsey: Crimes & Consequences*, Institute for Media Education, Crestwood USA, 1998.

Novak, Charles, *Jacob Frank. Le faux Messie'*, l'Harmattan, Paris, 2012.

Ryssen, Hervé, *Understanding the Jews*, Carlos W. Porter, 2014.

Jones, Michael E, *Libido Dominandi*, St Augustine's Press, South Bend, IN, 2000.

Shrimpton, Michael, *Spyhunter*, The June Press, Totnes, 2014.

Appendices

Appendix 1A: ATLAS Report (French)

Liège le 21/11/94
n° 3? /Ciel/ M

GENDARMERIE
District de Liège

B . S . R .
Rue Maghin, 50
4000   LIEGE
041/ 28.93.72

Au Chef Serv BSR de LIEGE

- *Au Magistrat National*
- *Au Comd BCR*

Objet : Criminalité organisée (*Mafia Russe et Autres*)
Réf   : Dossier ATLAS

0 ... *Prde Col.*
1 ... L'Col. *cHNTER*
2 ... *Deck* 11K
3 ... *Lattefer* 1Nk
4 ... *Col* *Grnff*

A- INTRODUCTION

A ce stade de la rédaction, certaines informations sont en cours de vérifications.

Plusieurs dossiers ont déjà été traités par divers services de Police qui ont pu quand-même démontrer certaines choses, même si la Justice ne les a pas toujours suivis.
L'histoire démontre tous les jours que de ces dossiers, certains n'ont jamais abouti et d'autres n'aboutiront sans doute jamais pour de multiples raisons.

Pour comprendre cette nébuleuse, il faut abandonner certaines logiques financières ou politiques, il n'est plus question de nation, de couleur de parti ou encore de cohérence économique.

Notre conclusion serait que depuis au moins vingt ans, des puissances économiques, dont certaines de type mafieux, alliées à des forces politiques et des structures criminelles organisées, ont atteint le 4° stade du blanchiment d'argent, à savoir, le Pouvoir Absolu.

Il nous est précisé qu'à l'heure actuelle ces personnages contrôleraient 50 % de l'économie mondiale.

B- INFORMATIONS

1. Il nous a été communiqué des renseignements sur *le personnage* qui semble être *un des dirigeants occultes de plusieurs Pays* (dont le nôtre)

Page - 1 -

Appendix 1B: ATLAS Report (English Translation)

CONFIDENTIAL REPORT-CANNOT BE USED IN COURT PROCEEDINGS

Liège, November 21, 1994 , nr 37, Ciel/M- Gendarmerie Liège District

To the head of BSR of Liège, to the National Magistrate, to the commander of BCR

Subject: Organized Crime (Russian mafia and other)
Ref: ATLAS file

> A. Introduction:
> At this stage of the redaction (of this report), some information is still being cross checked. Several files have already been examined by various police services, who have been able to corroborate some data, even if Justice has not always followed-up on them. Day to day events show us that some files never go anywhere and some others will no doubt never lead anywhere, for various reasons.
>
> To understand this 'Nebula', one has to abandon the established path of logic as far as finances and politics are concerned. No longer is there mention of nation states, of political party colors or of any economic coherence.

Our conclusion would be that, since over 20 years, some economical forces, some of which are of the maffia-type being linked to the political power and organized crime structures, have reached the 4th level of money laundering, in other words: Absolute Power.

It has been made clear to us that the persons cited below allegedly control 50% of the world economy.

> B. Information:
> 1. We have been informed about a person who appears to be one of the mysterious top leaders in several countries, (including ours).
> (Page 2)
> This person is portrayed as being the 'éminence grise', the de facto director of most of the big multinational companies whose structures are being used to Launder large capitals. This person is:

PRZEDBORSKI, Felix, born 12 december 1930, 'stateless', husband to Helène KRYGIER, formerly living in TERVUREN.

On the subject of this person, we have been told that:

– He has a double nationality: Belgium + Costa Rica.

We have been able to confirm that he obtained Belgium nationality on 6 September 1978, a few days before his emigration to Costa Rica. His wife, born 5 june 1931, obtained Belgium nationality on 28 December 1950.

– He is Ambassador of Costa Rica to IAEA in Vienna (anti-nuclear commission) and allegedly also holds the position of minister plenipotentiary of this same country at the European Economic Community as well as to France,(where has offices on Avenue Wilson, Paris).

– He actually lives in Costa Rica, where he owns the property BELLA VISTA in the San José Country Club, Escazu/ San José-Costa Rica.

– He regurly resides in our country, in Tervuren, Lorrainedreef n° ?, where he is the subscriber of telephone number 02/7679584 (secret).

– He has a brother (first name ???) who resides in New York, USA. He has nothing to do with the 'Nebula'. Felix is apparently hiding his brother from his partners and his enemies.

– Félix appears to heva two sons. (1) Named Serge, psychiatrist in New York, not involved in the 'Nebula', we have been able to find out his address: born 7 March 59 in Brussels, Belgian, Medical doctor, husband to Goldman, Sylvie, living since 22 december 88 in USA, 2000 Broadway Appartment 23D, 10023 NY-NY.

(2) Named Daniël. Lawyer in Brussels and Geneva. He allegedly wishes to take over the leadership of the 'Nebula'. His wife is said to be the daughter of a mafia godfather, close to CRAXHI (ex prime-minister of Italy, mentioned in operation MANI POLLUTI). Have found his address: (first names André-Marc, Daniel), born 7 May 1954 in Berchem-St-Agathe, Belgian, Lawyer, husband to BIALETTI, Alessandra, living in Switzerland since 11 December 84-Plateau de Frontanex nr 9Cin 1208 Geneva (extremely expensive/ up-scale quarter of Geneva). Subject still holds attorney officezs in Brussels, Avenue du Vert Chasseur nr 42 in 1180 Uccle (phone 02/3752408)

[Note of translator: The private residence of the US Ambassador to Belgium used to be in the same street]

2. The structure being headed by Félix PRZEDBORSKI is involved in trafficking various items worldwide:
DIAMONDS, WEAPONS, DRUGS, NUCLEAR MATERIAL, MONEY LAUNDERING, INFLUENCE PEDDLING.
(page 3)

To this end an economical-political structure has been erected in the last 40 years over which he reigns as the Absolute Master.

Although illiterate, he speaks 7 or 8 languages and is gifted with an extraordinary cunning intelligence, which has left him totally without any moral value whatsoever.

It is said that the financial foundation of his Group is estimated at 7 billion USD.

3. It is often said that to get on top of the hill, one has to surround himself with only the best. This is what Przedborski has practised, 'buying' the greatest economists, lawyers (attorneys) etc..pushing his friends into leadership positions in several countries.

For the security of his person and that of his group, Felix has called upon the security services of an ex-Mossad Colonel.

4. In order to understand this 'Nebula', one has to go back to the end of WWII, when PRZEDBORSKI allegedly was held prisoner in AUSCHWITZ , where he became friends with Belgian co-prisoners, among whom was the father of the late minister André Cools.

[Note from translator: other source says KZ Mauthausen, not Auschwitz.]

Apparently Przedborski was liberated by a Russian general, for whom Przedborski set up some black market trafficking (jeans, Rolex,..)

Around 1950 PRZEDBORSKI left Russia, but he always stayed in contact.

His Belgian co-prisoners have taken care of things so he could come over to our country. Even at this early stage, PRZEDBORSKI was in contact with:

-CIA (Vienna station, Rome station) (the CIA appears to still be playing a role in this Nebula, in particular in respect of arms smuggle, for which payments were transferred via GEOFFREY's Bank).

-The VATICAN

-Italian MAFFIA

5.In 1956, PRZEDBORSKI was arrested in Germany for his involvement in the trafficking of nuclear materials with some Chinese.Chancelor Adenauer apparently intervened personally to keep him out of jail. (The file on this subject was filed at the BKA Bundes Kriminal Amt under the codename SPRINGER). It is rather amazing to find that PRZEDBORSKI continued the nuclear deals even when being a member of the IAEA in Vienna in his capacity of Ambassdor of Costa Rica! Have confirmed that PRZEDBORSKI Félix was indeed listed in the IAEA in Vienna as being Ambassador of Costa Rica.

6.Toward the end of the 70s, beginning of the 80s, PRZEDBORSKI allegedly directed a Belgium-based international arms smuggle, in exchange of which drugs (heroin) were delivered.

PRZEDBORSKI was a friend Carlos MONGE (president of Coast Rica-deceded) who had made him honorary consul of this Central-American nation neighbouring NICARAGUA and PANAMA.

(page 4)

He [Przedborski] initially has set up a heroin smuggle with the help of the Ambassadors of this country, among whom the Ambassador to Luxembourg and Geneva. Same for the Ambassadors in Warsaw and Moscow (apprarently arrested with 24 kg of heroin)

-The weapons have been shipped from FN Fabrique Nationale via the airport of Bierset (Liège) being initially aircargoed to NANTES / FRANCE from where they were flown to Costa Rica (to SANTA ELENA, a vast region inside that country).

On the way back, drugs were flown in.

-In this arms traffick, we were told, following persons were involved:

    a. André COOLS, ex-minister, assassinated;

    b. Roger BOAS (ASCO company)

    c. Abraham SHAVIT- assistant to Roger BOAS-personal friend of Israel minister BEGIN. It is said that André Cools stayed at Shavit's place whenever he visited Israel.

    d. Guy Mathot, ex-minister

    e. Paul Vanden Boeynants, ex-premier

    f. Fernand Beaurir, general commandant of the gendarmerie.

Apparently Henri SIMONET (at the time has was Foreign Affairs minister and had Alfred CAHEN and Anne-Marie LIZIN working for him) was in the know of this.

It is said that some Irangate weapons transited through this network to the Contras in Nicaragua (In this context it appeared that PRZEDBORSKI adressed a US president by his first name).

7. Around 1983, PRZEDBORSKI hired an ex-Mossad colonel to ensure his security and that of his group.

PRZEDBORSKI had known this colonel, who, still working for Mossad, intervened inofficially to liberate the daughter of the international arms trafficker 'Raymond NAKACHIAN' (phonetical spelling). After which the colonel and his team quit the Mossad and started working for Przedborski.

This colonel served as a middleman to set-up shop in Belgium for Ketib-El-Ketib (Lebanese financier) deceased??, to set-up shop for the PLO in Brussels. He also took care of the military training of CONTRAS and CALI Cartel personnel.

8. Around 1985/86, Leon DEFERM (personal friend of Guy Mathot, Edmond Leburton and Michel Daerden etc..) was introduced to PRZEDBORSKI, for whom he started to launder large amounts of money.

(page 5)

(In this context we were told of the involvement of French CGE Compagnie Générale des Eaux and Lyonnaise des Eaux)

It is interesting to note that Przedborski and Deferm shared a mistress by the name of Helena KOHLBRUNER, who was recently arrested in Geneva in possession of (securities/shares/bonds/notes).

-The person who introduced DEFERM was the Brussels lawyer Marc KADANER who was instrumental in the Nebula operations. KADANER allegedly held control over Bernard ANSELME, francophone community minister, who, rumor has it, can often be found drunk at 10 a.m.

We were told that another lawyer working for the Nebula was Mr AFSCHRIFT whose services were highly appreciated by the Russians.

9. In 1993 , following the ratification of the GATT, the European Economic Community revised the banana import quota. This revision could have been effective had it not been for the omission of one country from the resolution: Germany, where the transit of bananas remained authorized.

This decision of the CEE was apparently influenced by a conference that Przedborski organized at the occasion of a reception party at his private home in TERVUREN.

Following people attended:

-the president of Colombia,

-the president of Honduras,

-the president of Nicaragua,

-Mr Jacques Delors (president of the EEC commission)

-Mr Frederic Velghe (director Caisse Privée Bank)

-a certain Le Hoday

All illegal transhipments were routed through the Zeebrugge Northsea terminal, via the Eurocomer company, whose main financier was Caisse Privée Bank.

An info is transmitted to us, we cannot link this with the banana-terminal at Zeebrugge. Rather it is to be stipulated that it was through the terminal of the GHENT port that about 5.000.000 $ were laundered with the help of Alain De Rouck of Ghent and more specifically through the ELECTRORAIL company. We were told that Jean-Pierre VAN ROSSEM had set-up this laundering structure and that part of the laundered money was transferred to the Cayman Islands via Banque Brussel Lambert.

10. We obtained information on various of PRZEDBORSKI's money laundering intermediaries.

a. BERCOVITCH (two brothers)

-the first being employed in the diamond business, not involved.

-the second is an art dealer, owner of the BERCO art galleries in ANTWERP, BRUSSELS and KNOKKE.

(page 6)

Their lawyer was Me ROGGEN, daughter of the next character.

b. ROGGEN, Yvan (ex-governor of the Brabant province)
-member of the Grande Loge
-also honorary consul of Costa Rica
-private secretary of PRZEDBORSKI

c. the KRIWIN family (ex bankers)
-of which one daughter Anne is a lawyer at the Brussels bar

d. the SCHEYVEN family (father and son)
-one of the richest families in Belgium;
-(covert?) financiers of the PSC party [Christian Popular Party]
-active member of the CEPIC and financier of the PSC via the

AMELINCKX construction company.

[CEPIC was an extreme right wing group centered on PSC minister Paul Vanden Boeynants-linked to Cercle Pinay]

e. Frederic VELGHE (Caisse Privée Bank)

f. Pierre SALIK (a big importer of money for PRZEDBORSKI)
-his daughters were once the fiancées of PRZEDBORSKI's sons. We do not know why they never married.
-this person obviously is very important within the Nebula, especially in respect of the operations conducted by his son-in-law Michel DWEK (Belgian aged ca. 35)
-works together with Ronald BRUCKNER (see below)
-works together with his nephew Serge BORENSTEIN, who takes care of money transfers via PRAGUE.

g. Serge BORENSTEIN (ca. 45 years of age-nephew of Pierre SALIK)
-residing in Prague, formerly the capital of Czechoslovakia. Initially this was the main route for Przedborski to launder the proceeds of his criminal activity.
-as to this figure, we got infos from the Chinese criminal milieu: he served as a middleman for the acquisition of a real estate complex including the restaurants CITY OF THE DRAGON in Brussels (17 mll $) and Liège (12 mll $)-(see YANG file)

h. A MIAMI company (Florida/USA): NEW REPUBLIC

This company had an account at the CGER [ASLK, Algemene Spaar-en Lijfrente Kas]
Managed exclusively by PRZEDBORSKI Felix (mentioned supra) and Farouk KHAN (of the KHAN-gang). This account was liquidated in 1990 (when the new law on money laundering took effect) and the funds -2 bn $- were transferred to IRAQ.

i. Another company was mentioned that apparently was one of the most important ones and that was recently acquired by the Russians: COMUELE S.A.

(page 7)

This company, acquired in the early 80s, held 'stock value' of about 1.3 M$.
Since then a total of 200 M $ has been transferred in particular by Serge BORENSTEIN in Prague.
The company holds offices in ZAIRE, NETHERLANDS, LUXEMOURG.
In this company the following persons hold a position (cross

checked with VAT number 403.340.648-Commerce Register nr Brussels 15.175-Capital 681.441.715 Belgian Francs= ca. 22 M $)

According to our informant:
X-Bruno GOLDBERGER

(According to National Registers born in Czechoslovakia on 20 October 1947, of American nationality, divorced from Susana KASZIRER in 1989-see below-stricken from the ANTWERP population registers on 16 December 1994)

Real estate agent in Brussels

-works for a certain 'GLOBUS GROUP' (??? Nationality unknown)

-he mediated the entry of the Russians into COMUELE co

-he was introduced to the Russians by Maurice TEMPELSMAN, widower of Jacqueline Kennedy, herself widow of the American president)

-he allegedly met the Russians on the occasion of (his or her) birthday party in Brussels in 1994. One of these Russians was Mike BRANDWAIN (director of the M&S International company of Antwerp, being mentioned in the BLACKSTONE file as well as in a file on the Russian Maffia in New York-US Customs, July 1994)

Another Russian was called ADIC from Antwerp.

-At this dinner, some serious threats were exchanged. The Russians had invested 100 M $ in the COMUELE SA, it was said that the source of the money was Israel.

The reason was (according to our info) that the company capital was increased in 1990 but the Americans refused to participate. It was on this occasion that the Russians were invited in and consequently were swindled out of the 100 M $ they had hoped to launder or to invest.

According to HELP , the cy capital was increased from 9 M $ to 22 M $ in 1992.

The previous increase in cy capital was in 1989, lifting it to 3 M $ only.

X-Michel WOLF

-Belgian living in the Liège region

-manager of a.o. the Michel Wolf & Brothers cy

-parkings, parking meters etc..

(page 8)

X-Arthur FOGEL

-presently president of the SOGEPA company (Chaussée de Vleurgat nr 243 in 1050 Brussels)

-it has been reported that Bruno GOLDBERGER and Arthur FOGEL were looking for new company associates for COMUELE, candidates being the WOLF brothers and a certain BAUMANN

-on BAUMANN we can testify that he actually lives in PULLY near LAUSANNE in Switzerland, Chemin Chamblande 19, employé of UNIMEDICA cy of Froideville (near Lausanne).

-owns a residence on the beachfront at Saint Jean Cap Ferrat (S France)

-his working permit is actually under scrutiny from the Swiss authorities

-has studied Law and Finances in Antwerp and in the USA

-works for fiduciary companies in France & Switzerland

-appears to have become enormously wealthy, setting up money laundering systems, takes care personally of money transfers for the Russians.

X-Daniel WEECKERS

-Brussels broker

-adress Avenue Fr Roosevelt 94, Brussels

-works for 'Groupe 'DEFI'

-has business relations with Max TERET of FNAC and CANAL + (it was apparently through this French television company and through LYONNAISE DES EAUX that large amounts of money have been laundered on behalf of PRZEDBORSKI and/or others among which CREDIT LYONNAIS)

-his name was dropped as a candidate successor to PRZEDBORSKI.

X-Pierre SALIK

-involved personally or via companies whose names start with JA or JU.

X-the Russians

-recently took up some positions in the cy; there is a certain ADIC of Antwerp.

-we're talking about Russian maffiosi here
-among who the famous Mike Brandwain

X-Shilo MILLER

-is not officially on the cy records

-he represented the Israeli partners (who provided the 100 M $???)

-no further info available on this person

j. A particular laundering network within the PRZEDBORSKI group has been brought to our attention: the DIAMOND network of Antwerp.

The basis of PRZEDBORSKI's wealth appears to have been the Diamond trade and smuggle. As early as the 50s, when he arrived in Belgium, PRZEDBORSKI reportedly already enjoyed the friendship of the King of KASAI [rich province of the Belgian Congo] (To this end a structure has been set-up via Antwerp by the aforementioned Maurice TEMPELSMAN, a certain GOLDFINGER and a certain Leo SIMON).

This network (see item J.) seems to exist independently and is only used on occasion by PRZEDBORSKI.

Involved in it are the following persons:

X-Sylvain LINKER

-Belgian, notary public at JUMET

-this person is the founder of the front companies used for money laundering

-had some trouble with justice after having orchestrated the theft of his own paintings

X-Richard DAVIDOVITCH

-diamond trader of Antwerp

X-Michel KÖNIG

-diamond trader of Antwerp

X-The TACHE brothers

-diamond traders of Antwerp

X-the GOLDBERG brothers

-diamond traders of Antwerp

-the wife of one of the brothers is a judge in Antwerp

X-the ex-director of Sociéte Nationale d'Aviation Française (UTA)

<u>X-the ex-director of IAL</u>, Israel Air Lines, Ben ARI (father), also on the board of directors of the Liège-Bierset Airport.

<u>X-Charles BORNET</u>, a Brussels lawyer

x-Xavier MAGNEE
-Brussels lawyer, ex- president of the bar

X-the JACKIAN family (father & son)
-both lawyers, the father being an ex-president of the bar

k. we have been informed of the names of the banks involved in the PRZEDBORSKI group for money laundering:
-COLBERT Bank (named after the ex-minister of France)
-GLOBAL Bank of DÜSSELDORF
-DISCOUNT Bank with offices in Luxemburg and Geneva
-NATIONAL REPUBLIC BANK with offices in Luxembourg and New York. It seems that a certain SAFRA is in charge of the special transfers.

(page 10)

We have noticed that this bank is also being used by:
a.Paul Vanden Boeynants, ex-minister, ex-prime minister
b.Roger BOAS, from the ASCO company
c.Abraham SHAVIT
d.The MOSSAD

11. It is reported that within his Group, PRZEDBORSKI is assisted by the following persons
a. Bruno GOLDBERGER (see above)
-ex-husband of Suzanna KASZYRER, daughter of Joseph
We have been informed that in the early 80s Bruno GOLD-BERGER has set-up a financial structure that later proved to be used a diamonds laundering operation by his father-in-law. When GOLDBERGER discovered this, he quit. Apparently there must have been a court case involving diamond traders and the ABN-AMRO Bank.
In the course of the proceeding someone must have spilled the beans. This person then 'jumped' to his death from the 47th floor a NY building. It is said that the killing was ordered by Joseph KASZYRER.
b. Pierre SALIK
-involved in the COMUELE Co directly or through front compa-

nies whose names start with JA or JU.

-is in contact with the Australian billionaire Allan BOND.

(Allan BOND: Australian aged ca. 50, acknowledged billionaire in Australia.

Owner of millions of hectares of property on which drugs cultures are grown.

Associate of Albert FRERE (who helped BOND penetrate the Belgian market;

Owns 4.8% of Groupe Bruxelles Lambert-since he holds <5%, no declaration is required under Belgian law. Has initiated very important company take-overs in the USA.)

c. Ronald BRUCKNER (Belgian ca. 35 years of age)
-works in Germany for the East-European countries, a.o. Russia

-works in direct liaison with Michel DWEK (son-in-law of Pierre SALIK)

d. CALUWE-PUTSEYS ass. lawyers
-a member of the CALUWE family is member of the Loge du Grand Orient.

-this cabinet took charge of the defense of Pierre SALIK and Roland BRUCKNER
Who got ensnared in some smuggling operation with the eastern countries. It is said that they induced a procedural error by having some documents stolen, thus claiming that the defense attorneys had been unable to study the evidence. The theft was arranged when the files were transferred. The investigating judge was Guido BELLEMANS.

e. VANDERELST, Brussels lawyers (father & son)
1.Raymond (father):
-PRZEDBORSKI's attorney,
-Attorney for the Loge du Grand Orient of Belgium of which he is a member.
-Personal advisor to King Albert II
-Works or has worked for the cabinet of Pierre LAMBERT

2. Michel (son)
-was arrested in the case of the kidnapping of ex-premier Paul Vanden Boeynants, with the HAEMERS-gang

f. Koen BLIJWEERT (Belgian)
-very active in the money laundering business

-son of Renaat BLIJWEERT, directorof the now bankrupt AMELINCKX construction cy.

g. Jacques MAISON
-Brussels political figure (involved in city finances)
-involved in the affair of the (securities / stocks / bonds / funds/ notes)
-is the point-of-contact for a Luxembourg-based ' godfather'
-actually engaged in organizing funds to the tune of 100-130 M $ for the 'Eastern Countries'

h. Lionel PERL
-ca 45 years of age
-has been awarded a honorary title 'Grande Distinction' by SOL-VAY Cy
-works from Antwerp, laundering Russian capital
-worked for several banks, was kicked out of Bank de GROOF after it was discovered that he had installed a laundering mechanism in the bank.

i. Cardinal BELLINI
-lives in Brussels, Avenue Bellevue 55 or 57
-Vatican representative for real estate matters outside of Italy

Please note: Pope Paul II, who is a friend of PRZEDBORSKI's, after his OPUS DEI sponsored ascent to the pontificat, has appointed cardinal Rossi as the manager of Vatican real estate in Italie. The right hand of ROSSI was none other than cardinal Marcinkus who himself got entangled in the securities (bonds, stock..) affair linked to the Banco Ambrosiano debacle.

1. j. Patrick FOCQUET (Belgian)
-ex employee of TUBEMEUSE cy
-held a position in the SOCOFIN cy and Bank NAEGELMAECK-ERS

2. k. David PINSENT (American)
-manager of the peanut company PLANTATION TRUST
(page 12)

12. PRZEDBORSKI , Grand Master of the Jewish Loge, very influential in the political world either by friendship or corruption.

3. His business relations were:

a. André COOLS
-Belgian ex-minister, assassinated;
-PRZEDBORSKI had a special relationship with Cools, given the old friendship with Cools senior.
-they frequently met and got into man-to-man talks in ANTIBES / FRANCE

b. Willy DECLERK
-Belgian ex-minister
-actually member of EEC
-it is said that he is at the orders of PRZEDBORSKI

c. Willy CLAES
-Belgian ex-minister of Foreign Affairs (last position held)
-actually Secretary General of NATO in Brussels

d. Alfred CAHEN
-Belgian Ambassador to FRANCE
-his spouse is Mme Nicole de BEAUVAY, formerly first honorary assistant to queen Fabiola. She left the royal court when her husband took up his diplomatic position in Paris.
-Master of the Loge
-friend of late King Baudouin
-friend of Willy CLAES
-ex secretary general of Foreign Affairs ministry (headed by Mr SIMONET) where he issued a diplomatic passport to PRZEDBORSKI in 1986.
-at that moment in time, Anne-Marie LIZIN worked with SIMONET as well. LIZIN, given her intimate relationship with SIMONET, had the opportunity to collect evidence about the aforementioned arms deals, which could have resulted in her 'immunity'. She was also the mistress of André COOLS.

e. François MITTERAND
-president of FRANCE

f. Pierre BEREGOVOY
-French ex-minister
-committed suicide last year

g. Jacques DELORS
-president of the ECC commission
-French ex-minister of finances
-possible candidate for the French presidential elections

-worked for Banque de France [France National Bank]

h. ?? MERLY
-mayor of the city of ANTIBES/ FRANCE
We have been told that nearly all of Cap d'Antibes is the personally owned by PRZEDBORSKI who lives in a stunning property in the street 'Impasse Félix', named after him.
Following persons have been reported there:
-André COOLS
-Baron EMPAIN
-Didier PINEAU VALENCIENNES of the SCHNEIDER GROUP, involved in money laundering affair.

13. Presently PRZEDBORSKI group is working on a large scale tourist real estate project (1800 square KM) in Costa Rica (SANTA ELENA), a 2 Bn $ investment.

Involved in this project:
-the chain CONRAD and Romi BARON (formerly of the MONI-TOR Cy and CENTRE ROGIER in Brussels)
-'GAONE' from Geneva
-Leon DEFERM

14.Felix PRZEDBORSKI is reported to be ill, so an internal succession struggle is developing.

Candidates:
a. Daniel PRZEDBORSKI (his son, lawyer in Brussels)
b. Daniel WEECKERS (broker, involved in COMUELE S.A.)
c. Two or three Frenchmen:
Among who Max TERET, friend of Felix PRZEDBORSKI, director of CANAL + (through which money was laundered in cooperation with Lyonnaise des Eaux)

15. We were able to piece together following chronology:

1984: association of A. FOGEL and B. GOLDBERGER on the one hand, and Joseph KASZIRER on the other.
They set-up a structure for real estate investment, founding a company for each acquisition, functioning as a recycling machine for cash derived from 'black' dealings in diamonds in Antwerp and NY.
The general set-up being taken care of by Charles DILLEY

(Brussels lawyer) via a Luxemburg holding cy , funds being transferred via ABN-AMRO Bank and NATIONAL REPUBLIC BANK of NY.

1987: splitting of association, but FOGEL and GOLDBERGER stick together.

Two events then follow:

1-they meet BAUM and STEINMETZ.

2-they get in touch with D. WEECKERS and through him with

PRZEDBORSKI Felix (his daughters being engaged to the SA-LIK sons)

SALIK, Pierre (associate of GOLDBERGER in SOGEPA Cy and others)

BORENSTEIN, Serge (nephew of SALIK)

COOLS André

1988/89. Big merger with COMUELE of which they grab control through Daniel WEECKERS.

1990. Felix PRZEDBORSKI has liquidated his account (the NEW REPUBLIC account) at CGER (ASLK) so 2 Bn $ are transferred and Serge BORENSTEIN gets the washing machine started in PRAGUE.

The COMUELE Cy is getting into financial trouble, needs capital urgently.

The Americans refuse to participate to increase capital.

C. GOLDBERGER enters the Russians via Maurice TEM-PELSMAN, they accept to invest 100 Mn $. It is stipulated that the capital originates from Israel. FOGEL and GOLDBERGER are aware of that.

The Americans exit the company.

By the end of 1994, COMUELE is unable to pay interests due.

October 1994: the Russians get real angry and threaten several people, they invite GOLDBERGER to UKRAINE for some explanations.

16. The reasons for our transmitting this report before having cross-checked are multiple.

-the most important reason, or so it appears to us, is that a group of journalists has obtained informations similar to ours, having obtained those through channels and by means differing from ours which results in their informations being more complete and verified in several countries.

-these journalist allegedly are very determined to bring it all out in their respective newspapers (the start of the revelations should have been scheduled for Saturday 18th march 1995 ... a verification problem, now solved, has caused the publication to be pushed back another week).

-we have been told that they would go so far as to cause a national strike of the journalists (note from the undersigned: which could eventually cause an incontrollable government crisis) if they were to be prohibited to publish their news articles. In case the pressure on the Belgian press would prove too strong, other journalists (French, Italian, American..) would take over and proceed to get these informations published. (note of undersigned: again situation incontrollable)

-we are in a position to get in touch with these journalists without really knowing what their demands are

-in any case, it seems that they have made great progress in their verifications, one being that the director of ISI-Limbourg in (city) Hasselt, Mister Stockman, allegedly has assisted Félix Przedborski (or his group) in figuring-out a construction that allows fiscal planning (which could of course also be used for money laundering).

-these journalists appear to have corroborated that the affairs [events, scandals] of the last few years are linked and in particular they seem to have obtained information on the investments, real estate and other, of Mr Willy Claes (and/or of his party [socialist]) in Spain.

17. Let's not forget that this Nebula controls most of the money transfers worldwide and also controls the highest political authorities.

This Nebula could, if so desired, put pressure on most of the important cities worldwide and get control over the almost everything (energy supply, water supply, environment), through corruption. This has been going on for several years.

Let's not forget that this same Nebula provides the security forces, Police and Military to several countries, including their equipment (weapons, communications etc..).

Listed as being part of this structure:

GEC General Electric Cy (weapons, water supply, etc..

ALSTHOM

BELL

ALCATEL: communications

SCHNEIDER

CGE COMPANIE GENERALE DES EAUX
LYONNAISE DES EAUX
Etc..

(signed)
HODY, Jean-Marie   DECK, Didier
1 MDL   1 MDL

Reviewed,
GRAFF, Commandant
Officer Resp BSR.

Appendix 2A: PV 18367 2001 (French)

Police Fédérale
Service judiciaire
ARRONDISSEMENT
de
BRUXELLES

Fraud Squad

Rue des Quatre Bras, 13
1000 - BRUXELLES

L'an deux mil un, le vingt-trois du mois d'août à 13,30 heures,

Nous, Bruno FAMENNE,

Inspecteur judiciaire divisionnaire, officier de Police judiciaire, auxiliaire de monsieur le procureur du Roi, exposons que dans le cadre de nos recherches tendant à établir la réalité des relations d'Eric VAN DE WEGHE et autres individus, il ressort ce qui suit.

Eric VDW nous a déclaré connaître et rencontrer actuellement le nommé PRZEDBORSKI Félix, il s'agit d'un ami de son père Edouard. Ils se sont rencontrés dans le milieu de Knokke qu'ils fréquentaient tous les deux.

***

Il s'identifie comme étant :
PRZEDBORSKI Félix, né en Pologne, le 12.12.1930, de nationalité belge, ép KRYGIER Hélène, administrateur de société, résidant depuis le 8.11.1960 au Costa Rica.
Lui et sa femme étaient rayés le 27.9.78 de son adresse en Belgique pour le Costa Rica.

Il apparaît toutefois que le précité est régulièrement installé en Belgique.

***

PRZEDBORSKI est connu de nos services.
Les éléments suivants ont été extraits de notre documentation nationale.

En 1954, il a été condamné à quatre mois d'emprisonnement avec amendes pour faux et usage de faux et port public de faux nom.

Par la suite, il est cité dans diverses affaires délictueuses, fraude fiscale, faux et usage de faux.

En 1979, il st signalé par les autorités américaines comme faisant partie d'un réseau mondial de trafic d'armes et de stupéfiants entre le Vietnam et les USA.

Λ

Appendix 2B: 2B-PV 18367 (English Translation)

Federal Police:

ANNEX 1 TO PROCES VERBAL 18367/2001 JUDICIARY SECTION
BRUSSELS DISTRICT
Fraud Squad
Rue des Quatrebras, 13
1000-Brussels

The year two thousand and one, twenty-third of august at 13.30hrs

I, Bruno Famenne, divisional judiciary inspector, judiciary police officer, assistant to the Public Prosecutor, bring to light that in the context of the investigations aiming at establishing the real connections of Eric VAN DE WEGHE and other individuals, the following has been discovered.

Eric VDW has acknowledged that he actually knows and presently has contact with an individual named Felix PRZEDBORSKI, a friend of his father Edouard. They met in the milieu of Knokke, which they both used to frequent.

* * *

Said person is identified as follows.
PRZEDBORSKI Felix, born in Poland on 12.12.1930, of Belgian nationality, married to KRYGIER Hélène, director of companies, residing in Costa Rica since 8th november 1960.
He and his wife officially checked out for Costa Rica on 27 september 1978.

Still, it could be established that the cited individuals frequently reside in Belgium.

* * *

PRZEDBORSKI is known by our services.
The following elements were taken from the national documentation.

In 1954, he was convicted to four months of imprisonment and fined for fiscal fraud, forgery and the use of forged documents.

In 1979 he was cited by the American authorities as being part of a global network of arms and drugs trafficking between Vietnam and the USA.

Annex 2 to Proces Verbal 18367/2001

In the same report the following individuals were cited: UNGAR Mauricio (° 24 feb 1919), LIPINSKY Jean (° in Frankfurt?), RABELBAUER Bela (°19 may 1934), BOURLA Michel (° in Paris?).

This network was allegedly controlled by an American, Roberto VESCO, who has taken refuge in Costa Rica.

At the time PRZEDBORSKI allegedly took advantage of his status of permanent representative of the Costa Rican government to the atomic agency in Vienna.

In 1981, in the context of dossier 33/81 of M. LAMBEAU, Brussels examining magistrate in the case of the forgery and the attempt to mislead the tax authorities, it has been established after a house search that the AMERICAN LEVANT INDUSTRIE company rented office space to the SERDAN company in order for this latter company to set up a fake mailbox office at Square de l'Aviation 2 in Anderlecht.

The SERDAN company is named after the sons of PRZEDBORSKI, Serge and Daniël. This company is involved in a giant tax fraud, as is the Anstalt TRADIN company, established in Liechtenstein. This company has offices in Auderghem, avenue des Traquets 38.

This company was involved in a fiscal fraud of several billion francs via a system of money transfers and invoices between LUFTHANSA and SERDAN. The latter company manufactured travel bags.

In the context of dossier 24/00 of M. VAN ESPEN, examining magistrate, it became clear that buildings 25-25-27, owned by ABRAHAM, were publicly auctioned in 1997 and sold to the CASSANDRA company for 27 million francs. The manager of this company is VANDEBERGH Johan (°17 April 1966), who admitted having acted as a puppet for Patrick ABRAHAM.

The SERDAN company is being managed by proxy by an individual named DELEEUW (°11 January 1914), manager of the COGESCO company.

The same investigation by M. LAMBEAU brought to light the existence of bank accounts in Düsseldorf, Germany, at the GLOBAL BANK, owned by TRADIN, SERDAN, PRZEDBORSKI Felix and KRYGIER Hélène. It also became clear that this bank extended a 150.000.000 francs loan to the TRADIN company.

From info collected at the official registry of real estate it appears that the buildings located at numbers 585 and 587 square du Bois in Brussels are the property of TRADIN ESTABLISHMENT, a foreign registered company with address in Tervuren, avenue Charles de Lorraine 13.

I attach to this PV a copy of an article about these buildings that was taken from the weekly magazine L' EVENTAIL .

ANNEX 3 TO PV 18367/2001

PRZEDBORSKI 's residential address in Belgium is avenue Charles de Lorraine 13.

Most of PRZEDBORSKI 's assets remain hidden behind fake companies and strawmen.

He enjoys the comfort of his villa in Knokke-Le-Zoute, Zwinlaan 18.

On 13 July 1981 the French police searched villa Campanelle in Antibes, domaine de la Garoupe, which was rented by the person in question.

On 18 July 1981 a search was completed in Tervuren, avenue Charles de Lorraine 13. A Costa Rican diplomatic passport with the picture and the name of Herbert Cullman was found.

One of the strawmen in his service was an ex-police officer by the name of Joseph Gilissen, born 8 June 1907, now deceased, who lived at Wezembeek-Oppem.

PRZEDBORSKI Felix entertains high level political contacts, on September 20, 1979 he received a diplomatic passport issued by the minister of Foreign Affairs. His wife KRYGIER Hélène received one as well.

These passports were issued on the direct orders of minister SIMONET, whose chef de cabinet was the late Alfred CAHEN.

The latter exerted considerable pressure to have passports of the same type issued to his sons Serge and Daniel.

These passports were called in by a civil servant by the name of M. Fernand DEWILDE (ambassador ?) after a series of punishable offences.

On 7 July 1981 these passport were re-issued on the direct request of Alfred CAHEN.

At this point it should be noted that the latter 's son is Max-Olivier CAHEN, an accomplice of Eric VDW.

During the investigation we discovered a copy of an informal letter from Alfred CAHEN to VDW about the past of Alexandre GALLEY. This letter was added to the files. Its authenticity could be doubtful.

Information collected from the Interpol files the following shows the following.
An investigation on the subject of PRZEDBORSKI Felix is conducted in 1997 by the OBSHAK group, the national ROC team of the Brigade Nationale, judiciary police.

PRZEDBORSKI allegedly is acting on behalf of a high level Russian criminal organisation of which Serguei MIKHAILOV is part.

Annex 4 to PV 18367/2001
He thereby puts to use the privileges accorded to him on behalf of his fake diplomatic status as honorary consul of Costa Rica.

These investigations are under the scrutiny of the national magistrate since 1995. Within this context, information is being spread internationally by Interpol at the request of inspector Pierre DELILEZ.

PRZEDBORSKI 's name appears in the André COOLS murder file.

It should be noted that Eric VAN DE WEGHE obviously dedicates particular attention to the person of MIKHAILOV, portrayed in this report.

Within the context of a different case we find the following.

In April 2000 the police authorities of Vaduz in Liechtenstein put forward a request concerning a large number of individuals and companies in several countries who are involved in a major money laundering operation.

From this we take the following names that could be relevant in this present case: PRZEDBORSKI Felix, UHODA Gabriel, MIKHAILOV Serguei and RICH Marc (°18 December 1934), an unknown Belgian national. The latter is not listed in the national registers.

Further investigation in our files revealed that RICH Marc is American, of Belgian descent, born in Antwerp. He was on the wanted list in our country in 2001, in accordance with a request from INTERPOL Washington and with an international arrest warrant. He was consequently delisted as requested by the Americans after he had been pardoned. No details provided. The grounds cited for the arrest warrant were fiscal fraud estimated at 100 million USD, embezzlement, extortion and conspiracy.

I attach to the present PV some excerpts from the collected financial documents in respect of the mandates held by Felix, Serge and Daniel PRZED-BORSKI, Eric DE CLERCQ as well as those pertaining to the companies TRADIN, SINT HUBERTUS RIDDERHOF and COGESCO.

Eric DE CLERCQ has taken over from Marc DELEEUW, who resigned from his job at COGESCO.

In the SINT HUBERTUS RIDDERHOF company the PRZEDBOR-SKIs are listed as stakeholders only, with the exception of Serge. The latter, a medical doctor, also heads the CENTRE HARVEY CUSHIN, 34 avenue des Archiducs in Watermael-Boitsfort, that takes care of people suffering from brain tumours and other brain deficiencies.

The financial information does not cover the SERDAN company.

Duly noted,

Appendix 3: MORGAN-GENERAL ELECTRIC-GERMAN BANKS-CGE1

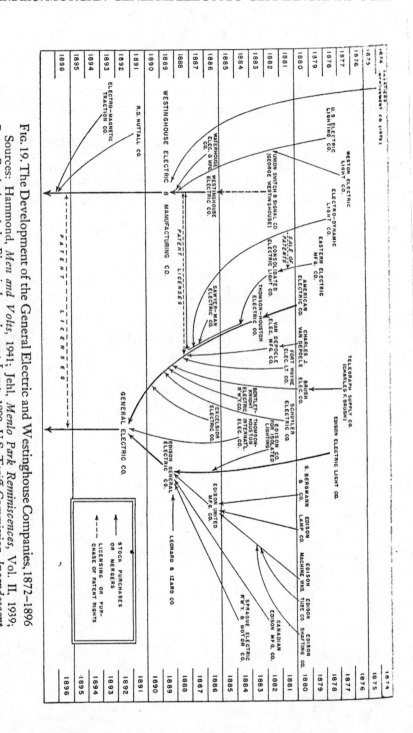

Fig. 19. The Development of the General Electric and Westinghouse Companies, 1872–1896
Sources: Hammond, *Men and Volts*, 1941; Jehl, *Menlo Park Reminiscences*, Vol. II, 1939;
Pope, *Evolution of the Electric Incandescent Lamp*, 1889; U.S. Tariff Commission, *Incandescent Electric Lamps*, 1939; and others.

Appendix 3: MORGAN-GENERAL ELECTRIC-GERMAN BANKS-CGE2

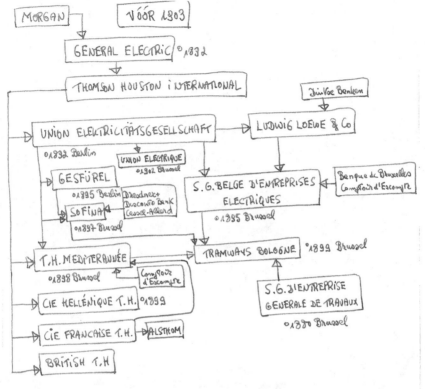

Appendix 4: PRZEDBORSKI-MERLI-MITTERRAND-POMPIDOU-ROTH-SCHILD

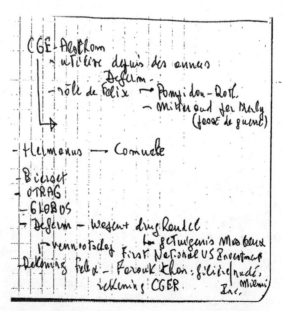

APPENDIX 5: PRZEDBORSKI-GARDEN PARTY-ANTIBES2-DEMORGEN 8APRIL95

APPENDIX 6: SPANDRE-LINK AGINTER PRESS-NATO-COUP 1974

1 RAGGRUPPAMENTO OPERATIVO SPECIALE CARABINIERI

Reparto Eversione

Nr.509/62 di prot. "P". Roma, 23 Luglio 1996.

OGGETTO: Procedimento penale contro Rognoni Giancarlo ed altri.

Annotazione sulle attività di guerra psicologica e non ortodossa, (psychological and low density warfare) compiute in Italia tra il 1969 e il 1974 attraverso l' "AGINTER PRESSE".

4. Ulteriore possibile connessione N.A.T.O. della Aginter Presse 12

4. ULTERIORE POSSIBILE CONNESSIONE N.A.T.O. DELLA "AGINTER PRESSE"

Essa è illustrata nella nota 509/6-1 del 10-01-1995 (All.11). L'esistenza di un canale belga di approvvigionamento di armi, pur senza la menzione del nominativo dell'Avv. SPANDRE, veniva confermata dal noto ETTORE MALCANGI nel verbale reso a personale di questo Reparto in data 28-11-1995 su delega della Procura di BRESCIA (All.12).

Nello stesso verbale il MALCANGI offre un duplice riscontro sull'identità tra il canale da lui menzionato e quello contenuto nella nota 509/6-1:

A) esso era utilizzato dal M.A.R.;

B) doveva venire utilizzato per il colpo di stato del 1974.

In data 14-03-1996 l'ORLANDO, in relazione alla nota 509/6-1, affermava che lo SPANDRE non aveva partecipato al pranzo presso il ristorante del Comando N.A.T.O. a Bruxelles ove erano presenti italiani ed Ufficiali americani conoscitori della lingua italiana. Sosteneva di non essere in grado di poter dire se lo SPANDRE sapesse della riunione o meno. Aveva compreso che l'Avvocato trafficava in armamenti pesanti. Ciò a verbale delegato dalle AA.GG. di Milano, Brescia e Bologna.

Appendix 7: Karfinco-Almany-Socialist Parties Funding

Source: Archives Walter De Bock

PRZEDBORSKi ⟶ Tradin

Ls louis Michel

(ancien président/PRL)

Almany NV

Karfinco   Structure Dufflot

Pacini Battaglia.

hydrocarbure de P.B

Dufdet

FIMO

ENi

SNAM

PS I.

PS F.

PS lux

PS

APPENDIX 8A: FAX JP VAN ROSSEM

25-APR-95 12:21   DRS FRANSSEN ARNAUD J P A   +32 089 714278   PAGINA 1

J.P. VAN ROSSEM   **KRANTENREDACTIE**

volksvertegenwoordiger   **BINNENLANDSE POLITIEK**

Leuvenseweg 14

1008 BRUSSEL

DE WAARHEID OVER AGUSTA en spreekverbod in de Kamer

Een dertigtal personen (allen personeelsleden van de Kamer van Volksvertegenwoordigers) waren vandaag getuige van een mooi staaltje democratie in het parlementaire halfrond. Toen volksvertegenwoordiger J.P. Van Rossem om 12.36 aan het spreekgestoelte het woord nam om belangrijke relevaties te doen in de zaak Agusta werd hem omwille van ordemaatregelen, na het noemen van de naam Felix Przedborski, door de plaatsvervangende voorzitter het woord ontnomen en dit in aanwezigheid van Minister Johan van de Lanotte. Zijn parlementaire medewerkers waren getuige van het feit dat de camera's van Reuter werden stilgelegd en de publieke tribune ontruimd. Tevens werd de microfoon uitgezet en op uitspraak van de waarnemende voorzitter zijn woorden uit het verslag geschrapt. omdat de Heer Van Rossem aldus de waarnemende Voorzitter zich niet hield aan de   punten van de dagorde zijnde de grondswetsartikelen die voor wijziging vatbaar waren. Toen Van Rossem weigerde om het spreekgestoelte te verlaten werd de vergadering geschorst. Het is ver gekomen in een parlementaire democratie wanneer een volksvertegenwoordiger in de Kamer zijn eigen mening niet meer mag verwoorden over corruptie en financiële schandalen van ex-regeringsleden. In bijlage treft U de volledige eindtoespraak van J.P. Van Rossem aan. Indien U uw lezers de waarheid niet wilt weerhouden inzake Agusta en de democratische beginselen van persvrijheid ondanks Uw overheidssubsidies nog hoog houdt kunt U wellicht in Uw volgende editie gewag maken van dit staaltje van spreekverbod. Hoogachtend.

J.P. Van Rossem

*+32089714278   25.04.95 13:09 P01

APPENDIX 8B-FAX JP VAN ROSSEM TRANSLATION

J.P. VAN ROSSEM   EDITORIAL OFFICE
Member of Parliament   DOMESTIC POLITICS
Leuvenseweg 14
1008 BRUSSELS

THE TRUTH ABOUT AUGUSTA and gag order in the Parliament

About thirty persons (all staff members of the Parliament) today wit-nessed a fine piece of democracy in the Parliamentary arena. MP J.P. Van Rossem took the stand at 12.36 hrs to reveal some important information on the subject of Agusta. When he named Felix Przedborski the President stopped him on account of the restoration of order in the Parliament. This happened in the presence of minister Johan Van De Lanotte. The latter 's parliamentiary assistants witnessed how the Reuters' cameras were switched off and the public benches evacuated. At the same time the mi-crophone was switched off and his statement deleted from the records, on order of the President.
[...]
When Van Rossem refused to leave the stand, the session was adjourned. What has come of our democracic system if an MP is not even allowed to voice his opinion about the corruption and financial scandals of ex-gov-ernment members?
[...]
In case you wouldn't want to withhold the truth about Agusta from your readers and respect the democratic principles of freedom of the press (de-spite your state subsidies), you might want to report about this case of state censorship in your next edition. Sincerely.

J.P. Van Rossem

APPENDIX 9- GBL-FRERE-DESMARAIS-LYONNAISE-TRACTEBEL

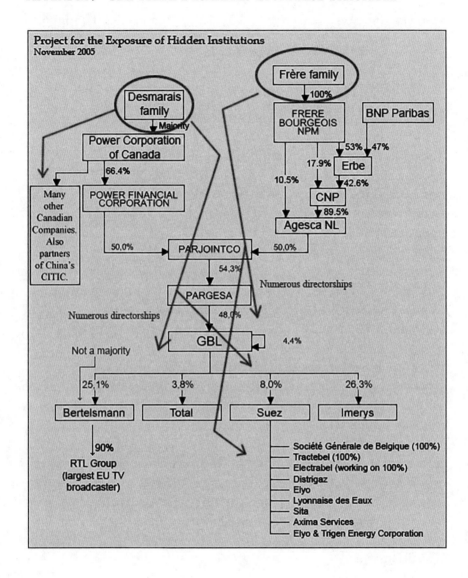

APPENDIX 9B-GBL-FRERE -DESMARAIS-SUEZ-PERNOD RICARD

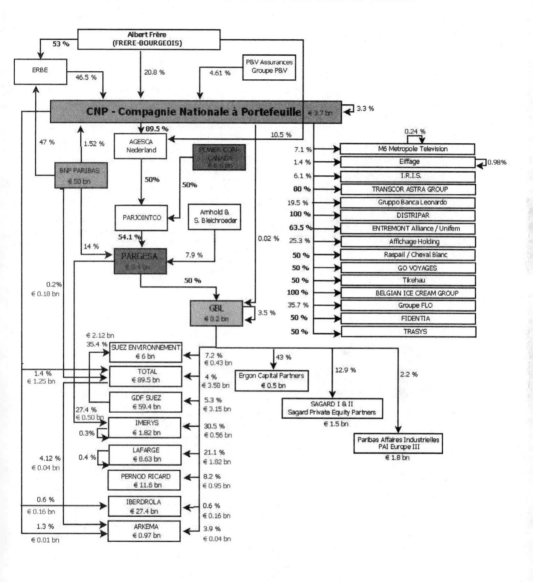

Appendix 10: Gunther Grass Poem

What must be said

Why have I kept silent, held back so long,
on something openly practised in
war games, at the end of which those of us
who survive will at best be footnotes?

It's the alleged right to a first strike
that could destroy an Iranian people
subjugated by a loudmouth
and gathered in organized rallies,
because an atom bomb may be being
developed within his arc of power.

Yet why do I hesitate to name
that other land in which
for years – although kept secret –
a growing nuclear power has existed
beyond supervision or verification,
subject to no inspection of any kind?

This general silence on the facts,
before which my own silence has bowed,
seems to me a troubling, enforced lie,
leading to a likely punishment
the moment it's broken:
the verdict "Anti-semitism" falls easily.

But now that my own country,
brought in time after time
for questioning about its own crimes,
profound and beyond compare,
has delivered yet another submarine to Israel,
(in what is purely a business transaction,
though glibly declared an act of reparation)
whose speciality consists in its ability
to direct nuclear warheads toward
an area in which not a single atom bomb
has yet been proved to exist, its feared
existence proof enough, I'll say what must be said.

But why have I kept silent till now?
Because I thought my own origins,
tarnished by a stain that can never be removed,
meant I could not expect Israel, a land
to which I am, and always will be, attached,
to accept this open declaration of the truth.

Why only now, grown old,
and with what ink remains, do I say:

Israel's atomic power endangers
an already fragile world peace?
Because what must be said
may be too late tomorrow;
and because – burdened enough as Germans –
we may be providing material for a crime
that is foreseeable, so that our complicity
will not be expunged by any
of the usual excuses.

And granted: I've broken my silence
because I'm sick of the West's hypocrisy;
and I hope too that many may be freed
from their silence, may demand
that those responsible for the open danger
we face renounce the use of force,
may insist that the governments of
both Iran and Israel allow an international authority
free and open inspection of
the nuclear potential and capability of both.
No other course offers help
to Israelis and Palestinians alike,
to all those living side by side in enmity
in this region occupied by illusions,
and ultimately, to all of us.

By Günther Grass

Appendix 11: Wanta-Cheney FAX-De Groot

<u>CC</u>: OFFICE OF THE PRESIDENT - WASHINGTON

14 Sep 11

legal Groups

TO: H.E. VICE PRESIDENT DICK CHENEY

H.E. AMB LEO E. WANTA   FAX:

was approached & my help was requested in moving large sums of cash into (Foundations) to be formed, for "charitable" work here in the Philippines. Approx. amount is 300T PHP of which 30% is offered as a "gift" to the USA. This lady is "Muslim" she is accompanied by a Major Dato who studied business/banking & flying in Afganistan!!, there are "dato's" with her!"

German m family has financed a large group who were recovering FRN boxes, which were taken to US, Germany & Moldova. Representatives of family are in Las Vegas, trying to collect, however, boxes in Germ. were allegedly confiscated! The group includes: Robert Haich, Bul Rahman of L. Vegas, Robert Wachtel, Brad K. Lee, Allan Nichols and many others in Manila, Francis Hernandez of CA now in Cebu, de Groot in Belg. & Peter Sermat in UK. They "family" want their boxes!! Things are getting out of hand!

Re: Francis Hernandez; look to Col. Vina who was prov. comm. of Cavite & Cebu, his boss was P. Lacson... all is interconnected... with the above people being small fry... look to chinese connection!!! Always!!

MIL needs the cash with which to purchase & remove these items... too much is in the wrong hands... & too much is going into the wrong hands!! If we are to be successful here, I have outlined how to do it. One other thing we must have is transportation "permits"...

(28)

TOTAL 2 PAGES Ben Yehuda Str. 25, Tel Aviv 63807, ISRAEL.
P.O.B. 4325, Tel Aviv 61 042, TLX:361319 ROSEN
Tel: (972) (3) 650831 FAX: 651452.

FAX Transmission

Tel Aviv:
Message No. 14-MAY 1990
TO Fax No.

RE: RM COMMODITY Att: MR LEO WANTS

SUBJECT TO CONTRACT CAN SUPPLY RM IN
POWDER FORM, THIS IS THE REGULAR TYPE,
AS LIQUID DOES NOT KEEP OVER A PERIOD
OF ONE YEAR X FROM POWDER MATERIAL
20.2 N 23 CAN BE DONE BY BUYER OR
ACC. SPEC OF THE BUYER SELLER WILL PRE-
PARE X

1) PRICE OF POWDER # 358 PER GRAM
NOT INCLUDING OUR COMMISSION
IF BUYER WANTS SELLER TO PREPARE LIQUID
FORM FROM THE POWDER PRICE # 335/GRAM
WITHOUT OUR COMMISSION

FROM ONE GRAM POWDER SUPPLIERS WILL
PREPARE ABOUT 1.3 GR LIQUID

WE WOULD LIKE TO GET INCASE BUSINESS
DEVELOP N P BOND. 2% OPENED, IF FOR
ANY REASON SUPPLIERS DOES NOT DELIVER
WE ENTITLED TO 1% OF THE P BOND.
ENCLOSE SPEC FOR THE POWDER N LIQUID
PLS ADVISE BEST REGARDS
ARIE

TELAVIV 17 MAY 1990

Ben Yehuda Str. 25, Tel Aviv 63807, ISRAEL.
P.O.B. 4325, Tel Aviv 61 042, TLX:361319 ROSE
Tel: (972) (3) 650831 FAX: 651452.

FAX Transmission

Tel Aviv:
Message No.
TO Fax No.

DEAR LEO,

Att: MR LEO WANTA

FURTHER (PREVIOUS) PREVIOUS EXCHANGE
OF CORRESPONDANCE &

SUBJECT TO CONTRACT, WE CAN SUPPLY
AS AGENTS EVERY WEEK 3 FLASKS &
PRICE DOLLARS 370 PER GRAM FOR
FIRST FLASK & AS YOU ARE AWARE
PRICES ARE MOVING ACC. TO MARKET.
THIS ACCORDING COLOUR YOU REQUESTED.
SELLERS SUGGEST YOU DEPOSITE FUNDS IN VIEN
FOR FIRST FLASKS IN BANK IN (ESCROW
ESCROW, THEN PROCEED TO FIRST CLASS
LAB. ACCORDING YOUR CHOICE IN A
NEIGHBOURING COUNTRY TO AUSTRIA,
GET LAB REPLY, RETURN TO VIENNA
RELEASE FUNDS AND GET GOODS &
THIS WAY YOU/BUYER WILL BE PROTECTED.
IN CASE YOU/NEED CONTRACT SELLERS/
BUYERS CAN MEET N DRAW CONTRACT.
PLS ADVISE WHEN CAN WE MEET IN VIENNA
TO MEET N START THE BALL ROLLING &

245

Appendix 13: Cesium133-Wanta-Tremonti Jack

Artikel   Jurgen — Mustefha
                                    AL KASTAWI
                           \ Felix artikel sturen

— Ro Premier Silaiev forceerde te Roebel-operatie
    om westerse consumgoederen te kunnen importeren

— Wanta met Silaiev in ongenade ± in 11.90

— Jack Tremonti Italo-amerikeen uit Detroit
        76 in Michigan veroordeeld wegens diefstal + hendel
        met gestolen goed

— Wanta arrestatie 20.7.93 in Genève — ± bedrog Charleston Bank
    — trou Wanta-groep   iom NR-USA aktiviteiten
    — in Vicenza Koericier met [Cesium 133] Rerhaeldelyk
        geancesteerd   in besteg genomen
    — leide naar internationale smokkel wegen + nukleeri
    — NR-USA levade nukleair material
    — Vanloa voor naar Tremonti
        25 miljoen doller ofte in rekeningen uitterdels
            bij "Handelsbeuk" v.d. chemische industrie
                                                van Rusland"
                    = HIMBANK
                    Moscou + Rochester (N.Y.)
                — blijkt ge witwesoperatie te syn
                    yd Russische + USA-mafia met Tremonti
                    volgens Russ + Ital

— Wanta benute firma Anthem in Roebeltransekties
— "   in Japen wegens devizen smokkel gesegnord
— "   _Oostenryk zwendel met kreditkaarta 7.90

— Sulevital medewerker van Tremonti

zeer gevaarlyk
afvelproduct
radioactief
etm.

APPENDIX 14: PRZEDBORSKI-NUCLEAR-AVVENIMENTI-FRANCO

07-MAG-1999 16:44   AVVENIMENTI 0657105212   0039 6 732489   P.02

Dear Jurgen, I'm sorry if I didn't answered before. Anyway, this is what I could find out at the moment.

1) There is one prosucutor in the north of Italy that is investigating about russian mafia. Among the subjects of the investigations there is also nuclear smuggling.

2) The Russian mafia have already invested in Italy some 100 billion of US dollars. The Russians would use Italy as a aircraft carrier to colonize western countries.

3) There is a Italian family who invested in Costa Rica. This family (Agusta) owned a company wich produced elicopters. In the early Ninghtees it was a scandal in Belgium about a sold of these elicopters. In the magistrature investigations there are some names who are linked to Przedborski. As you told me he also have investements in Costa Rica.

4) I didn't wrote articoles specificly about Przedborski. But I collected some informations about nuclear smuggling in Europe and in Russia. The problem is that I have the information in a file recorded in a floppy disk, wich is damaged. I asked to an computer expert who works in my newspaper to find out this file. I promised me to do it before tuesday. At that time I will send you as more detailed informations as I can.

5) When I was in South Africa I red his name in a investigation about smuggling of drugs and weapons in the Eightees. The problem is that I only could red this police statement, I haven't here in Italy. Anyway if you want specificly things about South Africa you could ask me.

One more time sorry for the late. I promise to send you the other informations tuesday. Best regards Franco.

APPENDIX 15: LIBERT MICHEL TESTIMONY-DINA-CHILE

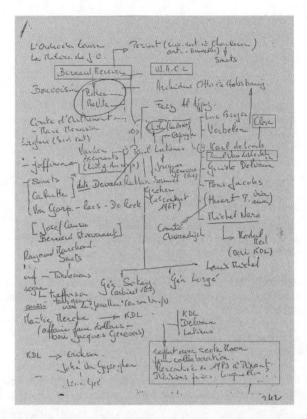

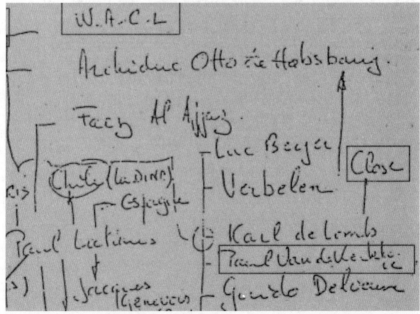

APPENDIX 16: SS WEWELSBURG SS

INCOMING CLASSIFIED MESSAGE   PAGE NO. _____

CENTRAL INTELLIGENCE GROUP

FROM: [   ]   PRIORITY

TO: SPECIAL OPERATIONS   14 APR 47

ACTION: COPS (1)   IN 12324

INFORMATION: ADSO (2)

PARAPHRASE NOT REQUIRED. HANDLE AS   SECRET
CORRESPONDENCE PER PARAS 81 (1) 60A AR-380-5.

SECRET   COPY 3

TO: WASH   CITE: M [   ] SOO: [   ] Evaluation   see KSM: 11 Apr 4

OAK [   ] RAMONA.

1. HC/351 HAS SUBMITTED DETAILED REPORT CONCERNING RECENT 11-DAY VISIT WITH ELLA TURNER. REPORT POUCHED TO WASH TODAY.

2. SHE HAS COMPLETE DOUBLE DOCUMENTATION IN NAME OF ELISA TURNER AND IVONE PANEA. THE ORGANIZATION HAS A LABORATORY LOCATED AT TORRE MONSERRAT, BARCELONA, WHERE THEY ARE WORKING INTENSELY ON INVESTIGATION AND MEANS OF PUTTING INTO PRACTICE BACTERIOLOGICAL WARFARE, WHICH THEY CONSIDER MORE IMPORTANT THAN ATOMIC ENERGY.

3. BC 364 STATES THEY INDICATED THAT MARTIN BORMANN IS NOW IN THE INTERIOR OF ARGENTINA AND HAS IN HIS POSSESSION THE TESTAMENT OF HITLER.

4. BC 364 DEDUCED FROM CONVERSATIONS CONCERNING LEON DEGRELLE THAT HE IS NOW IN THE INTERIOR OF SPANISH MOROCCO, AND THAT THE REAL ROBERT RIEGO HAD BEEN THERE WITH DEGRELLE FOR SOMETIME.

SECRET

APPENDIX 18: NAZI INTERNATIONAL-CIA DOC 1956

SECRET

NOFORN CONTINUED CONTROL

JX-8724

9 January 1956

MEMORANDUM FOR: RI Files

SUBJECT: The Fascist International

Attached is a report on Fascist organizations and personalities as provided by a sensitive and usually reliable source. It is requested that the names of organizations and individuals be indexed and the basic document be filed by you.

C/CI/SPD

NOFORN CONTINUED CONTROL

SECRET RI COPY

200-7-197-9-4

Declassified and Approved for Release
by the Central Intelligence Agency
Date: 2005

NAZI WAR CRIMES DISCLOSURE ACT

EXEMPTIONS Section 3(b)
Privacy
Methods/Sources
Foreign Relations

APPENDIX 18: NAZI INTERNATIONAL-CIA DOC 1956

- 2 -

15 P

THE FASCIST INTERNATIONAL

General

1. The European Popular Movement (EPM is an anti-American and an anti-Soviet fascist organization. Although the EPM is independent of the European Social Movement (ESM) and the European Liaison Office (ELO), some of the leading personalities of the EPM in France, such as Maurice BARDECHE, Henri BONIFACIO, and René BINET, are also members of the ESM or the ELO. Gaston RIOU, the honorary president of the EPM, lives at 42 Rue de l'Yvette, Paris XVe.

2. The Italian Social Movement (MSI), the EMP, and Otto STRASSER had planned to convene a congress in Rome; however, the congress will not meet because of a quarrel between the MSI and STRASSER over the issue of South Tyrol, the same issue which caused the conflict between STRASSER and the ESM.

3. On 1-2 October 1955 the German section of the ESM held its congress at Bad Homberg. The German authorities are making inquiries into the financial sources of the German section, since it has only 800 members, of whom 300 do not pay dues. Nonetheless, the German section is known to spend considerable sums of money, a portion of which comes from England (Oswald MOSELY) and from France.

4. The European-Arabian Study Commission was established in Vienna by Oskar HUSNER, member of the Austrian section of the ESM and a former member of the National Council, and (Dr.) Hans WILHELM, both of whom are from Vienna. While the official purpose of the Commission is listed as trade with Asia, it is merely a cover for ESM activities. No British, French, or Jewish firm may participate in the Commission's trade activities.

5. The ELO is in a difficult position following the resignation of Guy AMAUDRUZ as secretary-general and BINET has complained that the work of the French section, Comite National Francais, has become more and more difficult. The choice of the MSI to direct the work of the ELO has brought strong objections from both the German and Austrian sections. The German bloc in the ELO wishes to maintain at least the Swiss People's Party and the Austrian Freiheitliche Sammlung Oesterreichs as an ELO nucleus.

Organizations (with all six)
Austria:

6. Oesterreichische Soziale Bewegung: secretary-general Wilhelm LANDIG; in ESM; developed from League of Independents; collaborates with Germans.

Belgium:

7. Mouvement Social Europeen: led by Jean DEBBAUDT; expelled from ESM for excessive nazism and anti-semitism; now in ELO.

APPENDIX 18: NAZI INTERNATIONAL-CIA DOC 1956

- 5 -

Switzerland:

26. People's Party:
led by Erwin VOLLENWEIDER;
participated in Malmo congress;
separated from ESM because of excessive anti-semitism; has close
contacts with Germans and Swedes;
organs Volksruf and Appel Au Peuple.

Personalities

Austria:

27. Oskar HUEMER:
A leader of the League of Independents up
to 1953, co-founder of the Austrian section
of the ESM, member of the National Council
up to 1954.

28. Erich KERNMAIER:
former assistant to Gauleiter BUERCKEL,
author of neo-Nazi books, member of League
of Independents, contributor to Turmwart
and Nation Europa.

29. Wilhelm LANDIG:
secretary of Austrian section of the ESM.

30. Major LORENZ:
lives in Vienna, leading member of League
of Independents, executive member of the
Austrian section of the ESM.

31. Julius SCHACHNER:
leading member of the Austrian section of
the ESM, contributor to Natinform.

32. Fritz STEUBER:
former sub-editor of Voelkischer Beobachter,
member of League of Independents and its
National Council; cooperates with the ELO.

Belgium:

33. Jean DEBBAUDT:
leading member of the Belgian section of
the ELO, former member of the Waffen SS.

34. Leon DEGRELLE:
condemned to death by Belgian government,
now lives in Spain and plans to go to
Argentina, was leader of the Rexists, author
of "The Lost Legion", attended the celebra-
tion of the Blue Division in Madrid in 1954,
cooperates with the ESM and the ELO, has
contacts with Otto REMER and Otto SKORZENY.

200-7-197

APPENDIX 19-BURAFEX-BKA

Source: Notebook of Judge Willy Acke (Archives Walter De Bock)

APPENDIX 20: CIOLINI-PANORAMA MAG 22 SEPT 1982

Panorama

AFFARI ITALIANI

STRAGE DI BOLOGNA/1

Parla il supertestimone

servizi di Romano Cantore e Corrado Incerti

Elio Ciolini, agente segreto francese, rivela a «Panorama» come e perché ha messo i giudici in condizioni di riaprire l'inchiesta sulla strage di Bologna. La parte della P2 e quella di Delle Chiaie. Il polverone dei documenti falsi. Il ruolo ambiguo dei «servizi».

Due anni dopo l'attentato più feroce mai compiuto in Italia, quelli che hanno messo la bomba fra la folla della stazione di Bologna hanno adesso un nome e un cognome. I magistrati sono arrivati a loro grazie alle rivelazioni di un agente dei servizi segreti francesi, Elio Ciolini. I cinque autori della strage sono Stefano Delle Chiaie, il più importante latitante del terrorismo nero, Maurizio Giorgi, Pierluigi Pagliai, il tedesco Joachim Fiebelkorn, il francese Olivier Danet. Non è escluso che altri nomi vengano fuori. Quelli dei mandanti, per esempio.

Panorama ha rintracciato, fra la Francia e la Svizzera, il «supertestimone» Elio Ciolini. E si è fatto raccontare, per filo e per segno, come è arrivato a sapere i particolari di questa orribile storia.

Domanda. Dicono che lei sia il «testimone principe» nell'inchiesta sulla strage alla stazione di Bologna. È vero?

Risposta. È vero. E aggiungo che proprio grazie alle rivelazioni che ho fatto ai giudici bolognesi la magistratura conosce i veri organizzatori della strage.

D. Si rende conto di quello che sta dicendo?

R. Certamente. Non credo di essere un pazzo. E per convincervi racconterò tutto, per filo e per segno, anche a *Panorama*.

D. Come è venuto a conoscenza di quello che ha rivelato ai giudici?

R. Grazie ai miei lunghi, non di-

Licio Gelli. Sopra, le «credenziali» di Ciolini

sinteressati e avventurosi rapporti che ho avuto con l'avvocato Federico Federici di Firenze, con Umberto Ortolani, Licio Gelli e Stefano Delle Chiaie, attori e comprimari di una organizzazione terroristica cui convenzionalmente ho attribuito la sigla di Ot. In pratica una organizzazione che ha preso corpo accanto alla famosa e ancora segreta Loggia di Montecarlo, e che conosco bene perché io c'ero dentro.

D. Quando e come vi aderì?

R. È una storia molto lunga. Per chiarezza vorrei raccontarla seguendo il filo cronologico.

D. Benissimo. Cominciamo allora dal principio. Chi è Elio Ciolini? Chi è lei?

R. Un agente segreto di 36 anni.

D. Come ha cominciato?

R. Negli anni Sessanta, a Firenze, la mia città, conobbi un tedesco, un uomo importante legato agli ambienti spionistico-militari. Io facevo il funzionario alle poste e il mio lavoro non mi piaceva. Nel 1970 a Baden Baden, in

APPENDIX 21: CIOLINI ELIO-ARAB TERROR- EL CHOUK

NR 114
URGI..T   26/08/78   1100

RPPORT NR D/3139

SUJET: TERRORISME/ ELIO CIOLINI

SENATO DELLA REPUBBLICA
CAMERA DEI DEPUTATI
000339
COMMISSIONE MITRUKHIN
UFFICIO STRALCIS'

1. UN RESSORTISSANT ITALIEN S'EST PRESENTE RECEMMENT A NOUS
ET NOUS A FAIT SAVOIR QU'UN ARABE, LIE AUX ORGANISATIONS
TERRORISTES ARABES, DU NOM DE SALAH YASSINE EL-CHOUK, SURNOMME
EGALEMENT LORENZ, ET DEMEURANT A GENEVE.
LUI AVAIT PROPOSE DE S'ENROLERDANS LES RANGS TERRORISTES, ET
DE PARTIR SUIVRE UN ENTPAINEMENT EN SYRIE. PAR LA SUITE IL DEVRA
SE RENDRE EN ISRAEL POUR Y PERPETRER PROBABLEMENT DES ATTENTATS.

2. CI-APRES LES RENSEIGNEMENTS PERSONNELS DU SUJET ITALIEN:

- DATE DE NAISSANCE   : 18/8/46

- PRENOM DU PERE   : ROLANDO - ETAIT OUVRIER-IMPRIMEUR -
                          DECEDE EN 1967.

- SA MERE   : BRUNA, AGEE DE 62 ANS, VIT A FLORENCE-
                          8 VIA LANBAUSCHINI.

- ADRESSE PERSONNELLE   : 2 PUE GRANGE LEVRIER AVANCHET PARC-

- ADRESSE BUREAU   : STE RENOVIM (SEMBLE-T-IL) 4 RUE CHAMPOULET
                          GENEVE.

- SIGNALEMENT DU SUJET : TAILLE 1,78 M., STATURE MOYENNE, CHEVEUX
                          NOIRS, CALVITIE FRONTALE. PETITE
                          PROEMINENCE SUR LA PARTIE SUPERIEURE DU NEZ.
                          A EPOUSE EN 1976 UNE RESSORTISSANTE SUISSE
                          NOMMEE RFANCOISE BOLLE, AVEC LEQUELLE IL

CIA-agent Ciolini wordt in 1978 gelieerd aan het internationaal terrorisme en infiltreer
vanaf 1984 in de bende-Haemers.

APPENDIX 22: CIOLINI AKA COL BACCIONI – SIS PASS

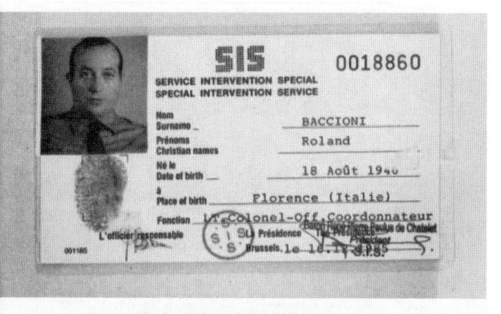

Signé par le baron Paulus De Chatelet...

Index